ALBRECHT DÜRER

COLLECTION

A CURATED ARCHIVE OF 162 DOWNLOADABLE MASTERPIECES

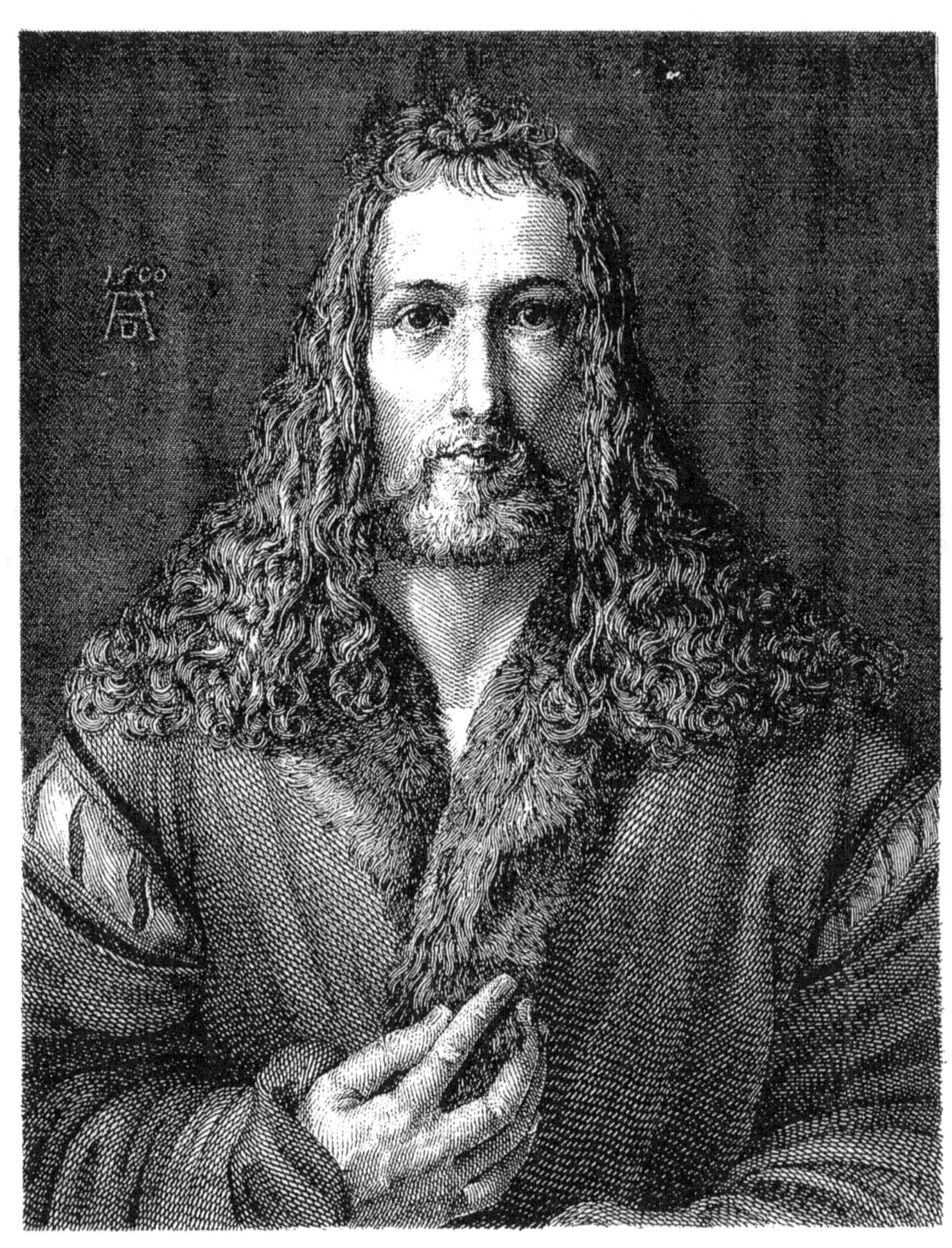

ALBRECHT DÜRER

21 MAY 1471 – 6 APRIL 1528

ISBN: 978-1-922966-42-1

TABLE OF CONTENTS

1

INTRODUCTION

"As I grew older, I realised that it was much better to insist on the genuine forms of nature, for simplicity is the greatest adornment of art"
-Albrecht Dürer

Albrecht Dürer, born on May 21, 1471, in Nuremberg, Germany, is one of the most significant figures in art history. He was a master of multiple media, including painting and printmaking as well as authoring several books. Dürer's work exemplifies the Renaissance's artistic, scientific, and intellectual spirit.

Dürer's father was a goldsmith, and he was an apprentice in his father's workshop. However, his extraordinary talent in drawing became apparent from a young age and is particularly evident in the work known as *'Self-Portrait at the age of 13'*. At 15, he became an apprentice to Michael Wolgemut, a leading Nuremberg artist. Under his guidance, Dürer gained an introduction to the visual arts, particularly in printmaking techniques, an area in which he would eventually have a significant impact.

In 1494, Albrecht Dürer embarked on a transformative journey to Italy, a pivotal moment that profoundly influenced his style. There, he encountered the works of the Italian Renaissance masters, a revelation that merged his Northern European detail and precision with the proportions, perspectives, and classical themes of Italian art. Dürer's works, such as the Meisterstiche (master engravings) *'Knight, Death, and the Devil'* (1513), *'Saint Jerome in His Study'* (1514), and *'Melencolia I'* (1514) exhibit these influences and are celebrated for their technical brilliance and depth of meaning.

Dürer's timeless engravings, woodblocks, and etchings demonstrate his exceptional skill in creating detailed line work and innovative approach to composition and subject matter.

His series of prints, including *'The Apocalypse'* (1498) and *'The Large Passion'* (1511), revolutionised the art of printmaking. These works were not only artistic achievements but also accessible forms of art that could be widely distributed, contributing significantly to the spread of Renaissance ideas across Europe.

This book extensively explores Dürer's prolific output in these mediums. Each piece has been carefully curated to showcase the breadth and depth of his work, from his early woodcuts to his mature engravings and etchings. This archive not only presents high-quality reproductions of Dürer's prints but also provides a unique opportunity for art enthusiasts and scholars to delve into the intricacies of his craftsmanship.

This book includes a download link granting access to high-resolution files of all the images featured. This digital archive allows a closer examination of Dürer's techniques and the details in his artwork, enabling a deeper appreciation of his genius. Whether you are a seasoned art historian or a curious newcomer, this collection serves as a valuable resource for understanding the lasting impact of Dürer's work.

Through this compilation, we celebrate the enduring legacy of Albrecht Dürer, whose art continues to inspire and captivate audiences more than five centuries after they were created. His contributions to art are immeasurable, and this book aims to honour his mastery by making his works accessible to a broader audience, ensuring that his genius is recognised and appreciated for generations to come.

01

BIBLICAL SCENES AND SAINTS

'Biblical Scenes and Saints' includes three of Dürer's biblical series: *'The Apocalypse'*, *'The Great Passion'*, and *'The Small Passion'*. It also contains interpretations of biblical scenes, characters, and depictions of various Christian saints.

'The Apocalypse' (full title: *'The Apocalypse with Pictures'*) is a series of fifteen woodcuts depicting various scenes from the Bible's *The Book of Revelation*. In 1498, Albrecht Dürer embarked on his first major book project, publishing these images with accompanying Biblical text. The book was released during a period of intense doomsday fixation in Europe, fueled by interpretations of a verse in the *Book of Revelation* that led many to believe the year 1500 marked the end of the world. This series was immensely popular and established Dürer's fame.

Dürer's *'The Great Passion'* and *'The Small Passion'* series tell the Biblical story of the events leading up to, and including the crucifixion and resurrection of Jesus Christ. *'The Great Passion'* features eleven woodcuts plus a frontispiece and was produced between 1497 and 1510. *'The Small Passion'* was published in 1511. It contains 36 woodcuts and a frontispiece. It tells an expanded version of the life of Jesus Christ. Dürer's atmospheric images are full of fascinating, complex details, making them as compelling to viewers today as they were hundreds of years ago.

01

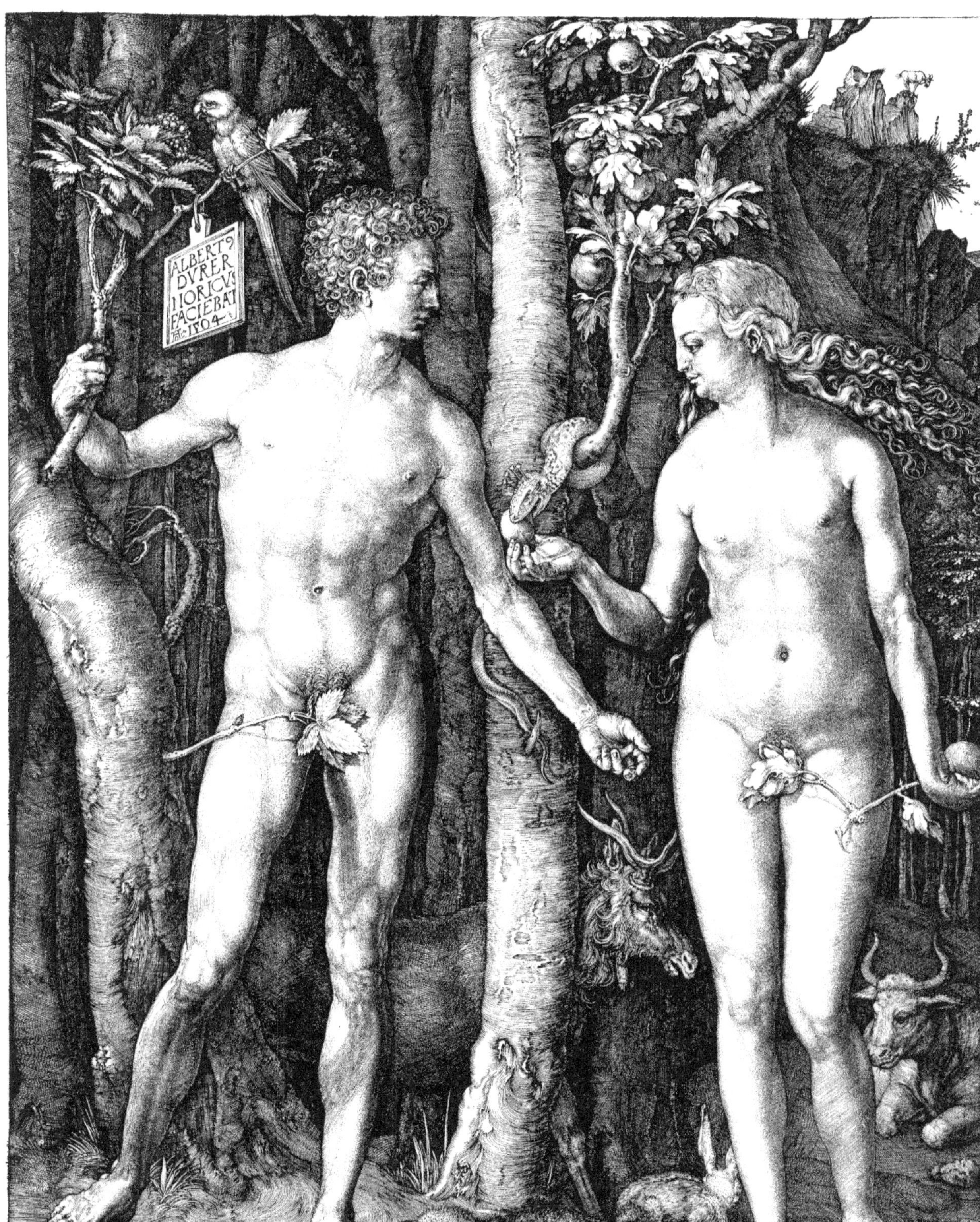

ALBRECHT DÜRER

02

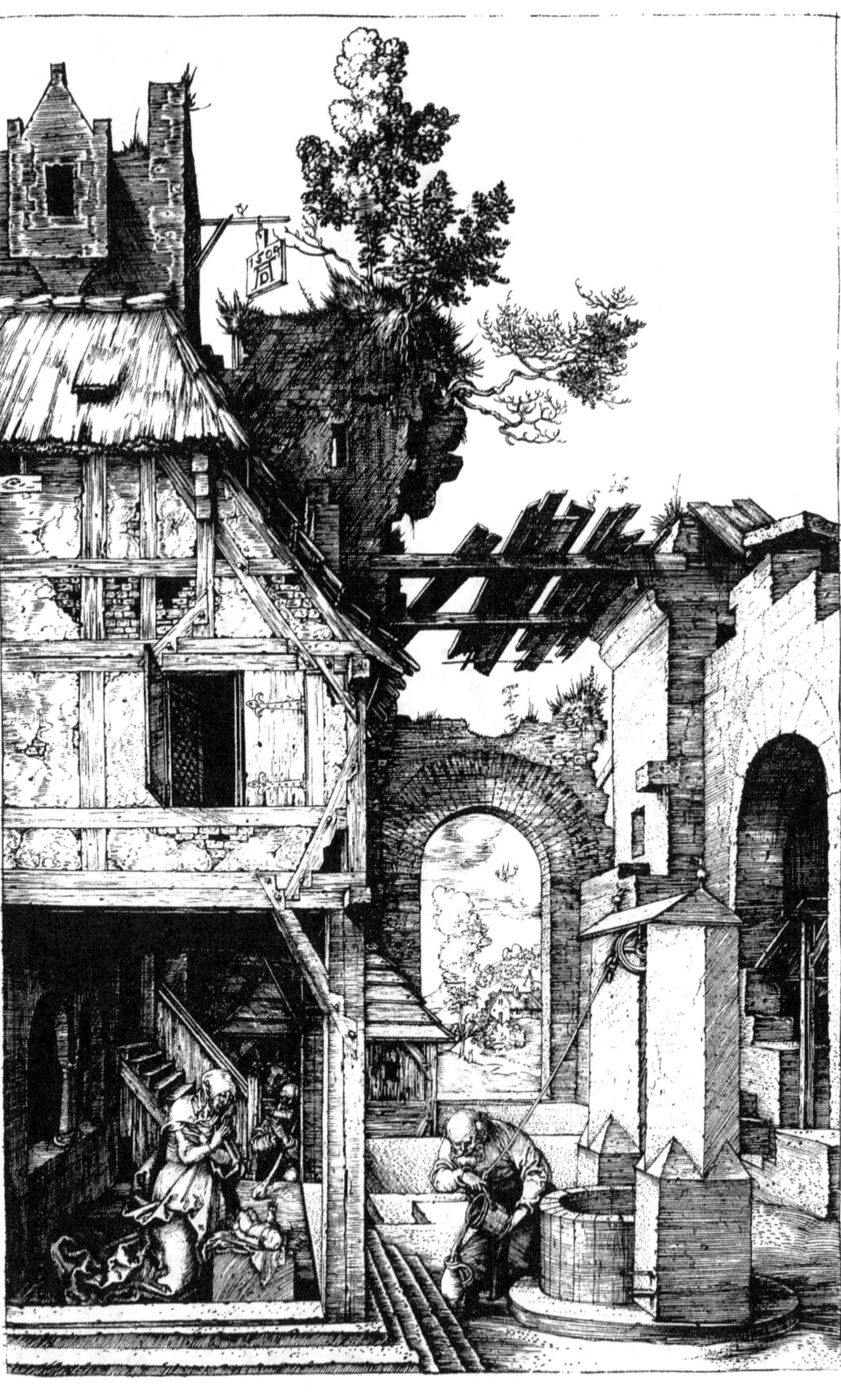

02. The Nativity, Albrecht Dürer, 1504

03

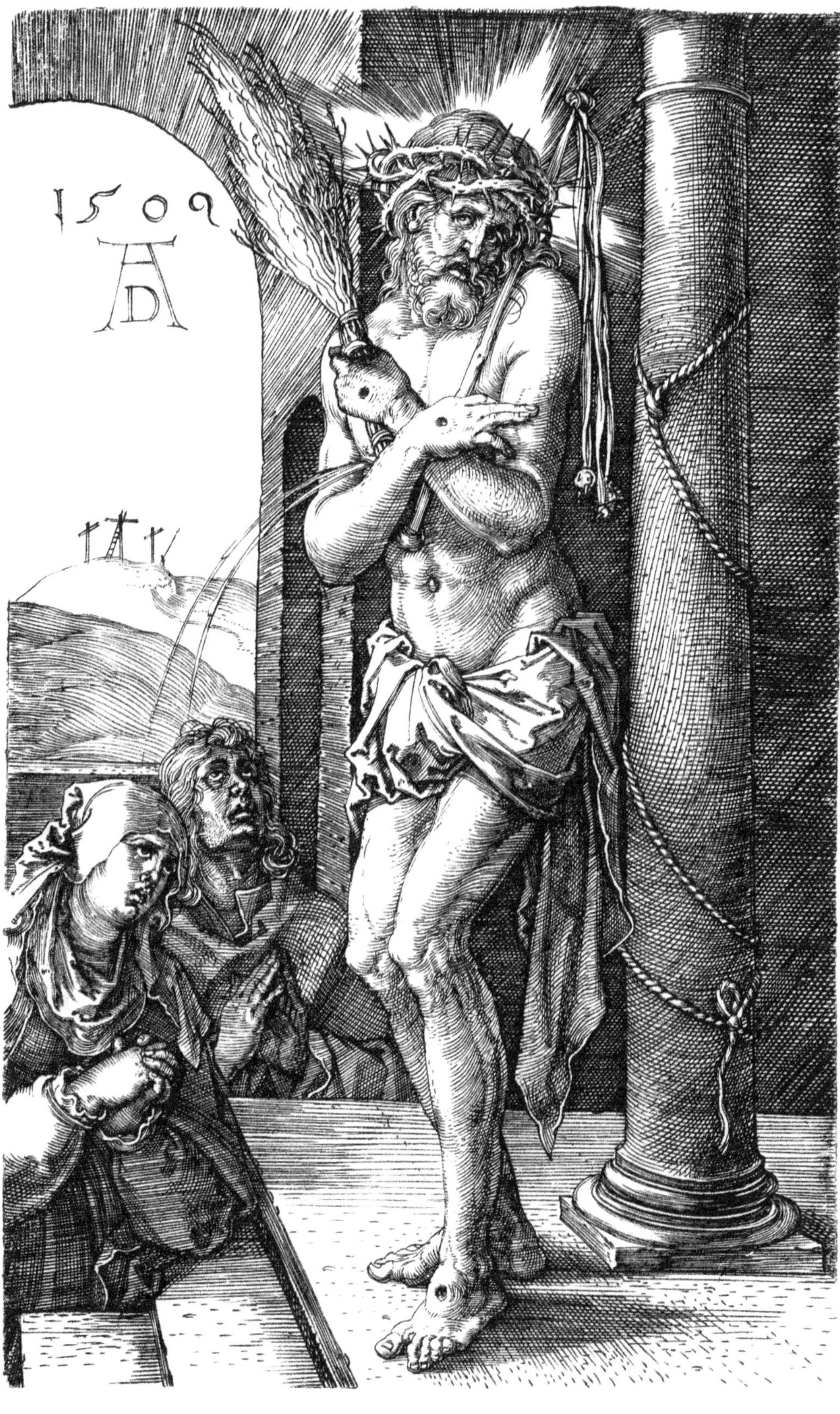

ALBRECHT DÜRER

03. Christ as Man of Sorrows at the Column,
Albrecht Dürer, 1509

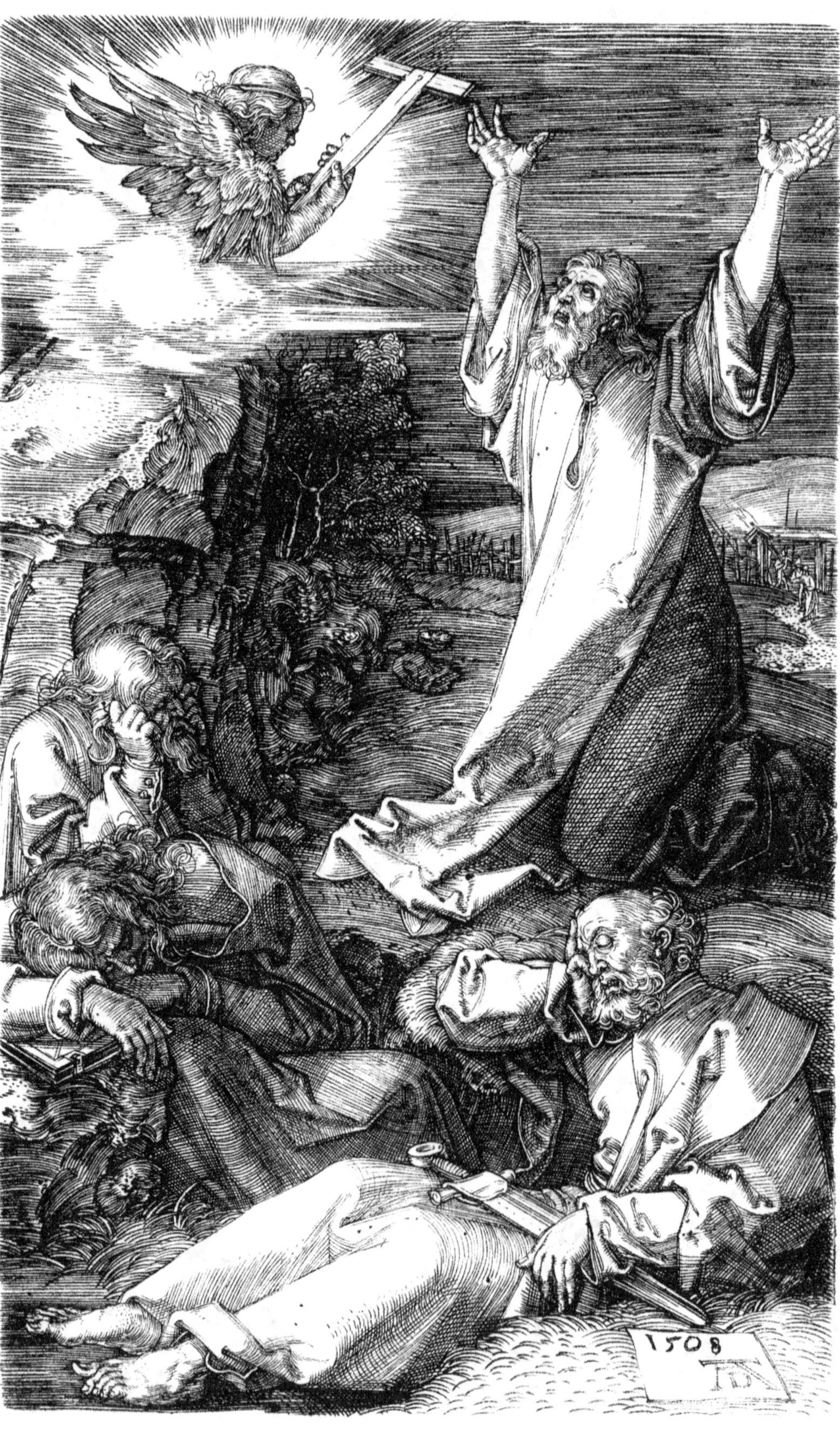

*04. Christ on the Mount of Olives, Albrecht
Dürer, 1508*

05

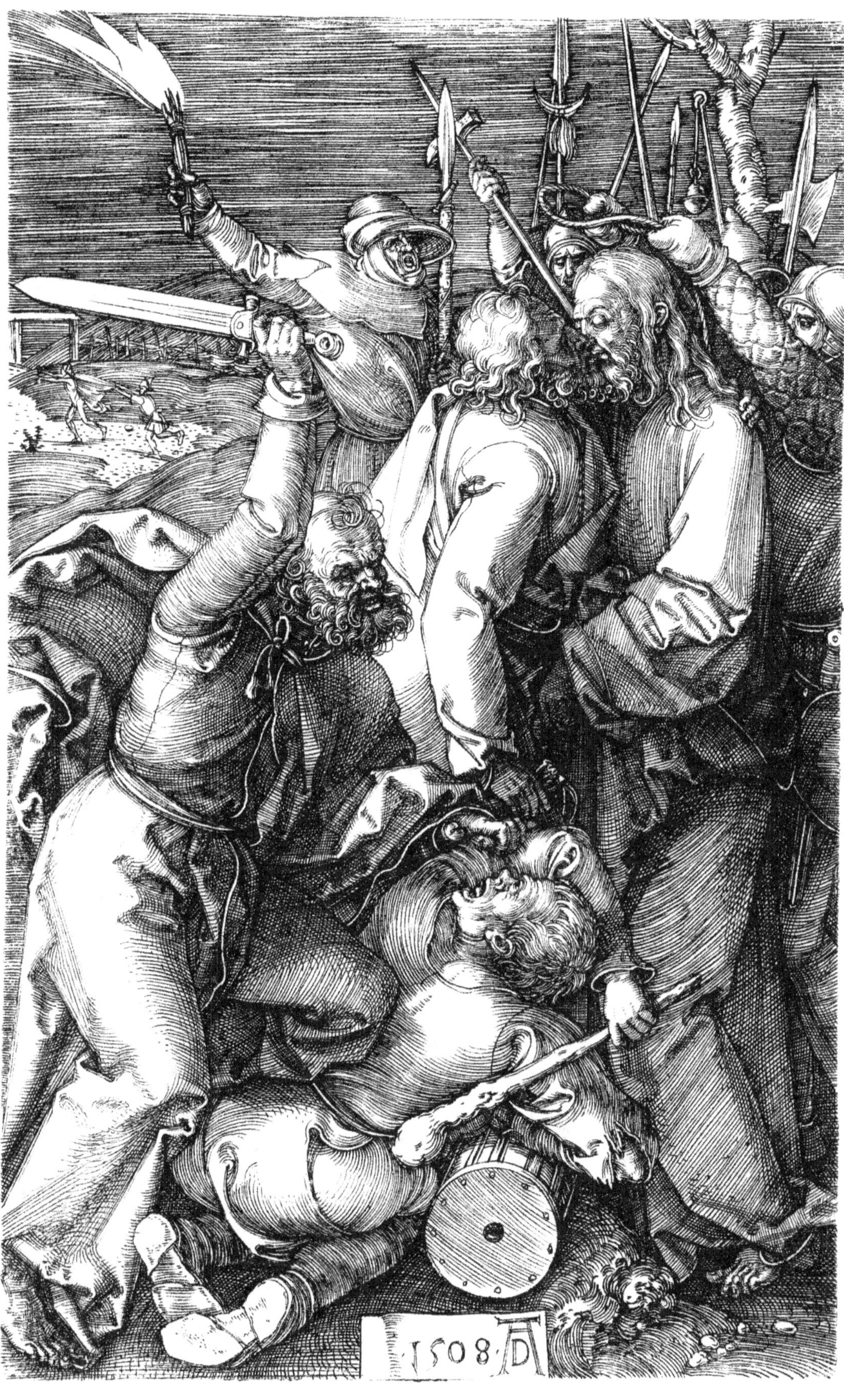

ALBRECHT DÜRER

ALBRECHT DÜRER

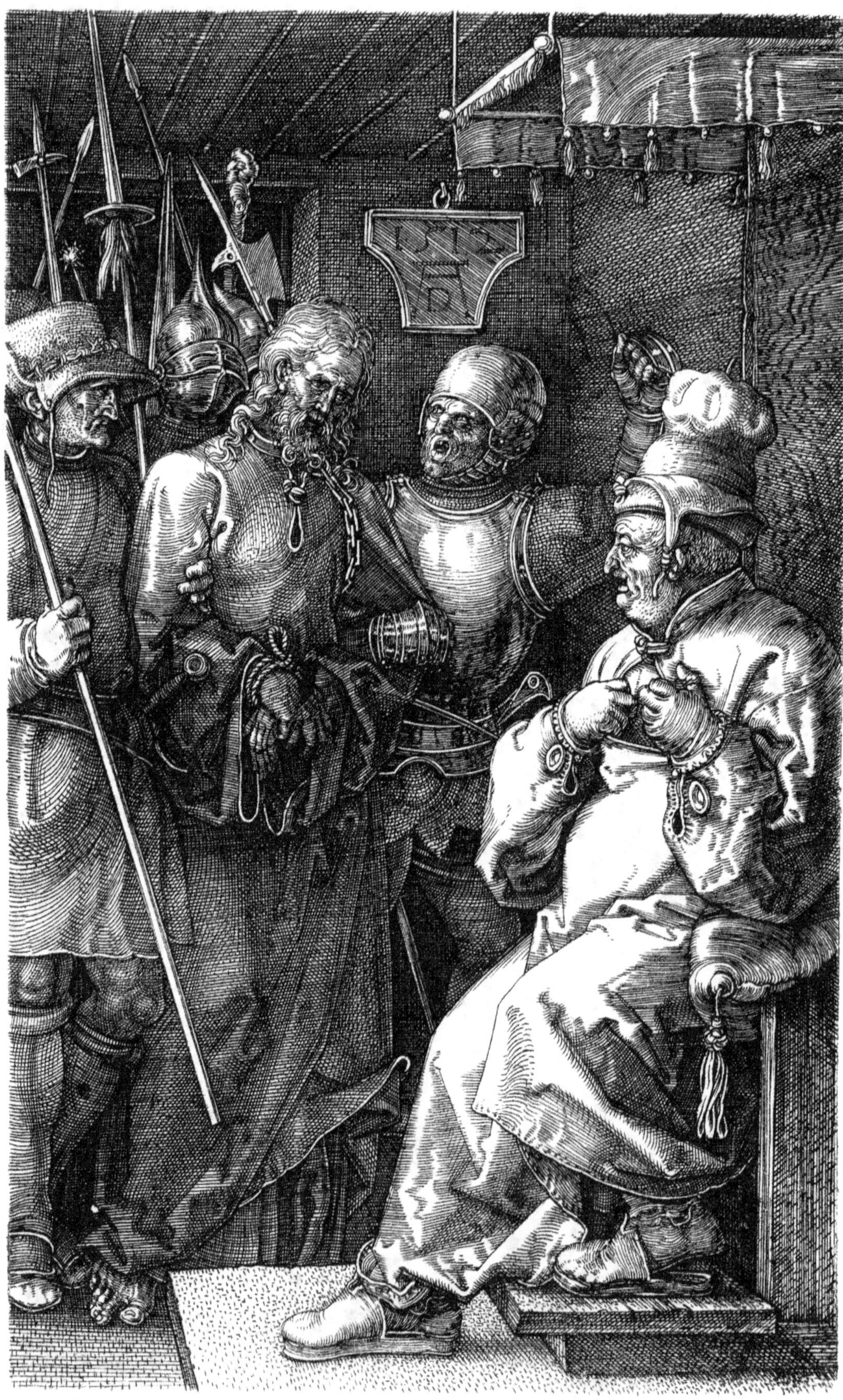

06. Christ before Caiaphas, Albrecht Dürer, 1512

07

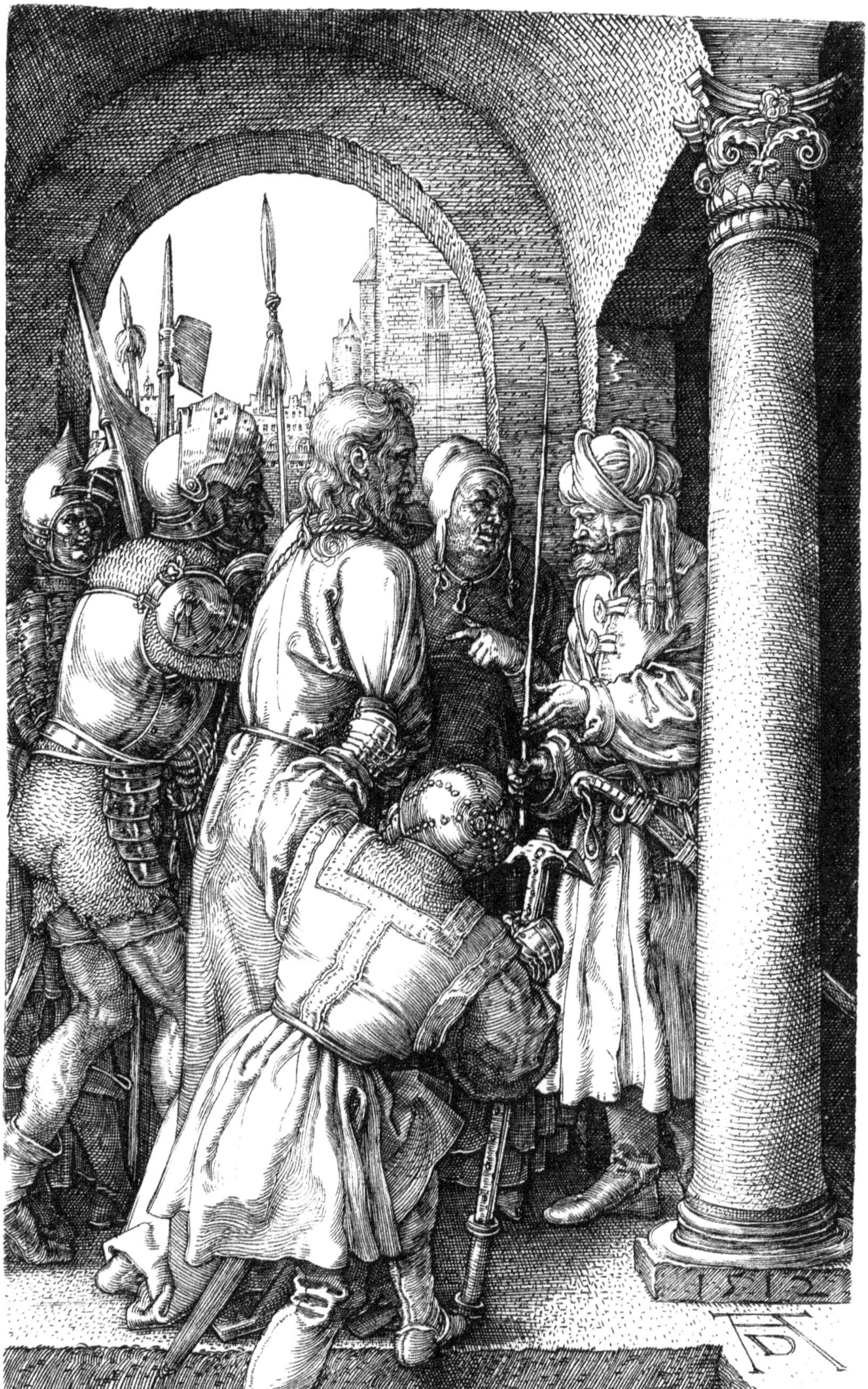

07. Christ before Pilate. Albrecht Dürer, 1512.

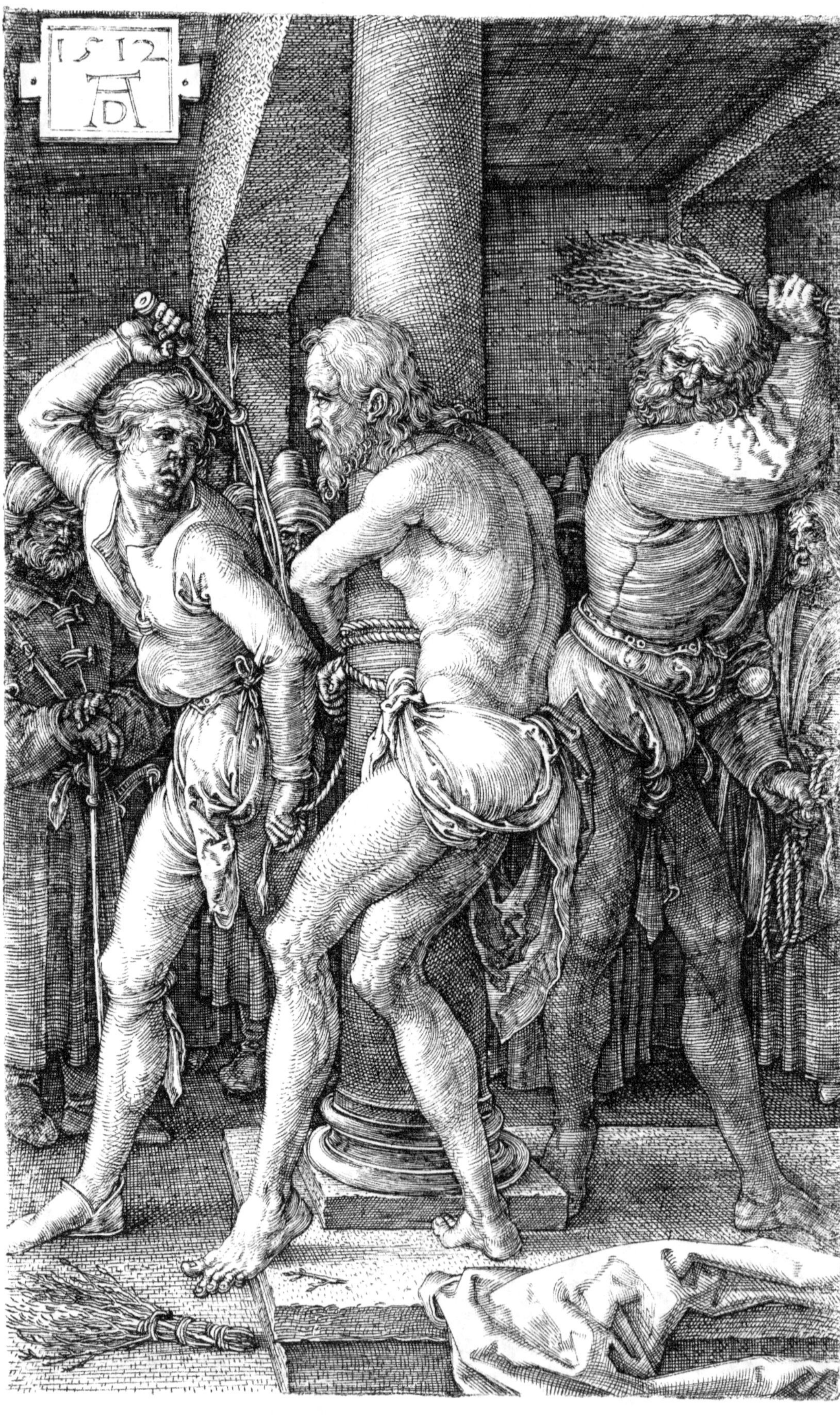

08. *The Flagellation, Albrecht Dürer, 1512*

09

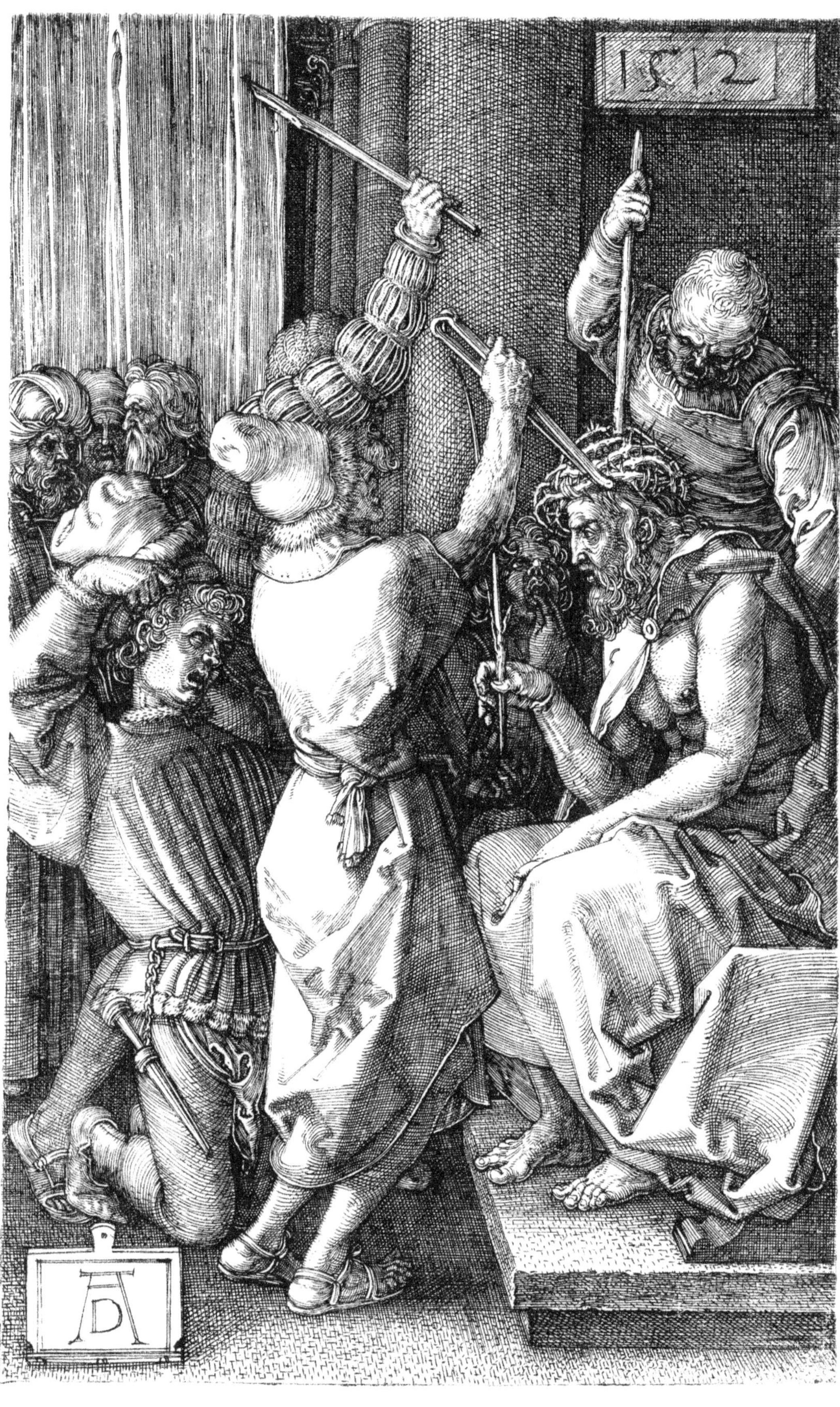

09. The Crowning with Thorns. Albrecht Dürer.
1512

10

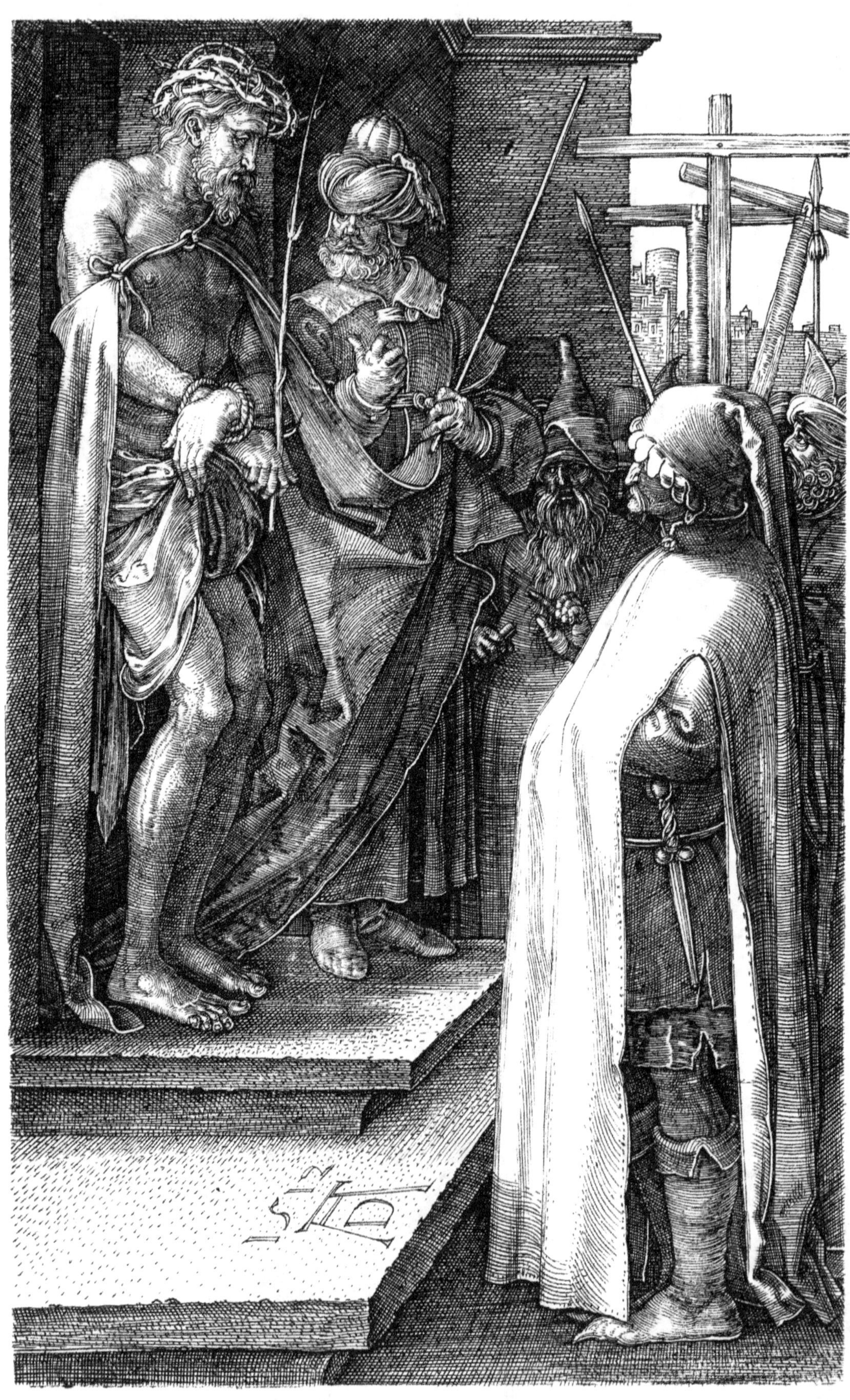

10. Christ Shown to the People (Ecce homo),
Albrecht Dürer, 1512

11

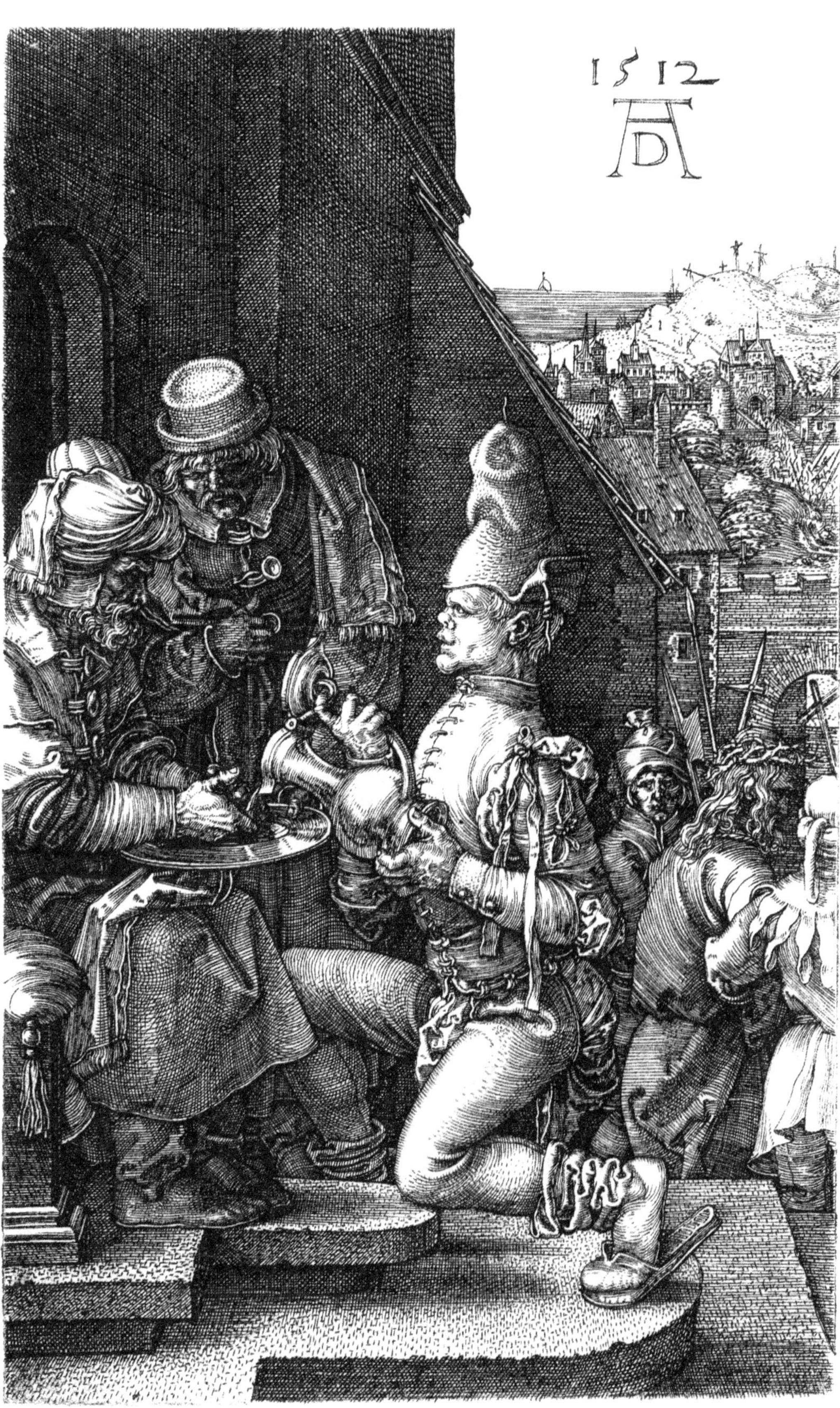

ALBRECHT DÜRER

11. Pilate washes his hands in innocence.
Albrecht Dürer, 1512

12

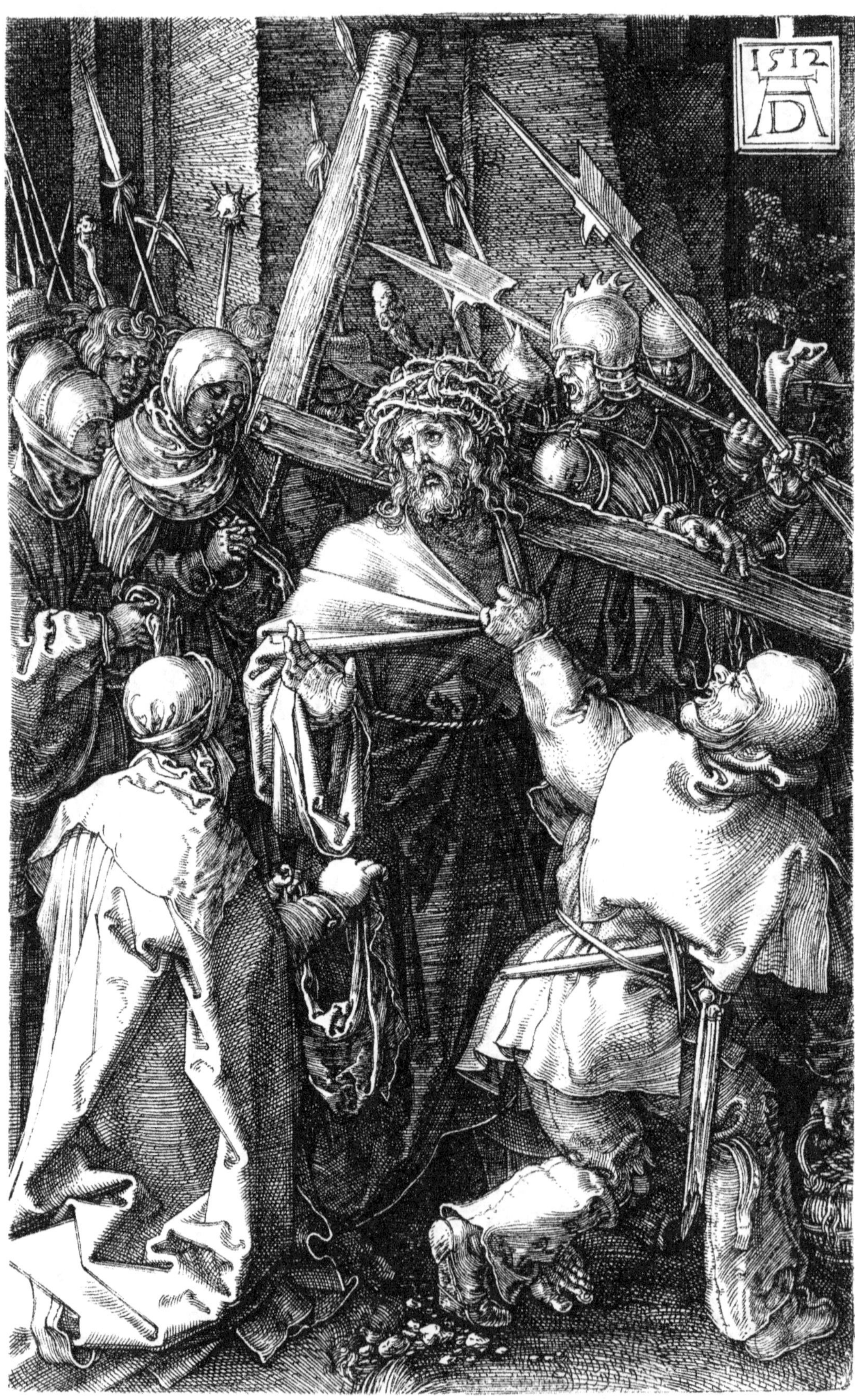

12. *The Carrying of the Cross. Albrecht Dürer.*
1512

13

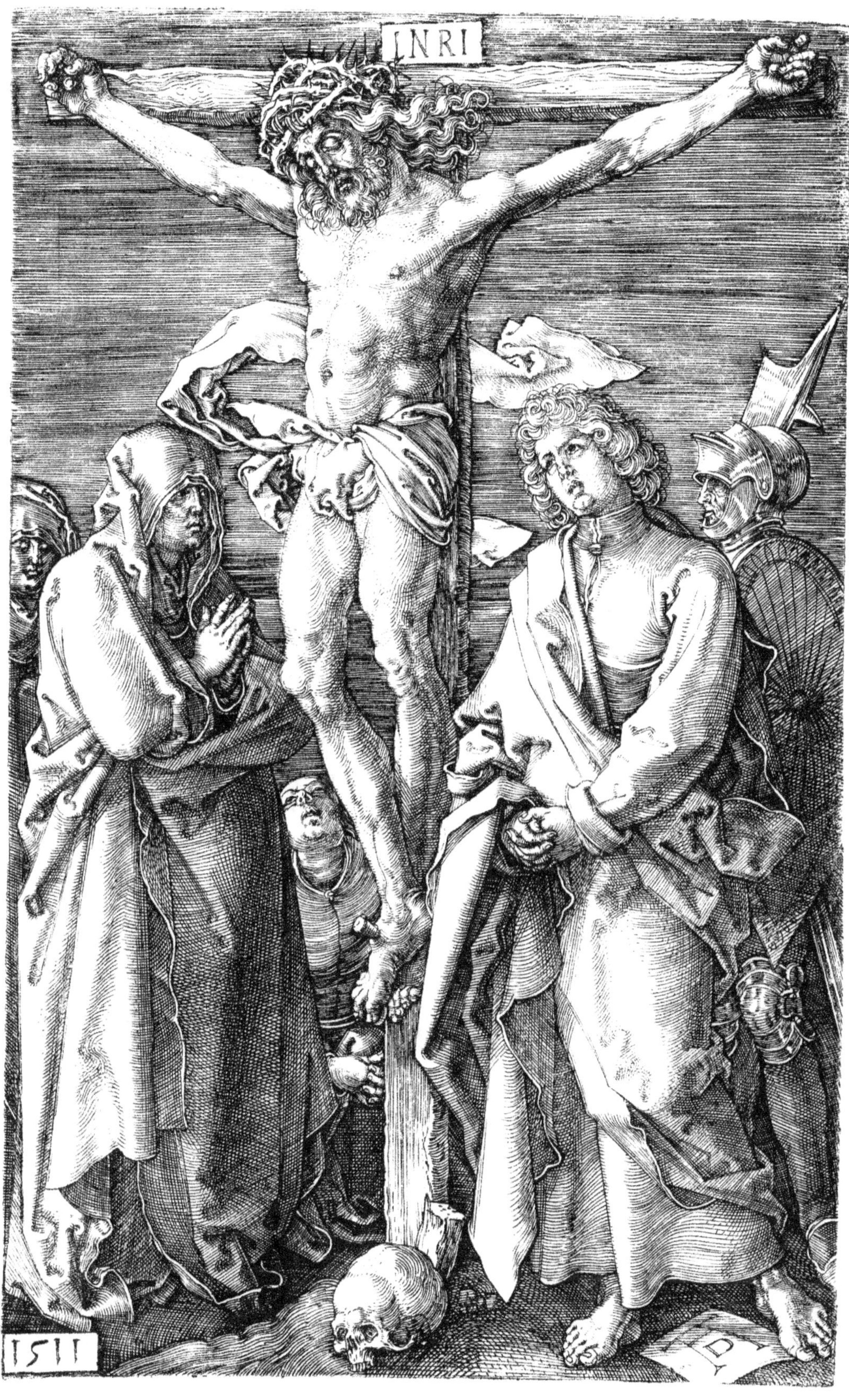

ALBRECHT DÜRER

14

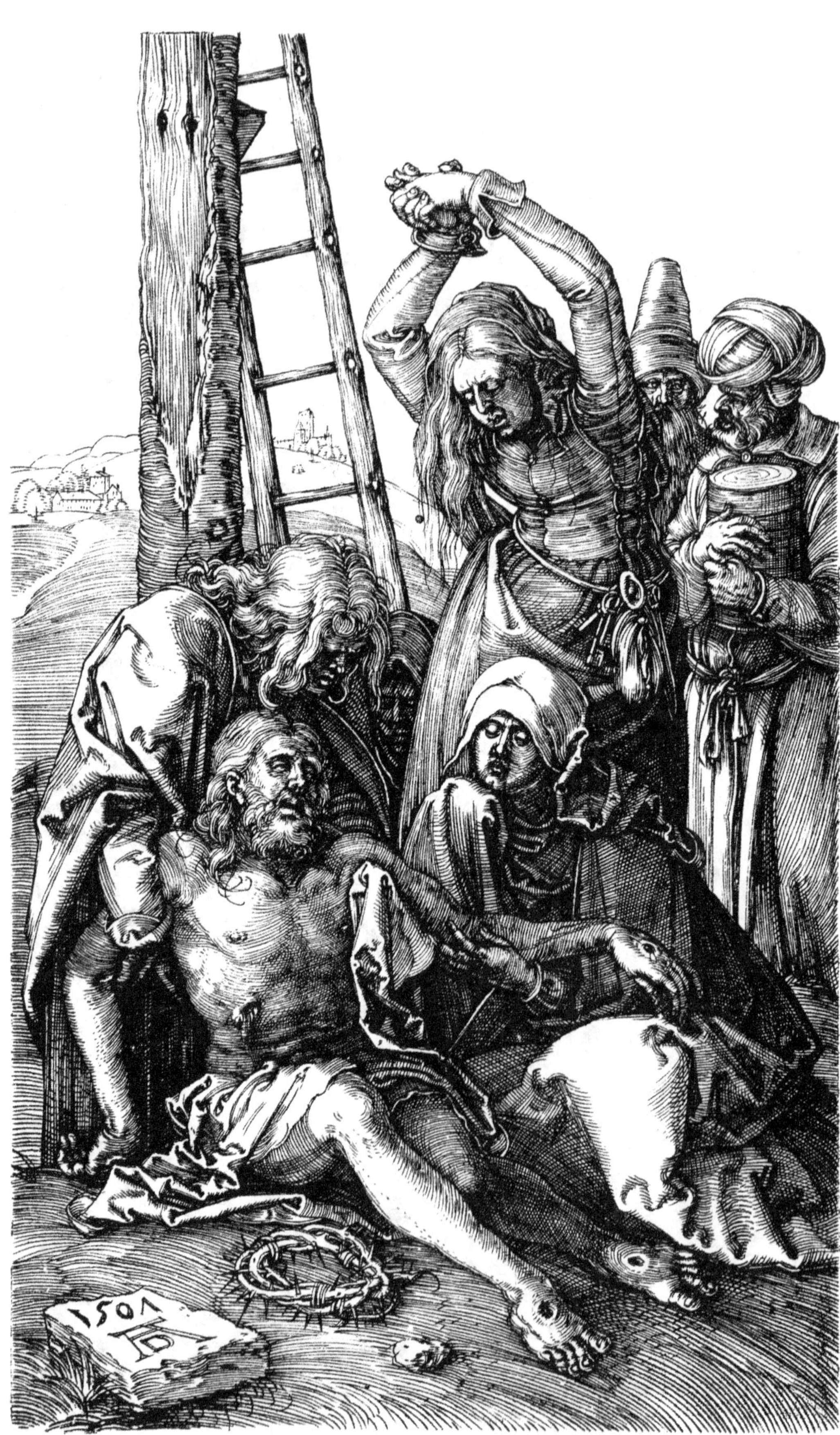

14. Lamentation, Albrecht Dürer, 1507

15

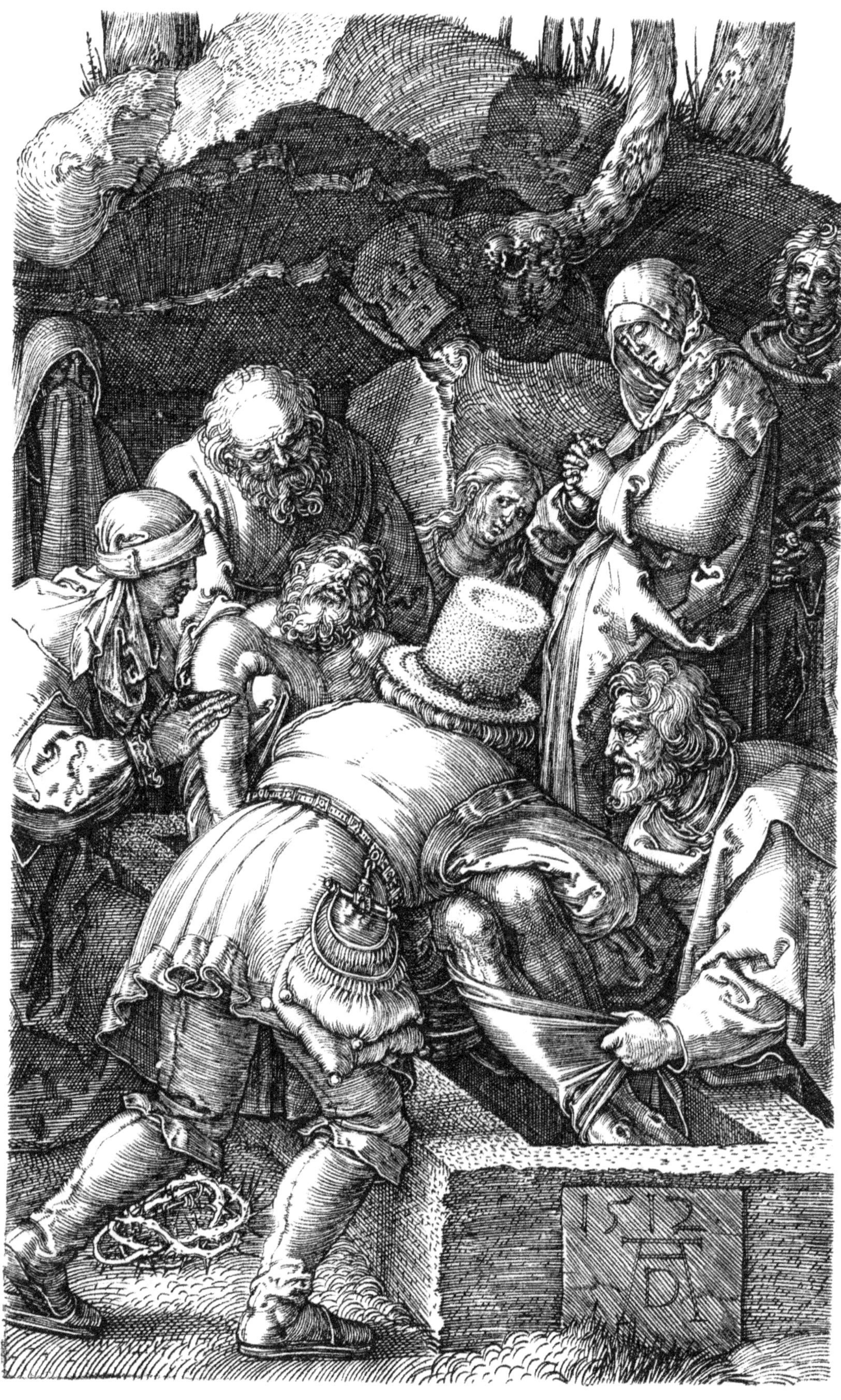

ALBRECHT DÜRER

16

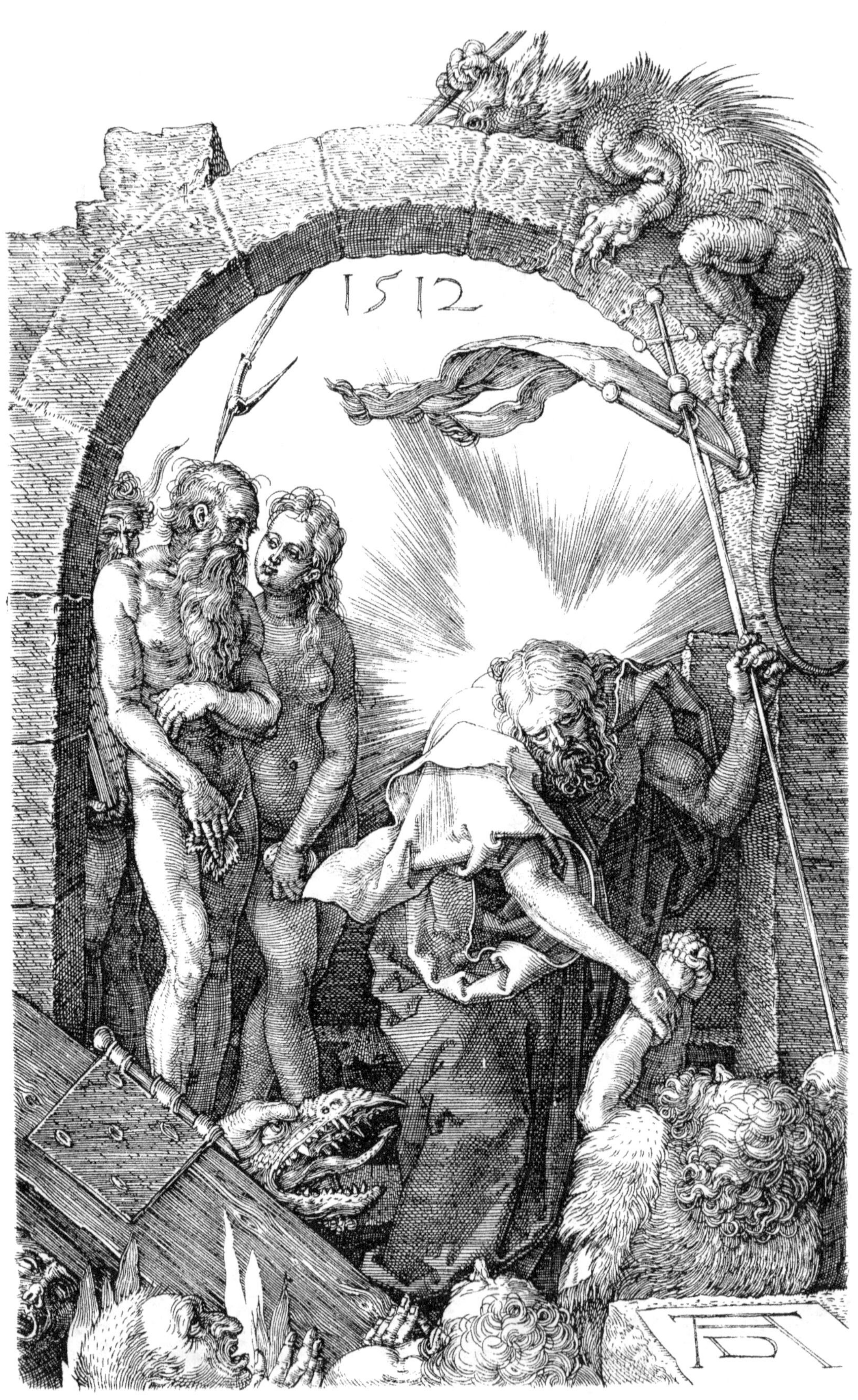

16. *The Descent into Limbo, Albrecht Dürer, 1512*

17

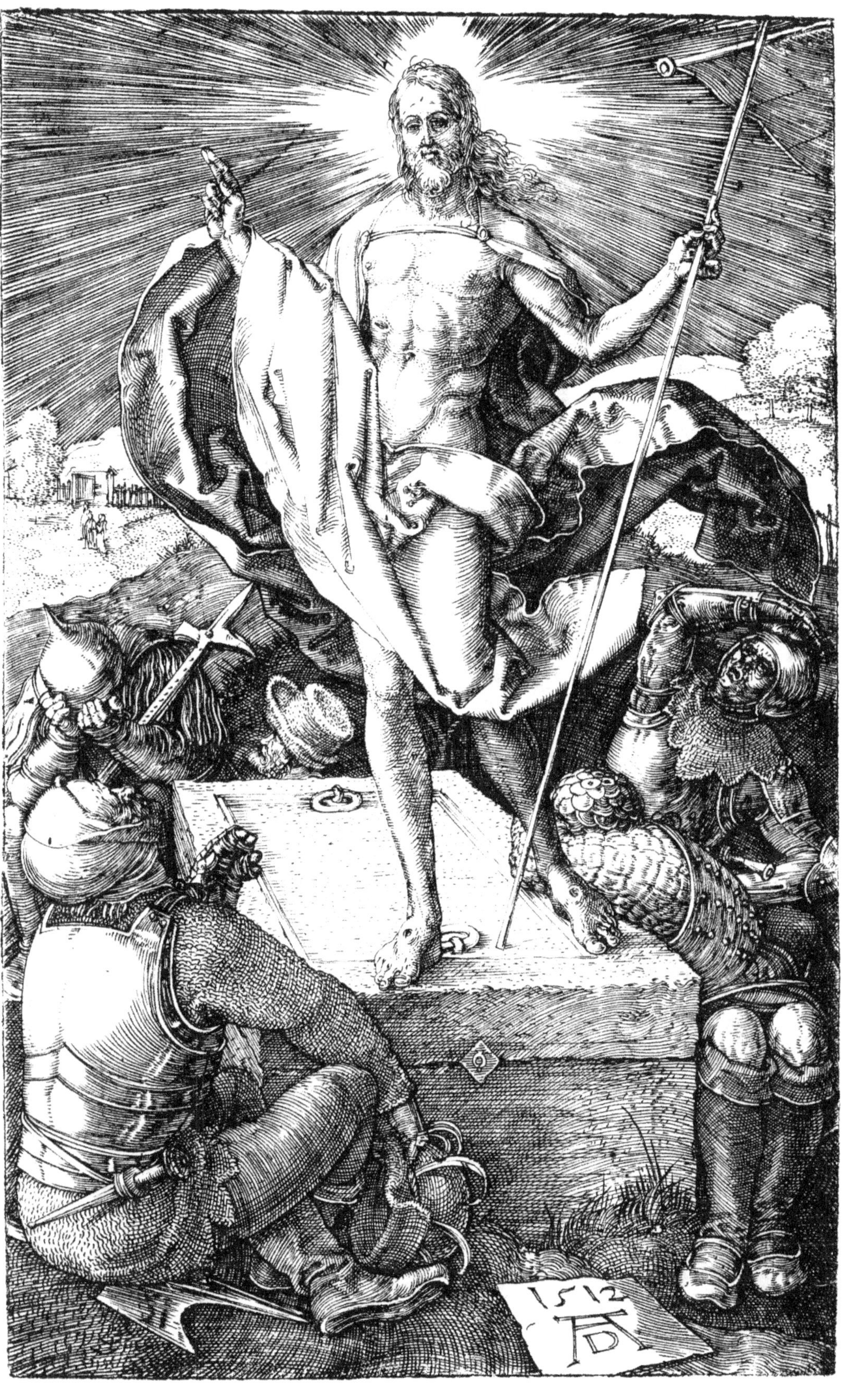

17. The Resurrection, Albrecht Dürer, 1512

18

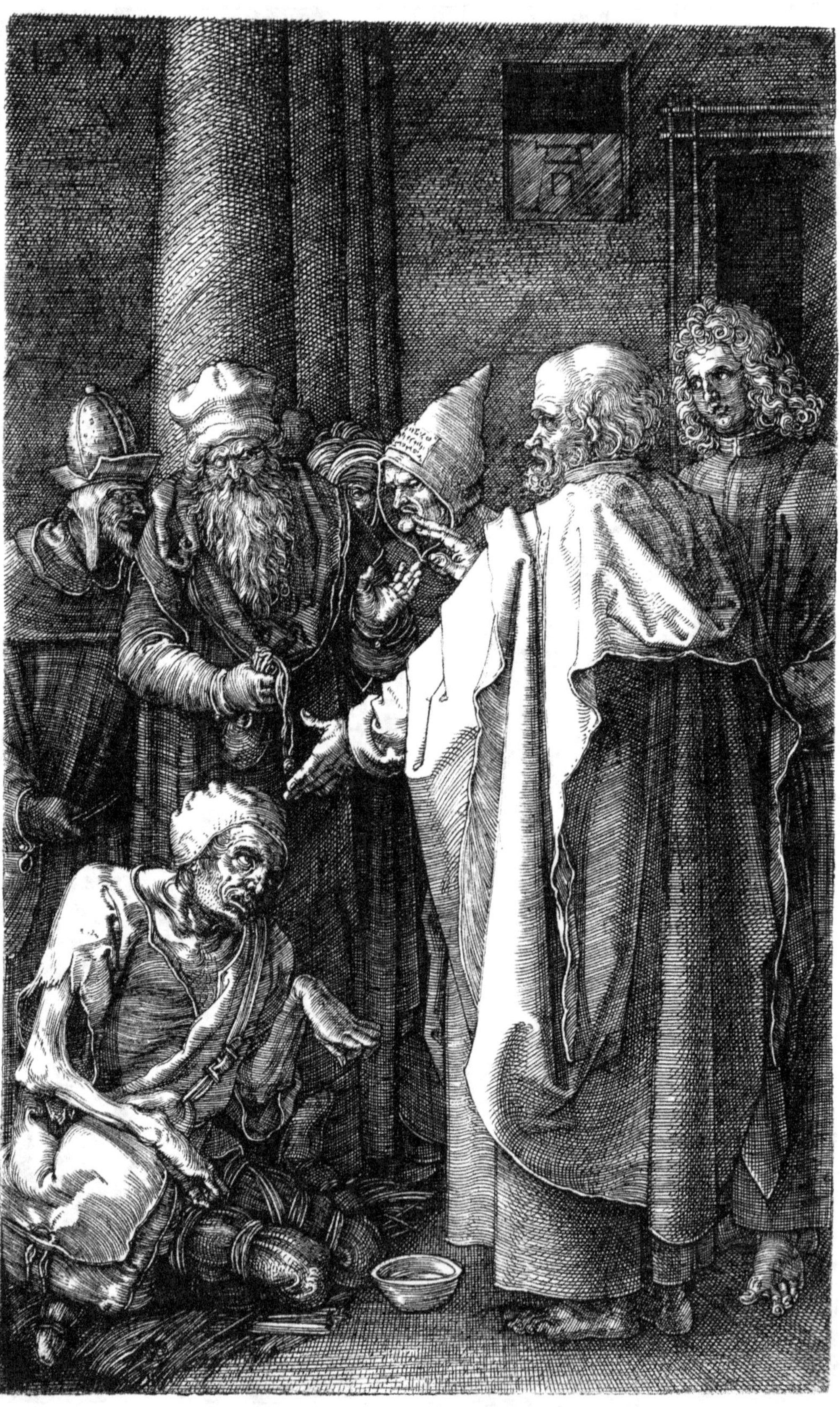

*18. Peter and John heal a paralyzed man at the
temple gate, Albrecht Dürer, 1513*

19

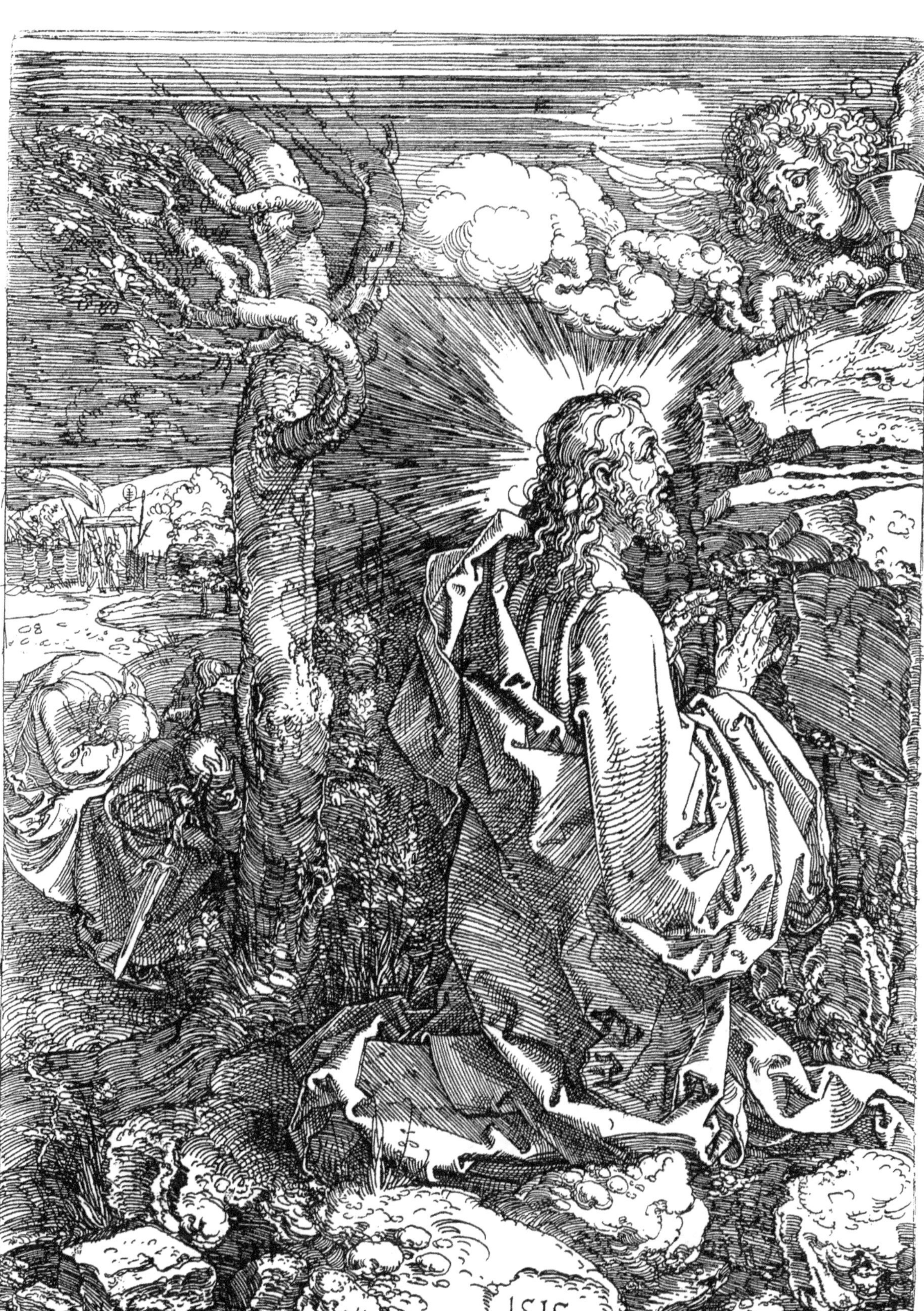

19. *Christ on the Mount of Olives*, Albrecht
Dürer, 1515

20

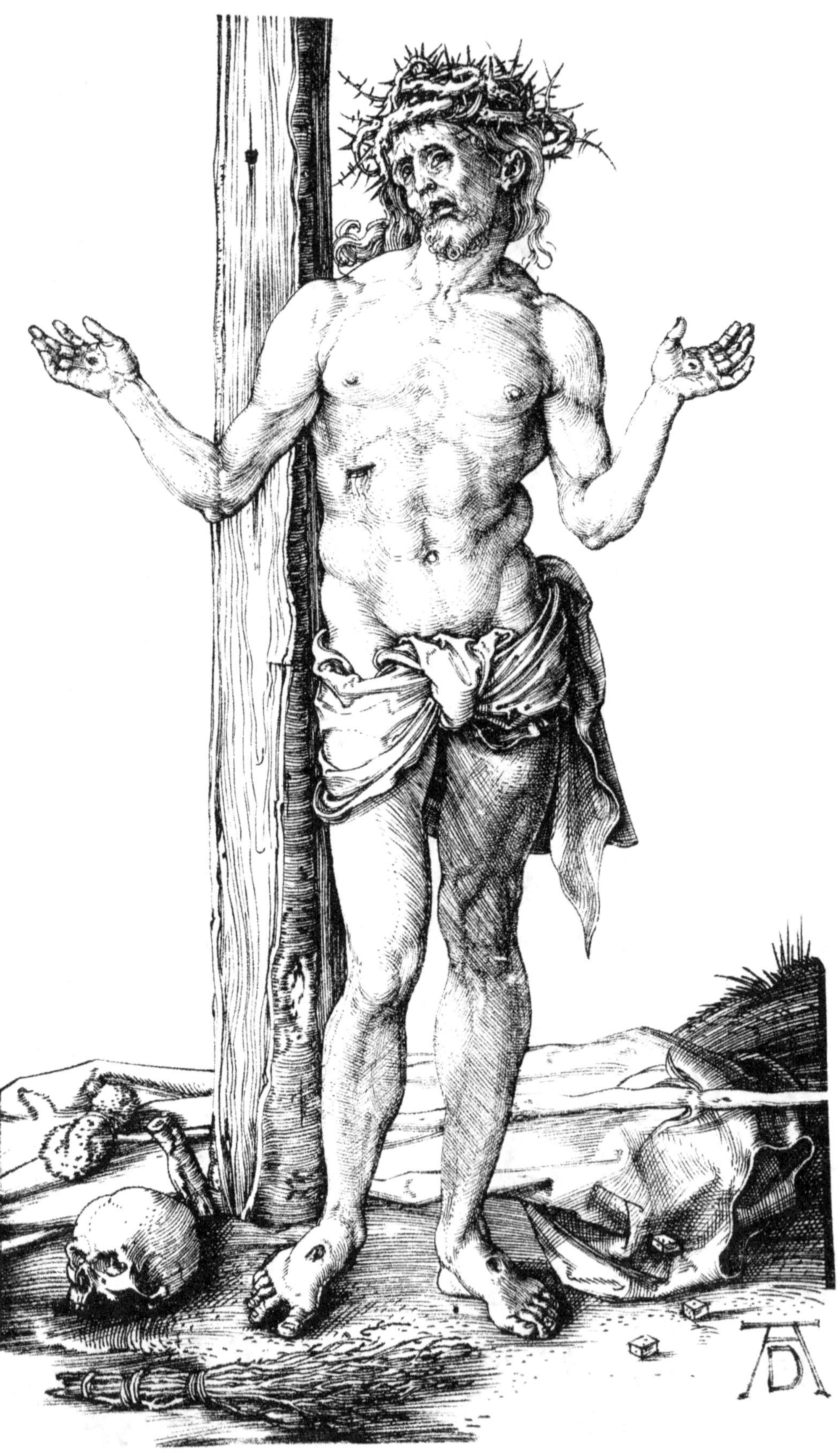

20. Christ as Man of Sorrows, with raised hands.
Albrecht Dürer, 1498 - 1502

21

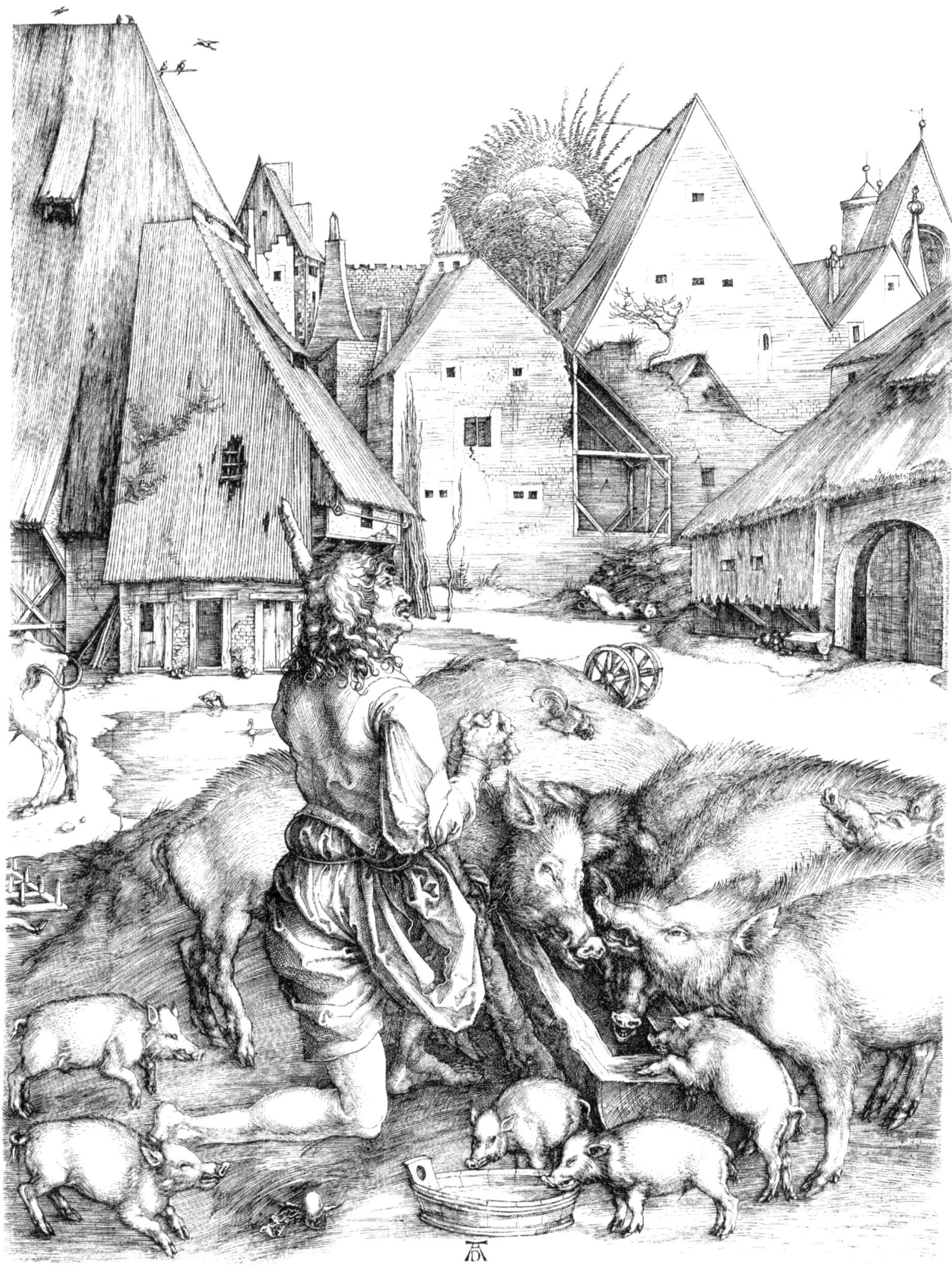

ALBRECHT DÜRER

22

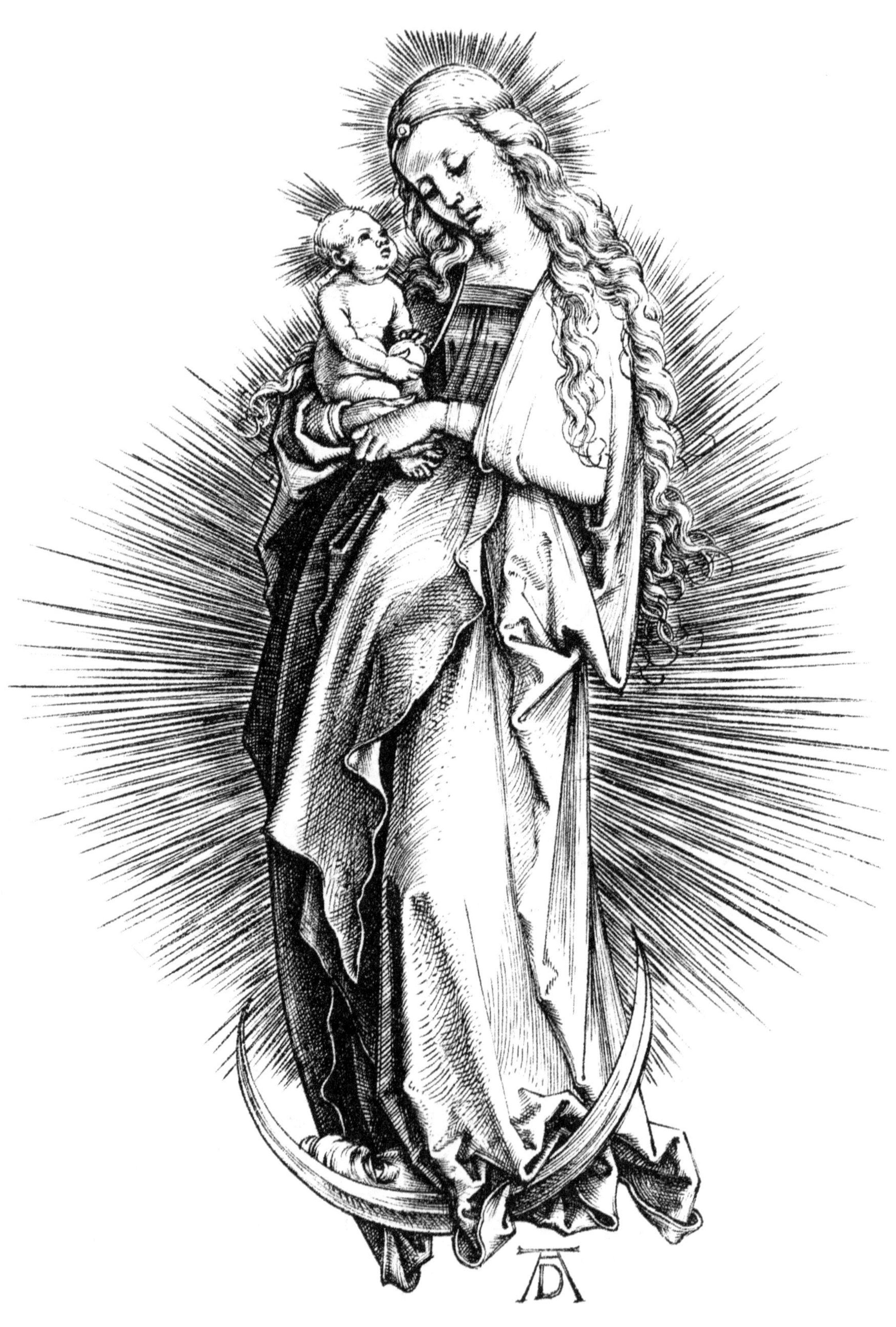

*22. Mary with Child on the Crescent Moon,
Albrecht Dürer, 1497 - 1501*

23

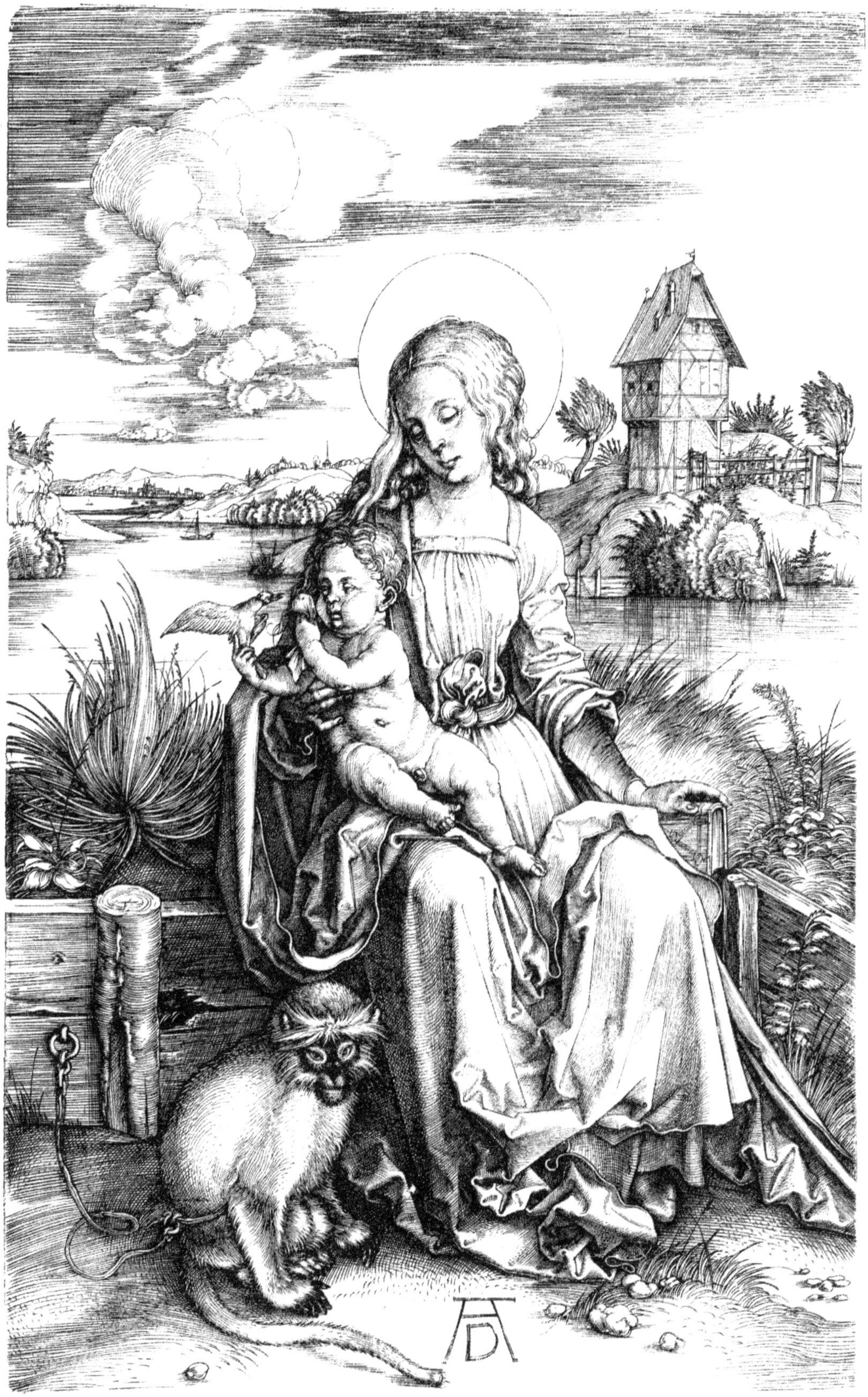

ALBRECHT DÜRER

24

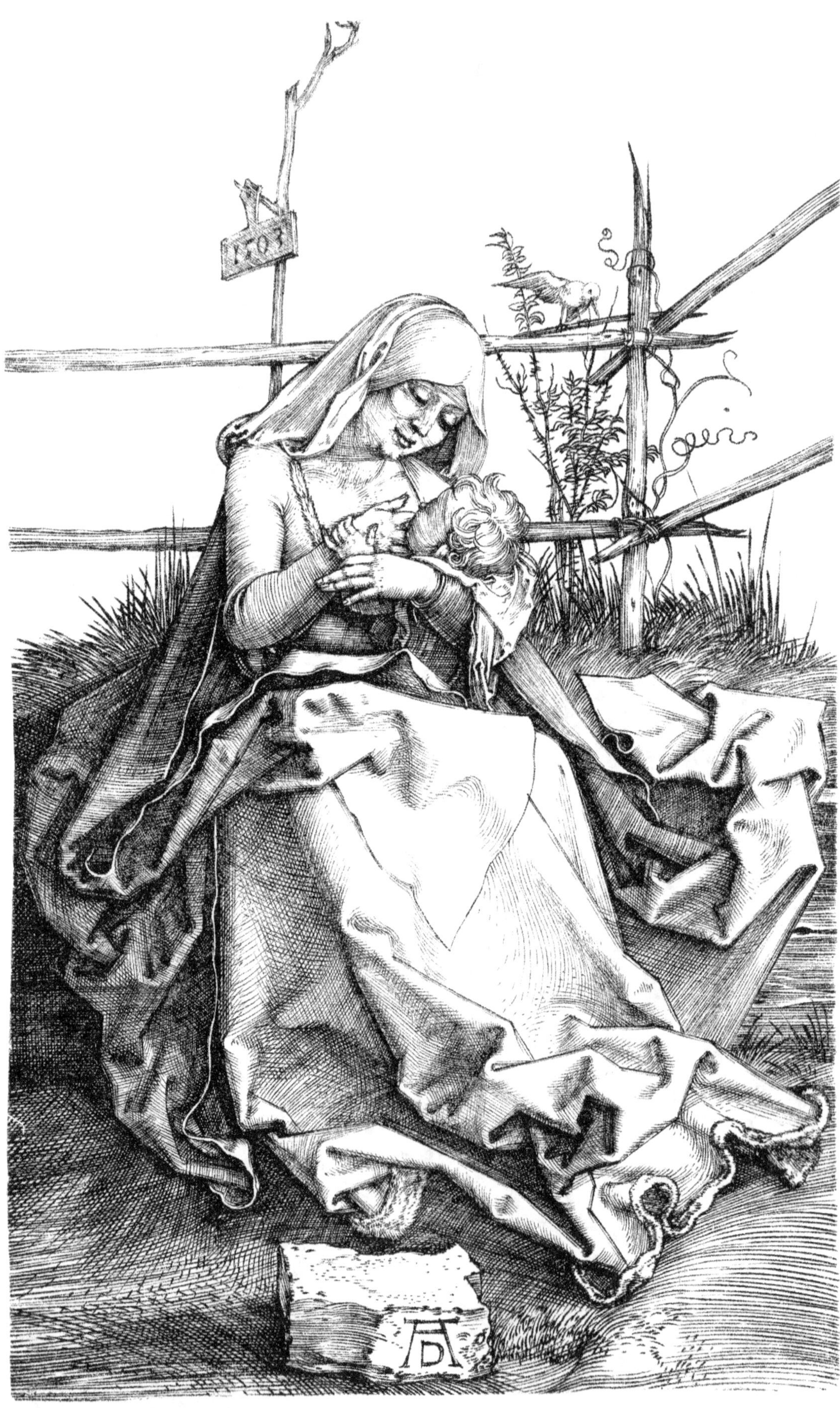

24 Mary with Child at the Breast at a Gate.
Albrecht Dürer, 1503

25

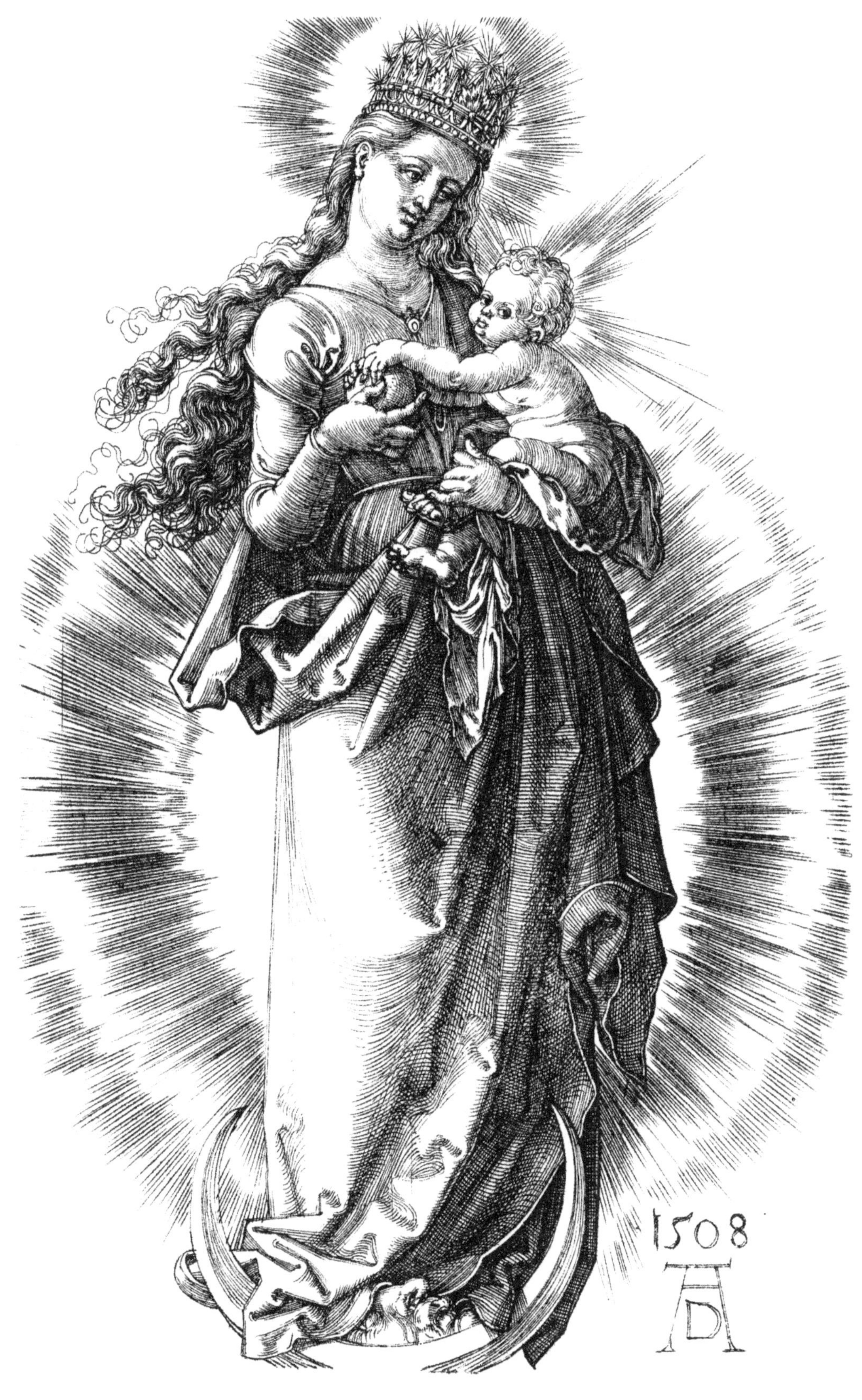

25. Mary, a starry crown on the head, with child
on the crescent moon. Albrecht Dürer, 1508

26

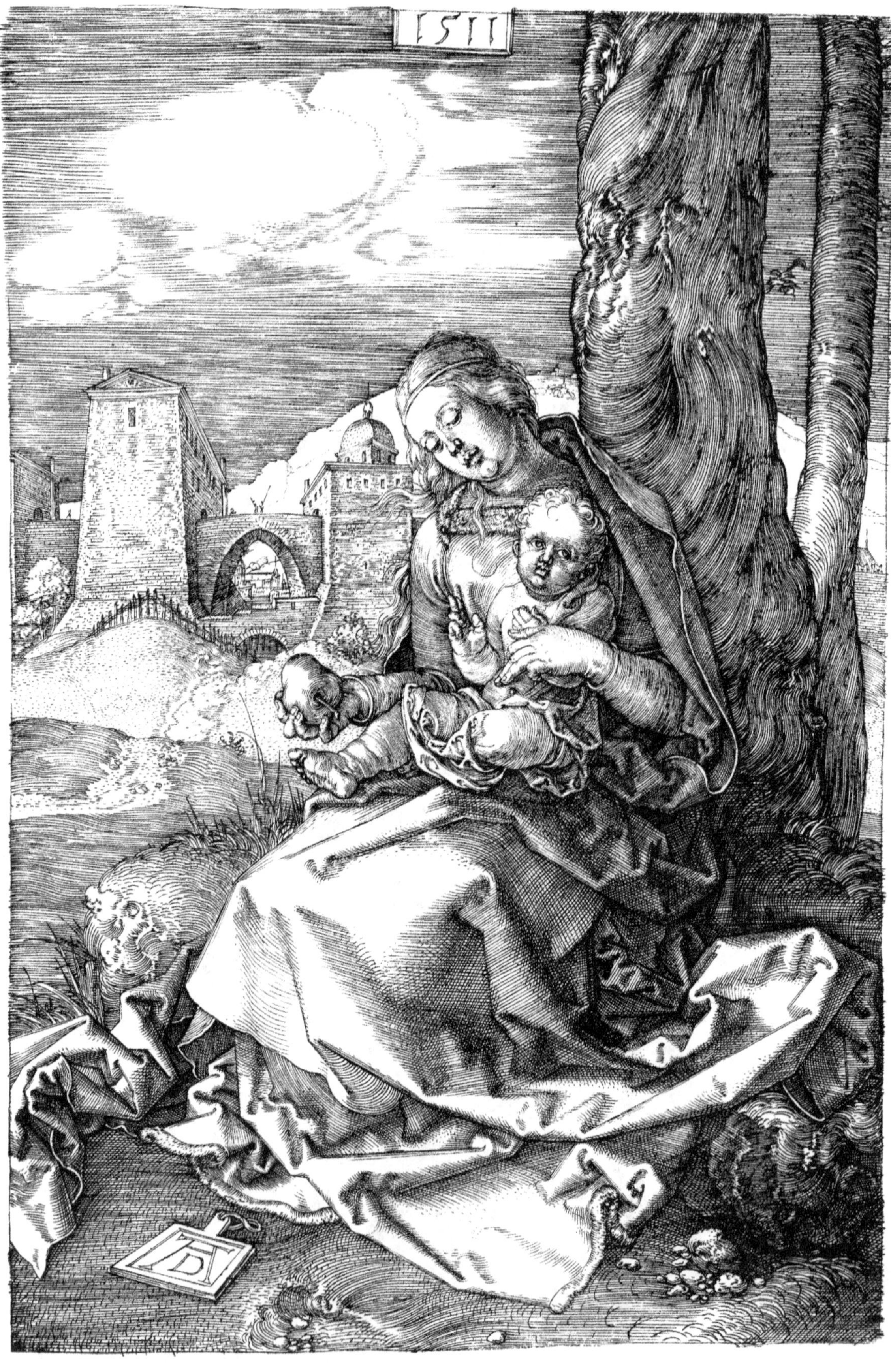

26. Mary with Child and a Pear. Albrecht Dürer, 1511

27

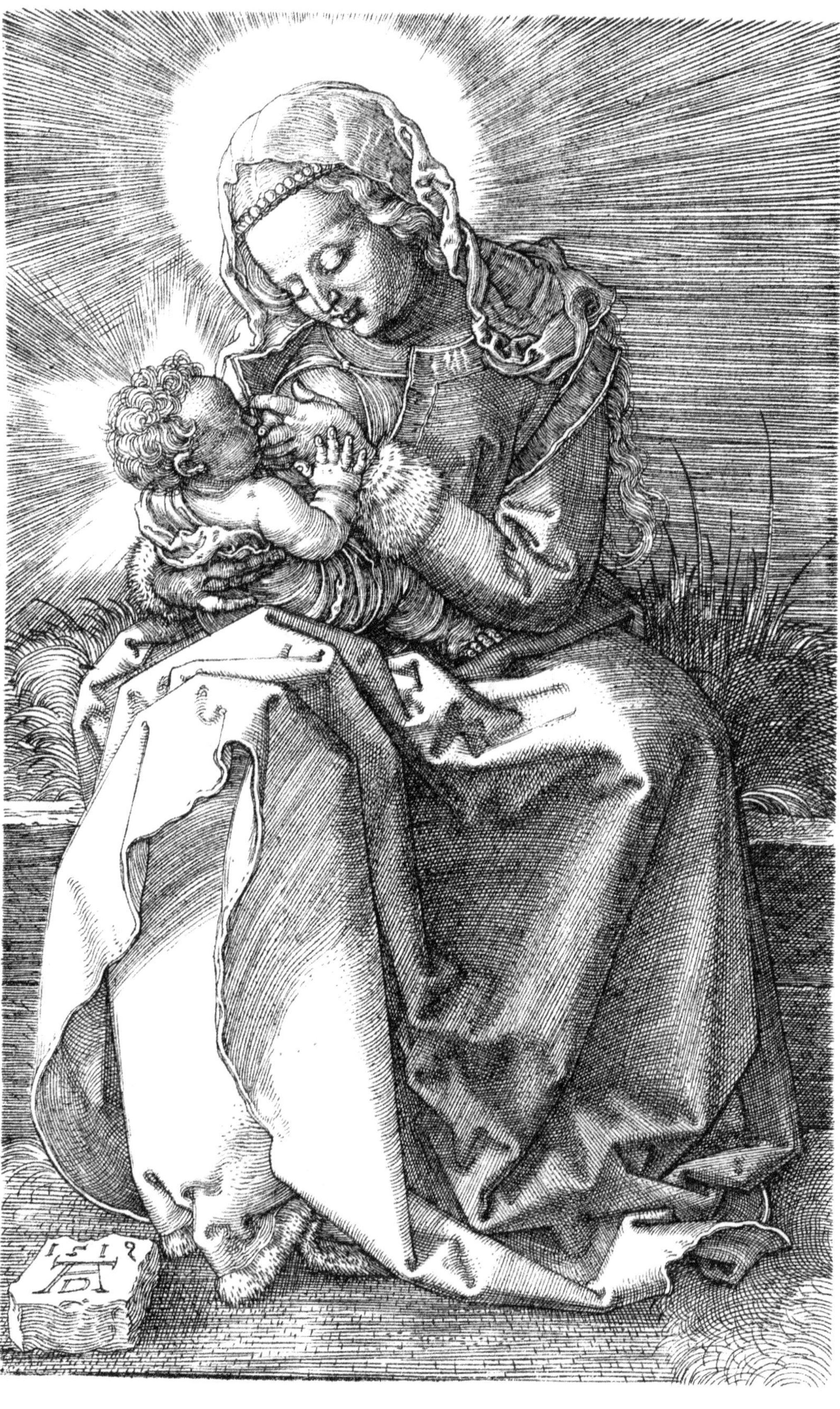

ALBRECHT DÜRER

27. Mary with Child at the Breast, Albrecht
Dürer, 1519

28

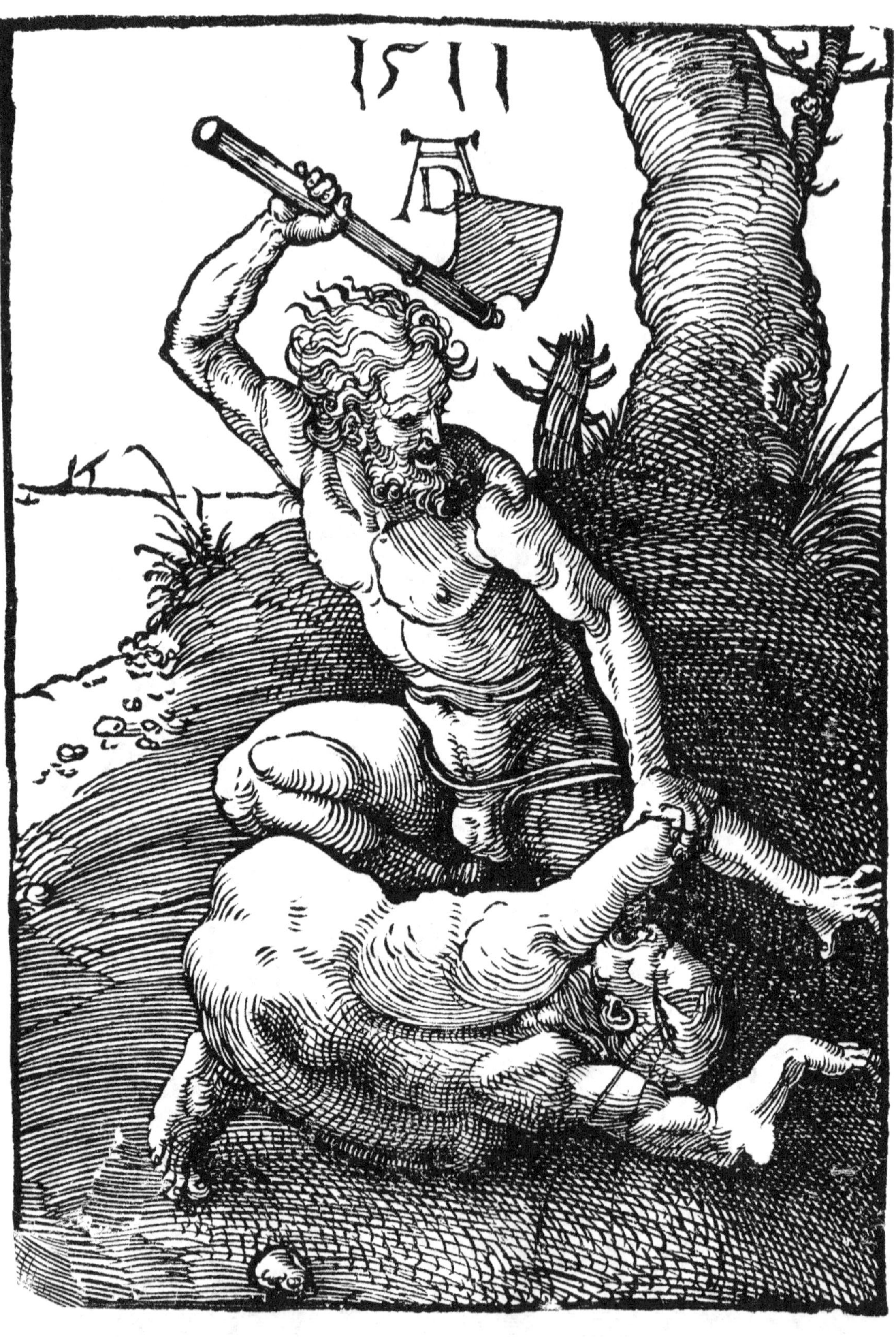

28. Cain kills Abel, Albrecht Dürer, 1511

29

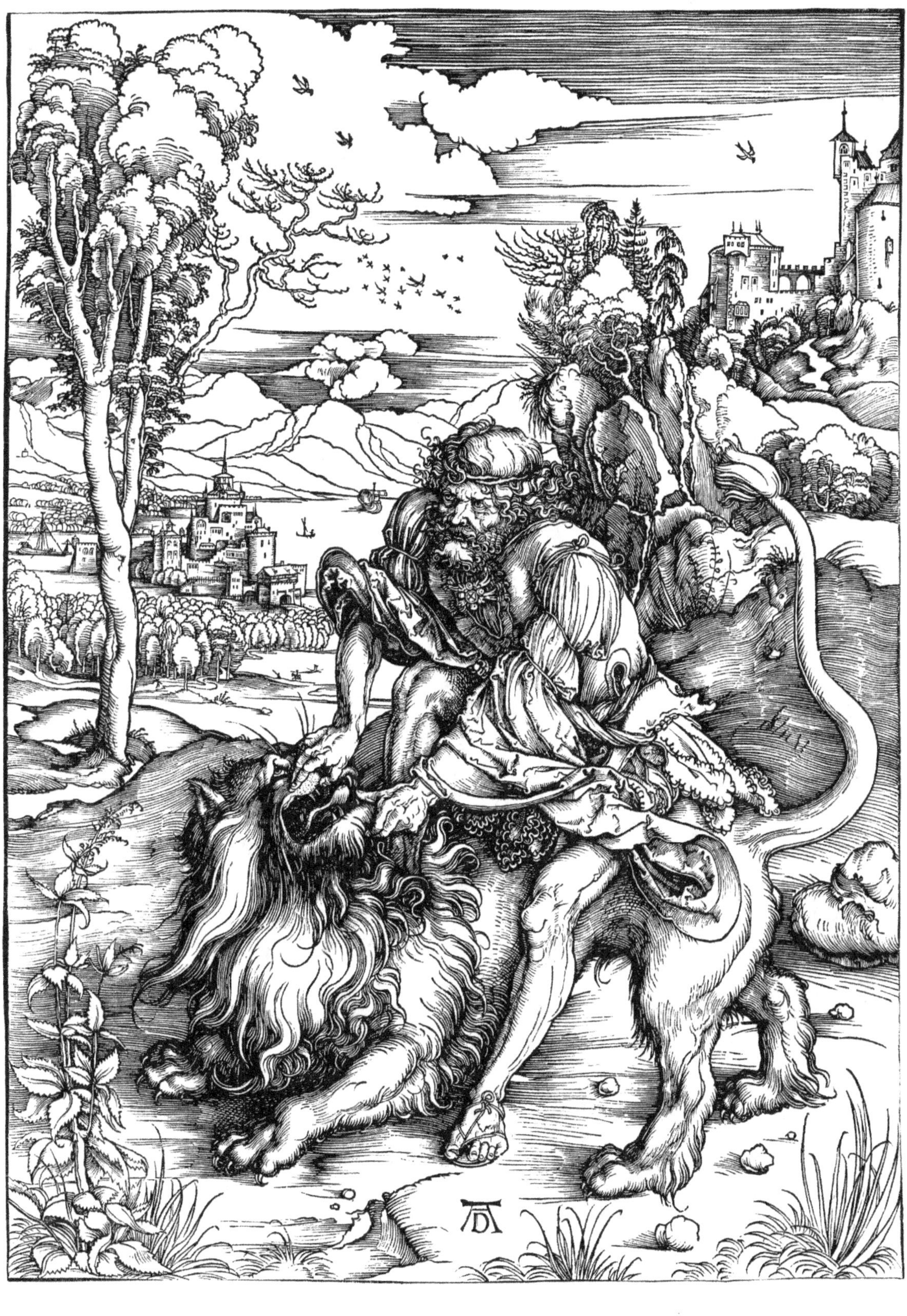

29. Samson Fighting the Lion, Albrecht Dürer.
1494 - 1498

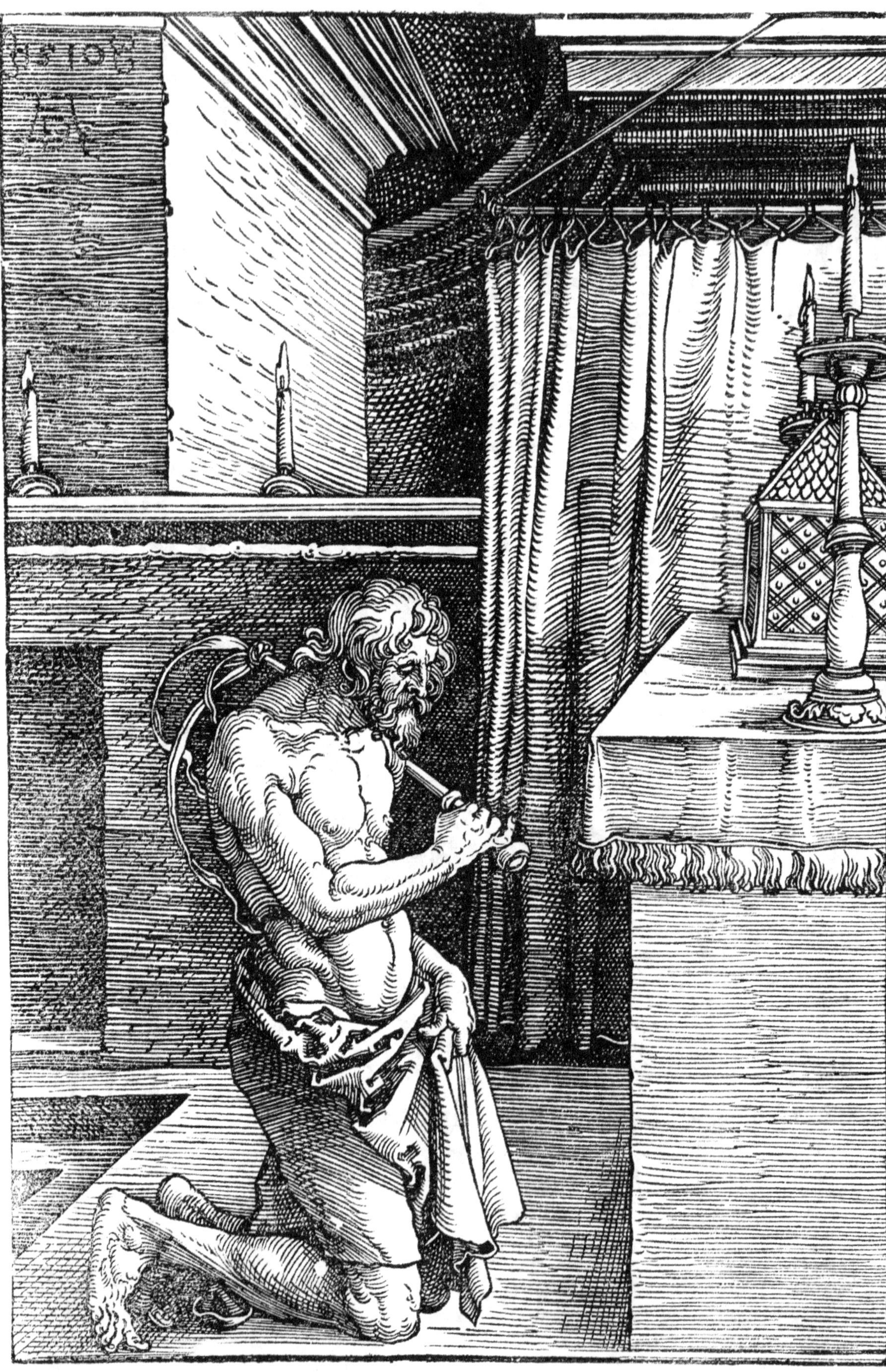

30. *The Penitent Man (King David), Albrecht*
Dürer, 1535 - 1545

31

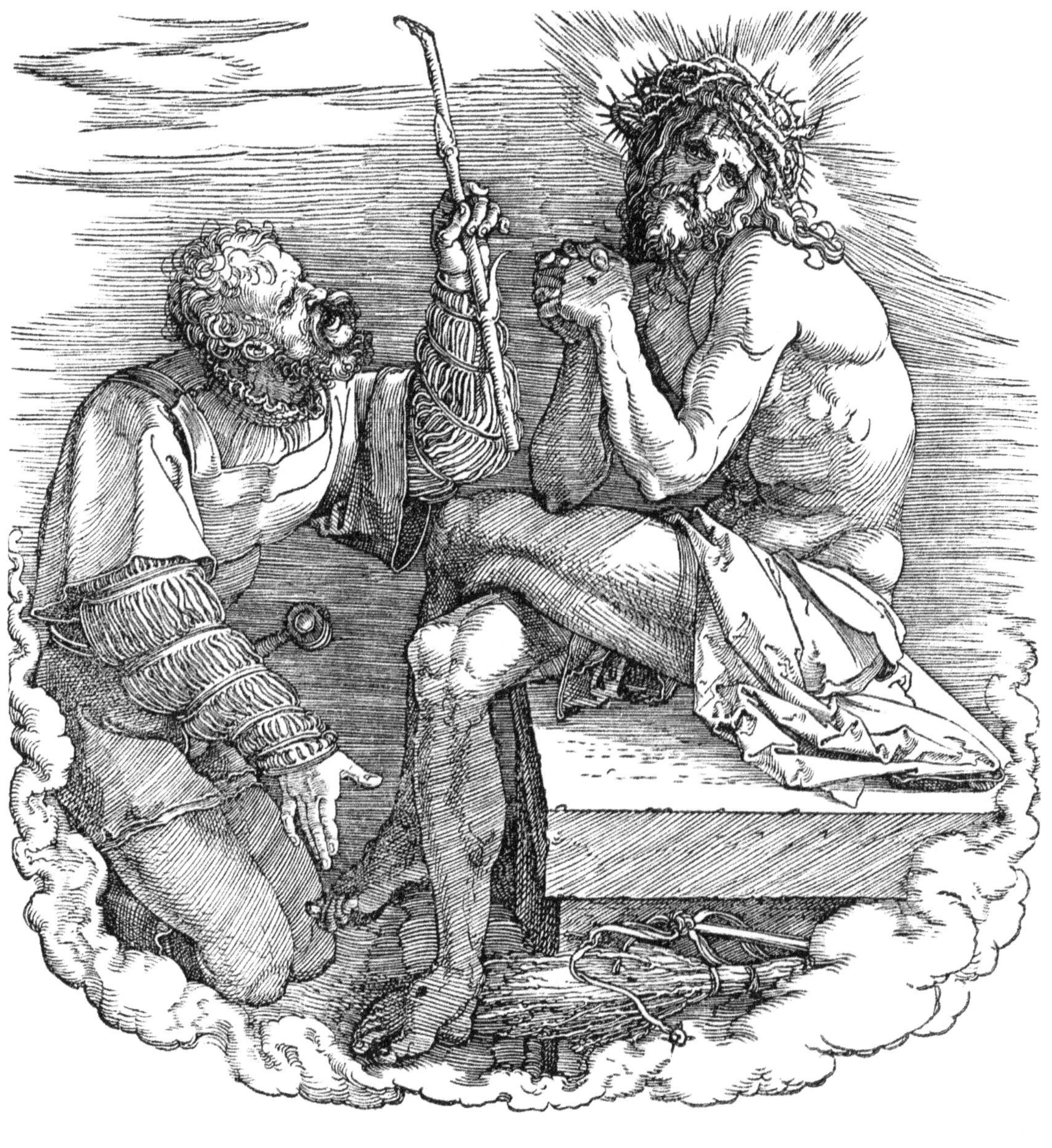

ALBRECHT DÜRER

32

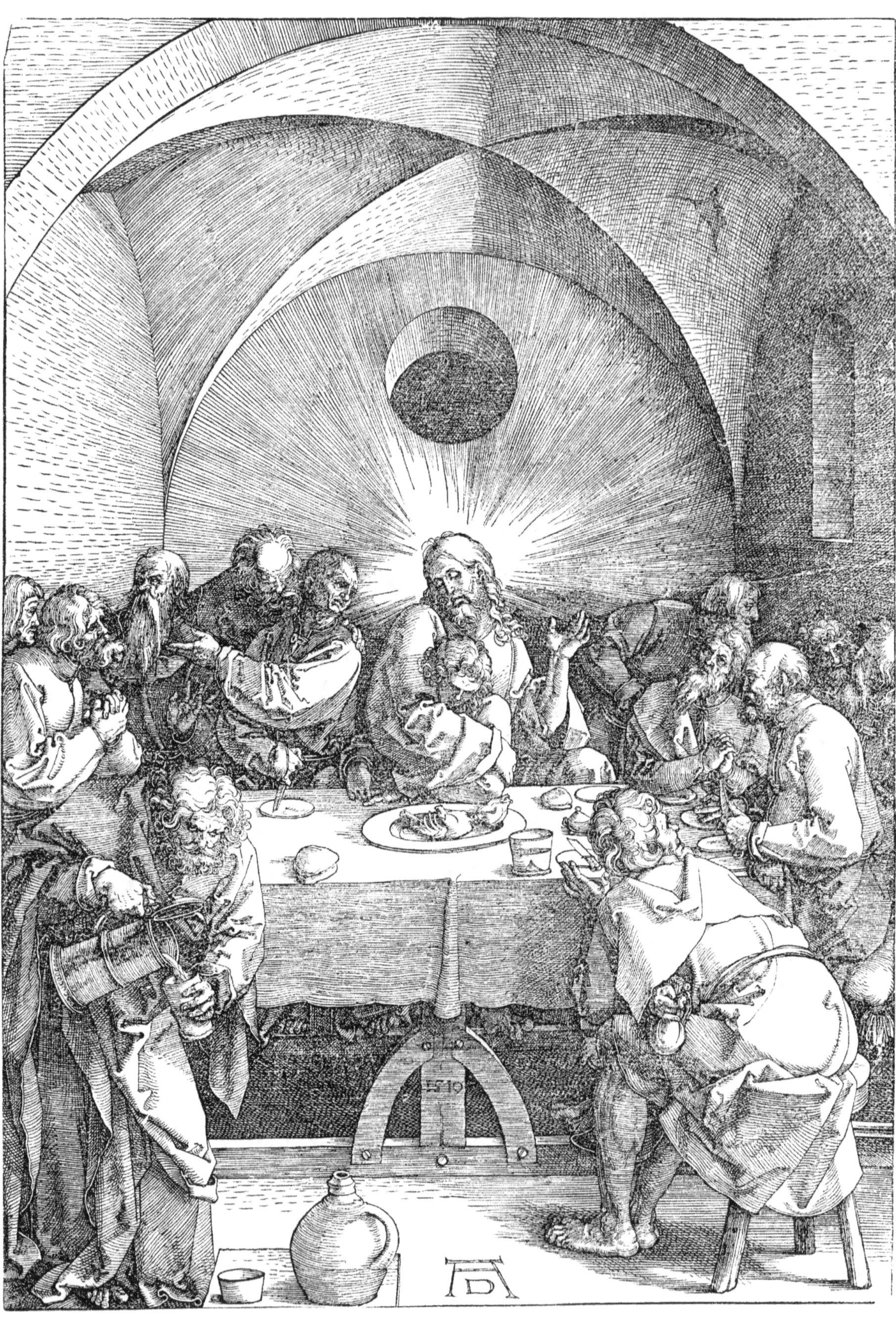

ALBRECHT DÜRER

33

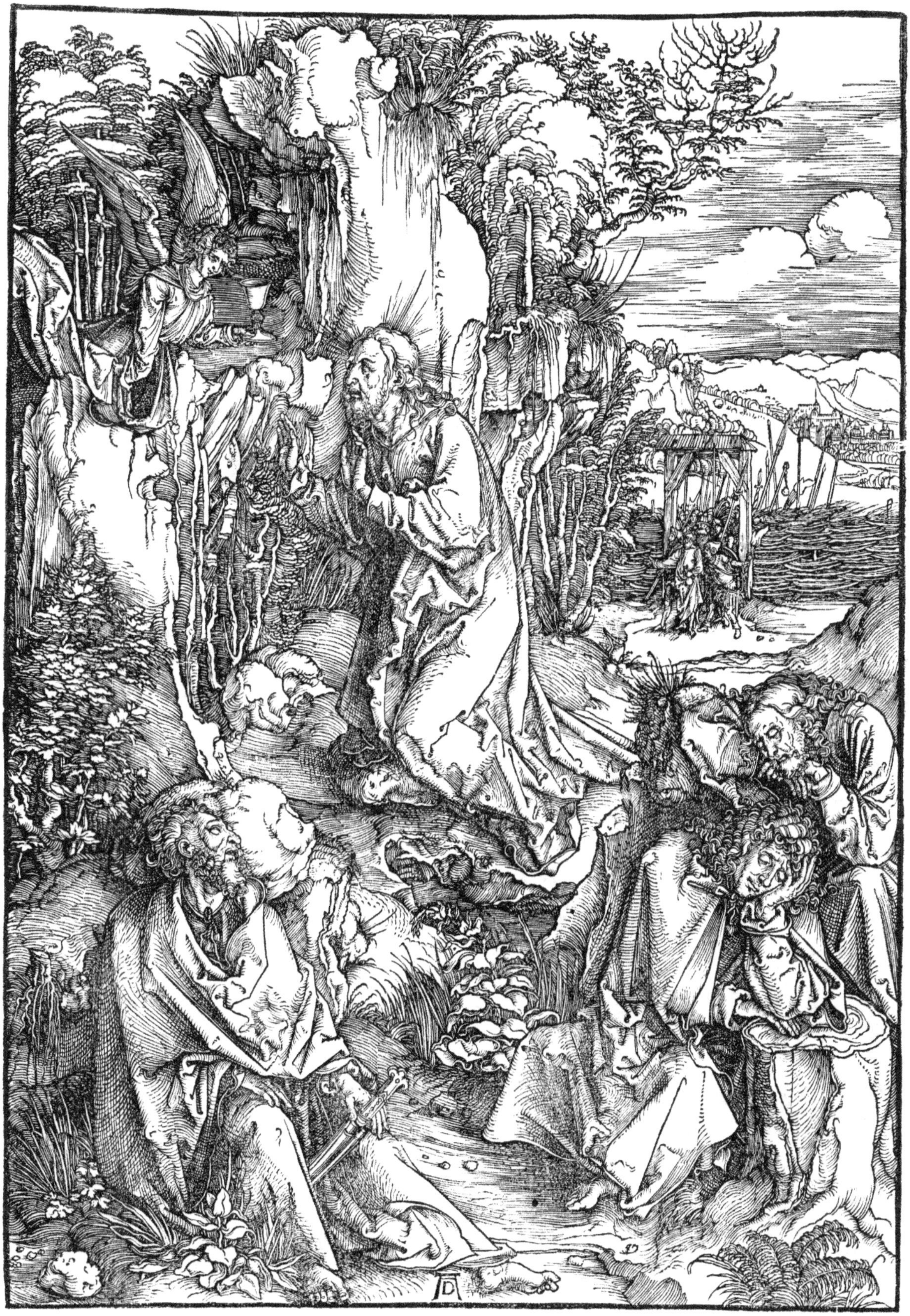

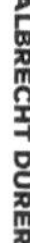

ALBRECHT DÜRER

33 Christ on the Mount of Olives, Albrecht
Dürer, 1496 - 1497

34

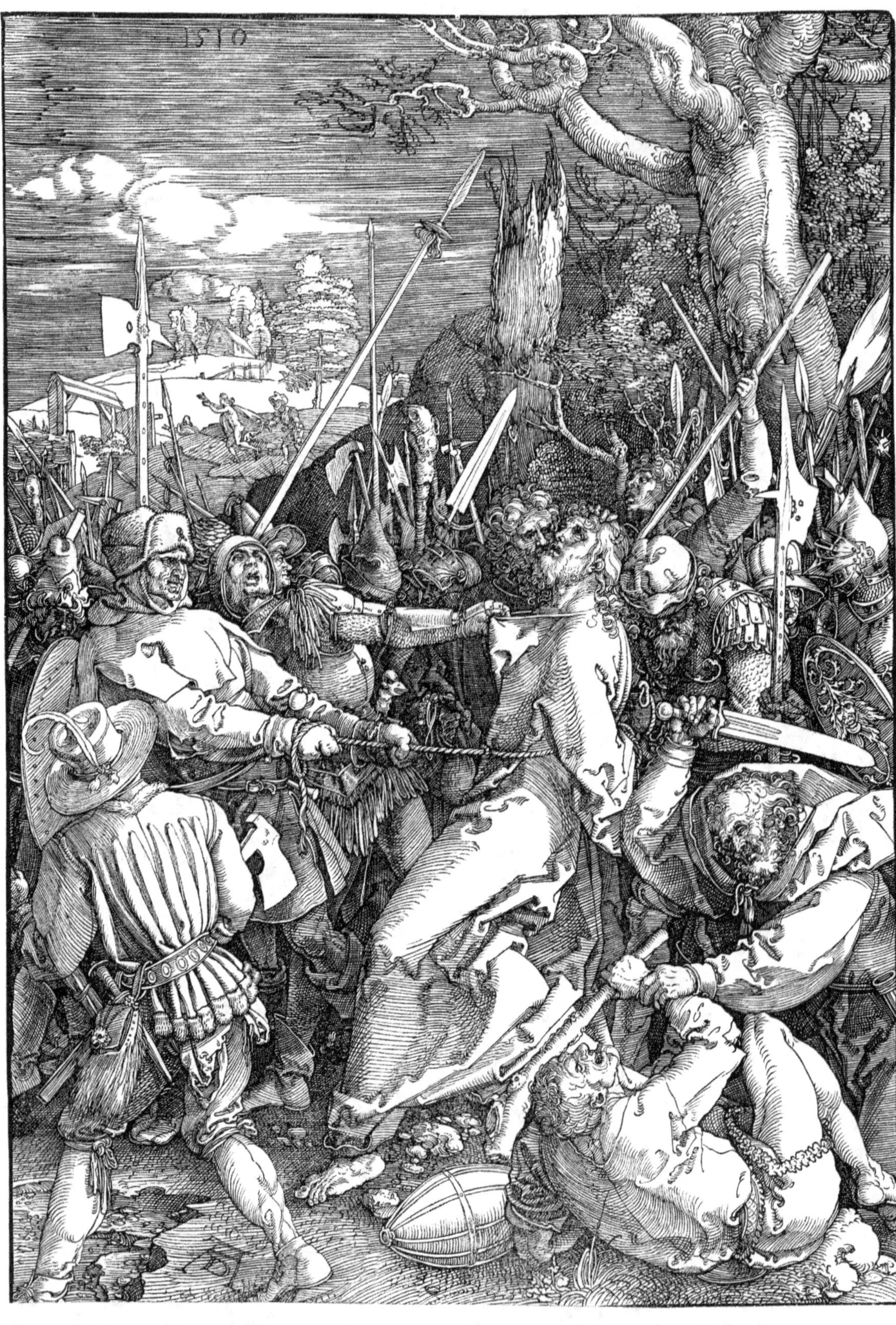

34. Capture, Albrecht Dürer, 1510

35

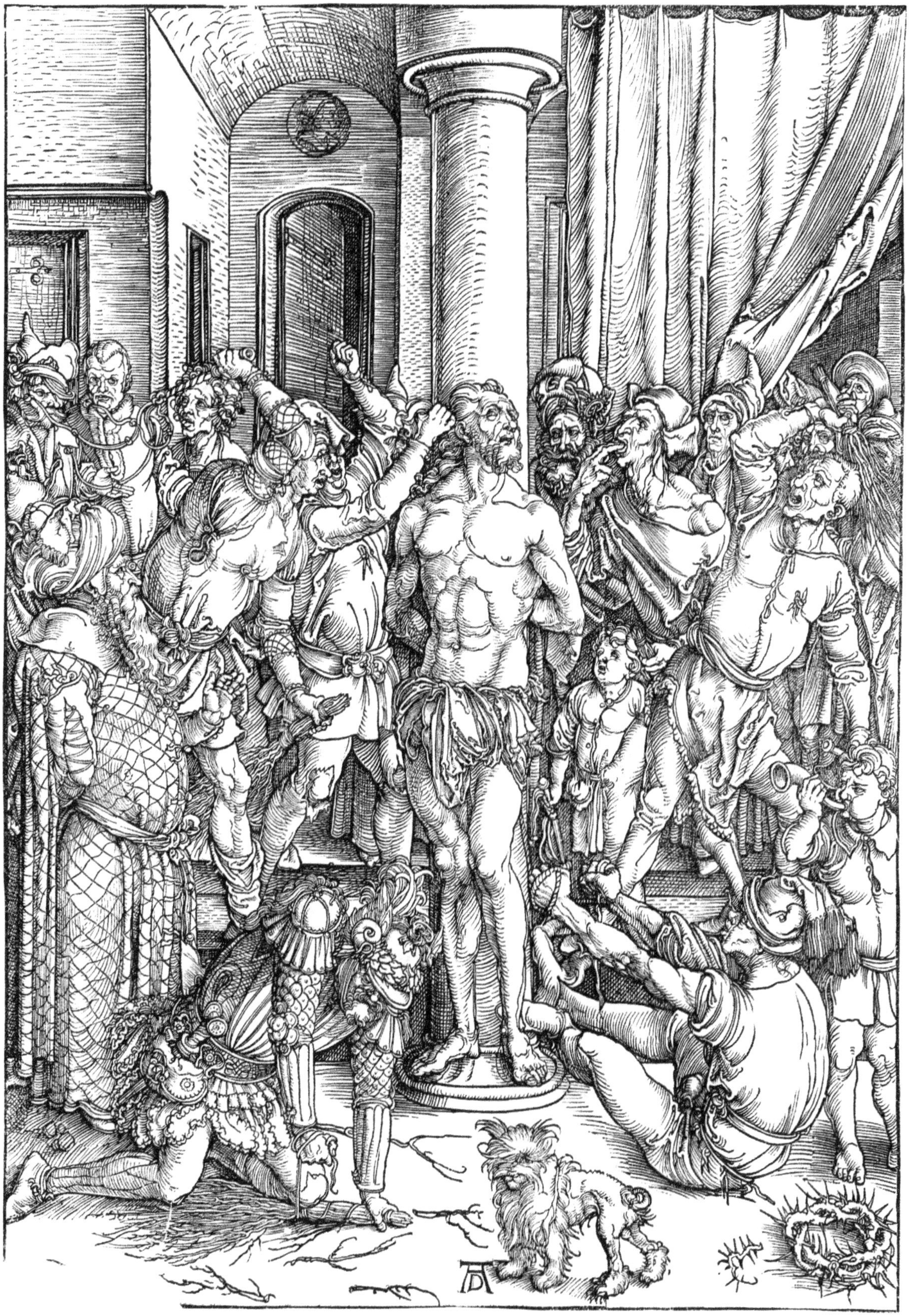

ALBRECHT DÜRER

35. Flagellation of Christ. Albrecht Dürer.
1496 - 1497.

36

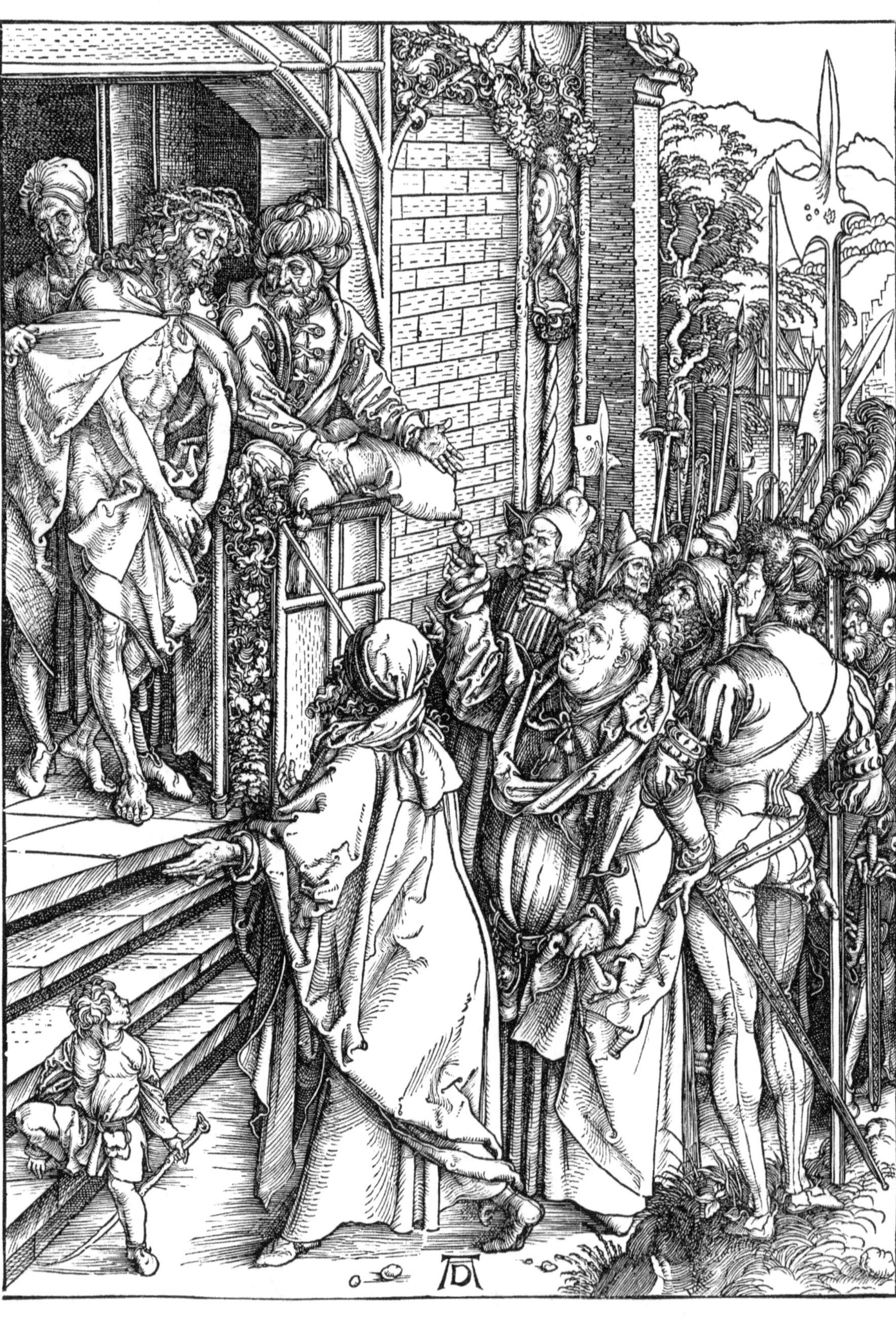

36. Christ Shown to the People (Ecce homo),
Albrecht Dürer, 1498

37

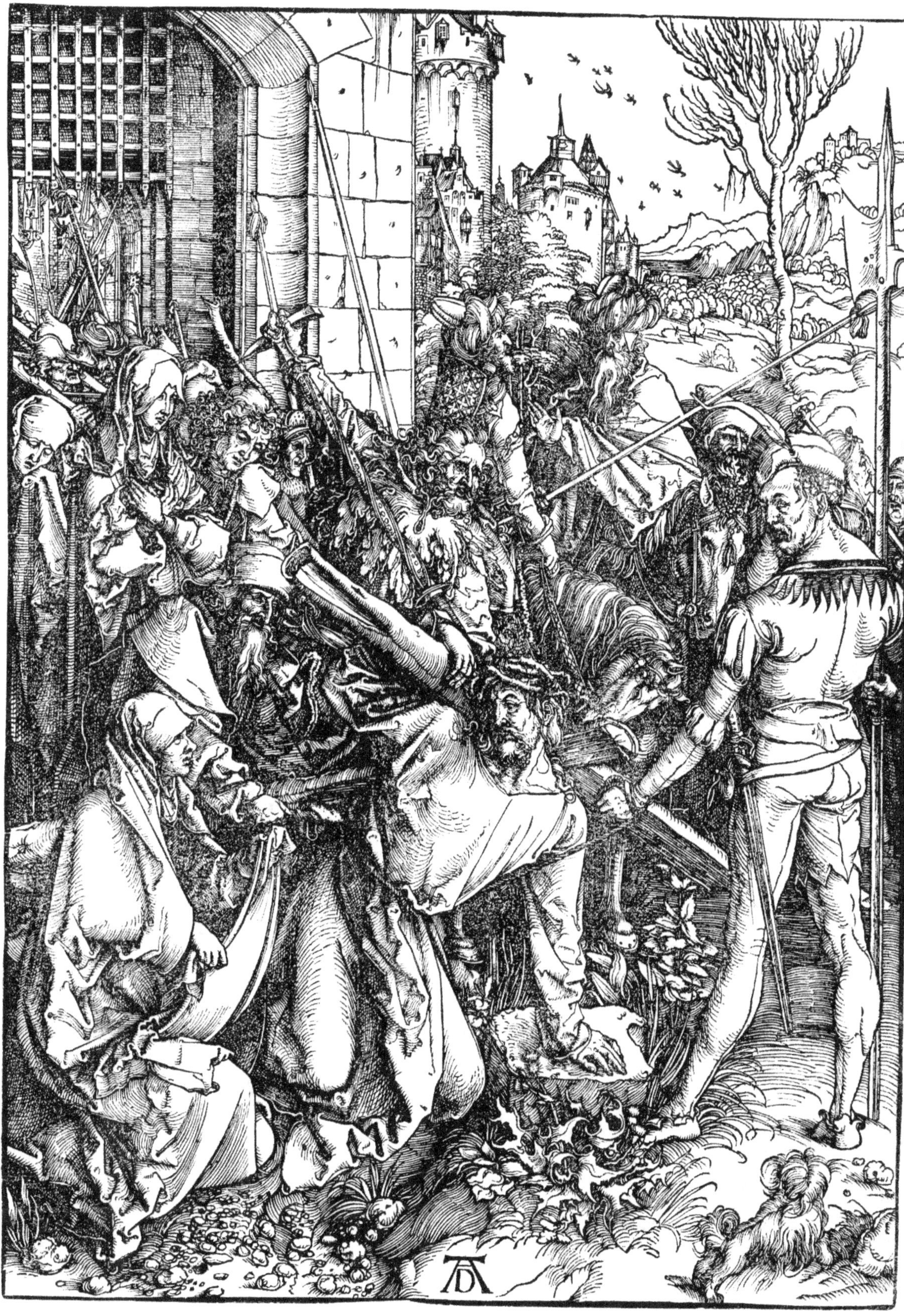

ALBRECHT DÜRER

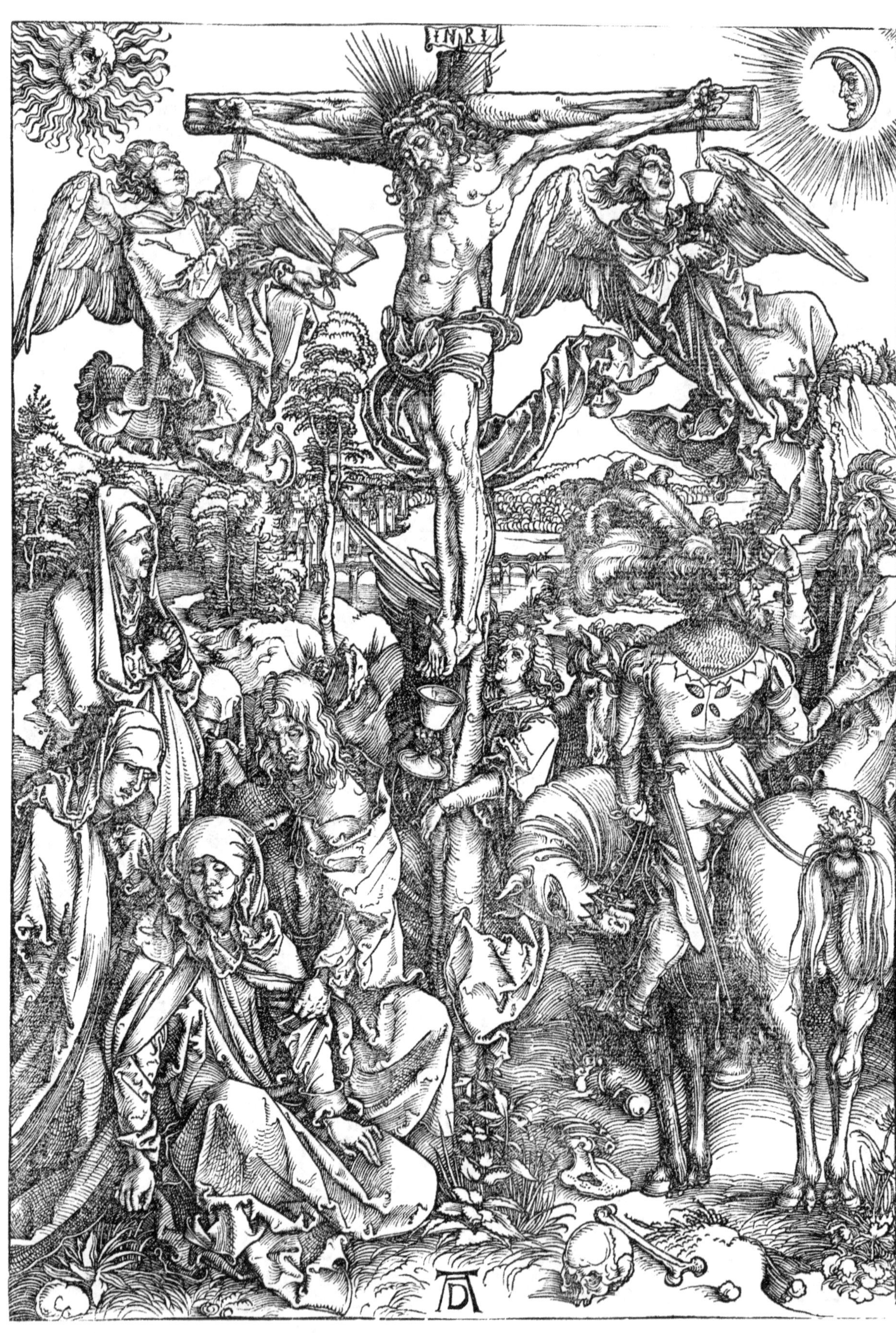

38. The Crucifiction, Albrecht Dürer, 1511

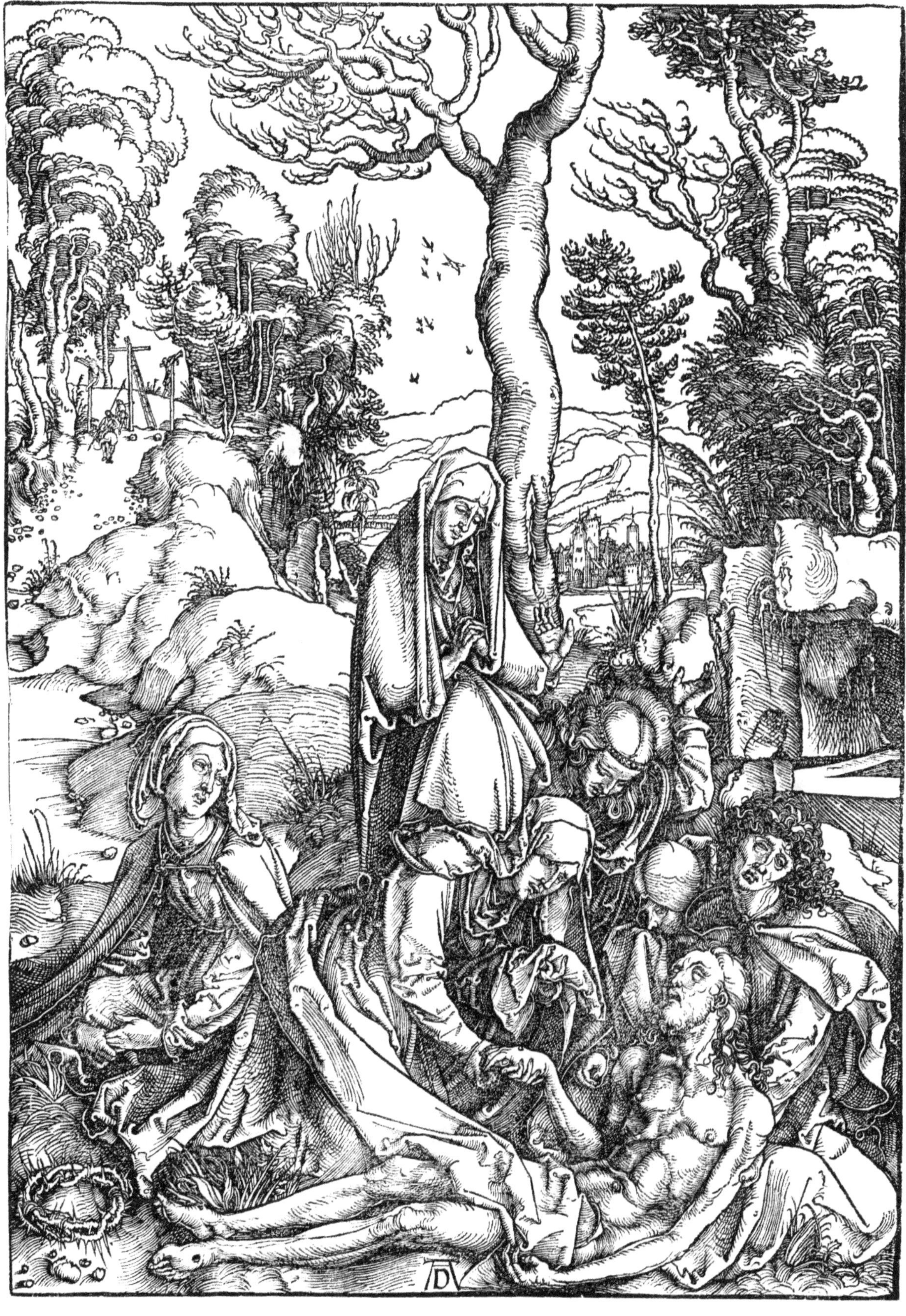

39. Lamentation, Albrecht Dürer, 1511

40

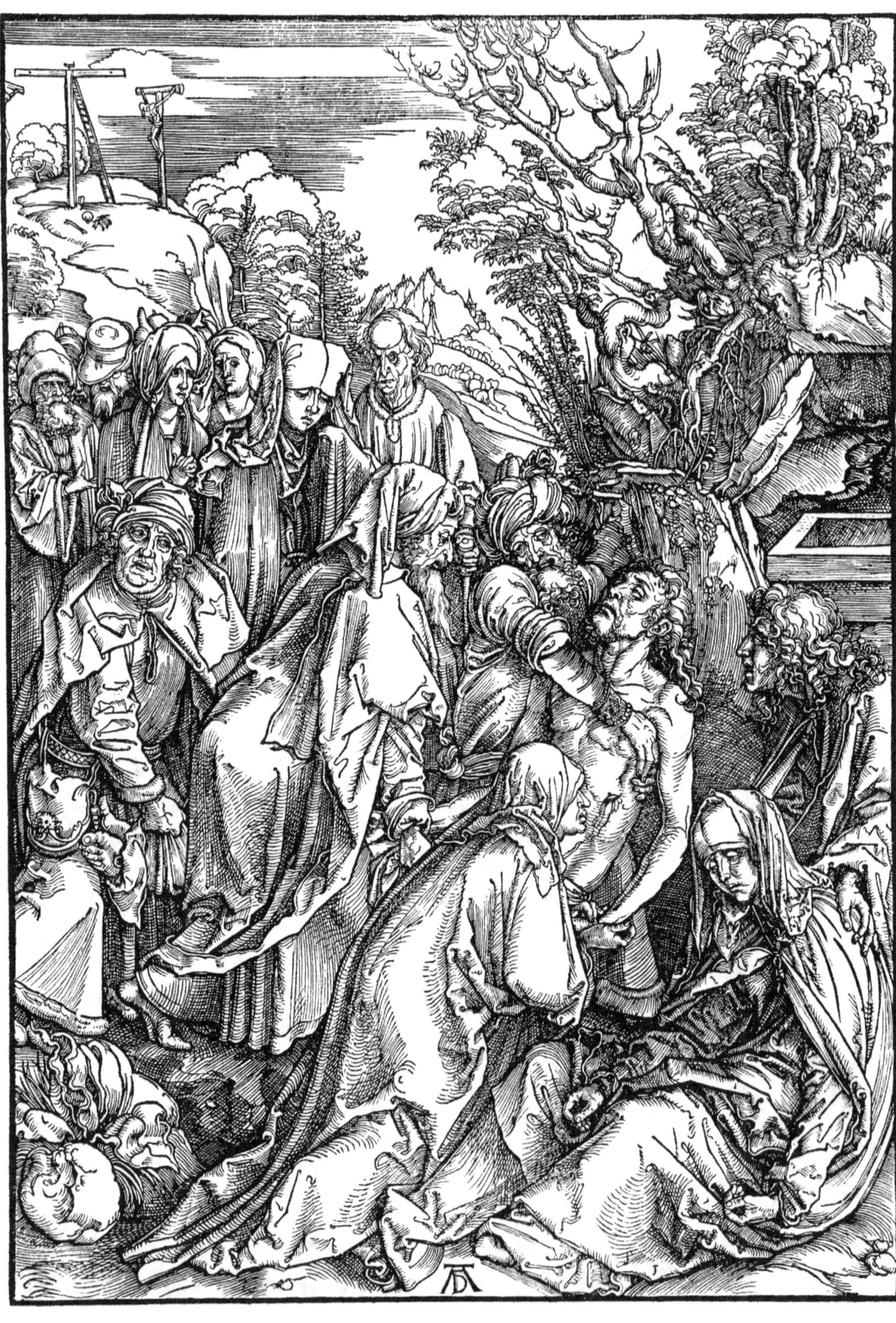

40. *The Entombment, Albrecht Dürer*

41

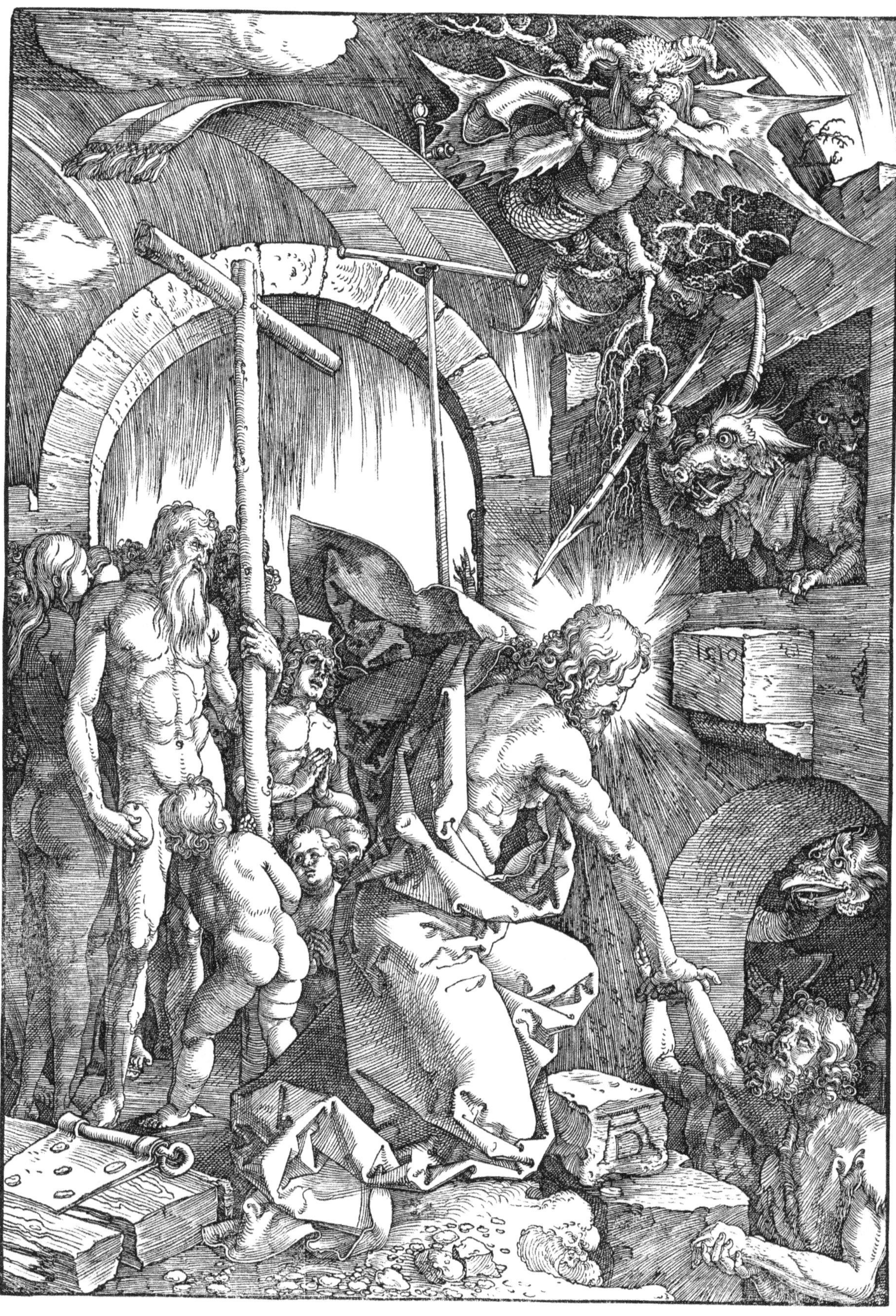

ALBRECHT DÜRER

41. Descent into Limbo, Albrecht Dürer, 1510.

42

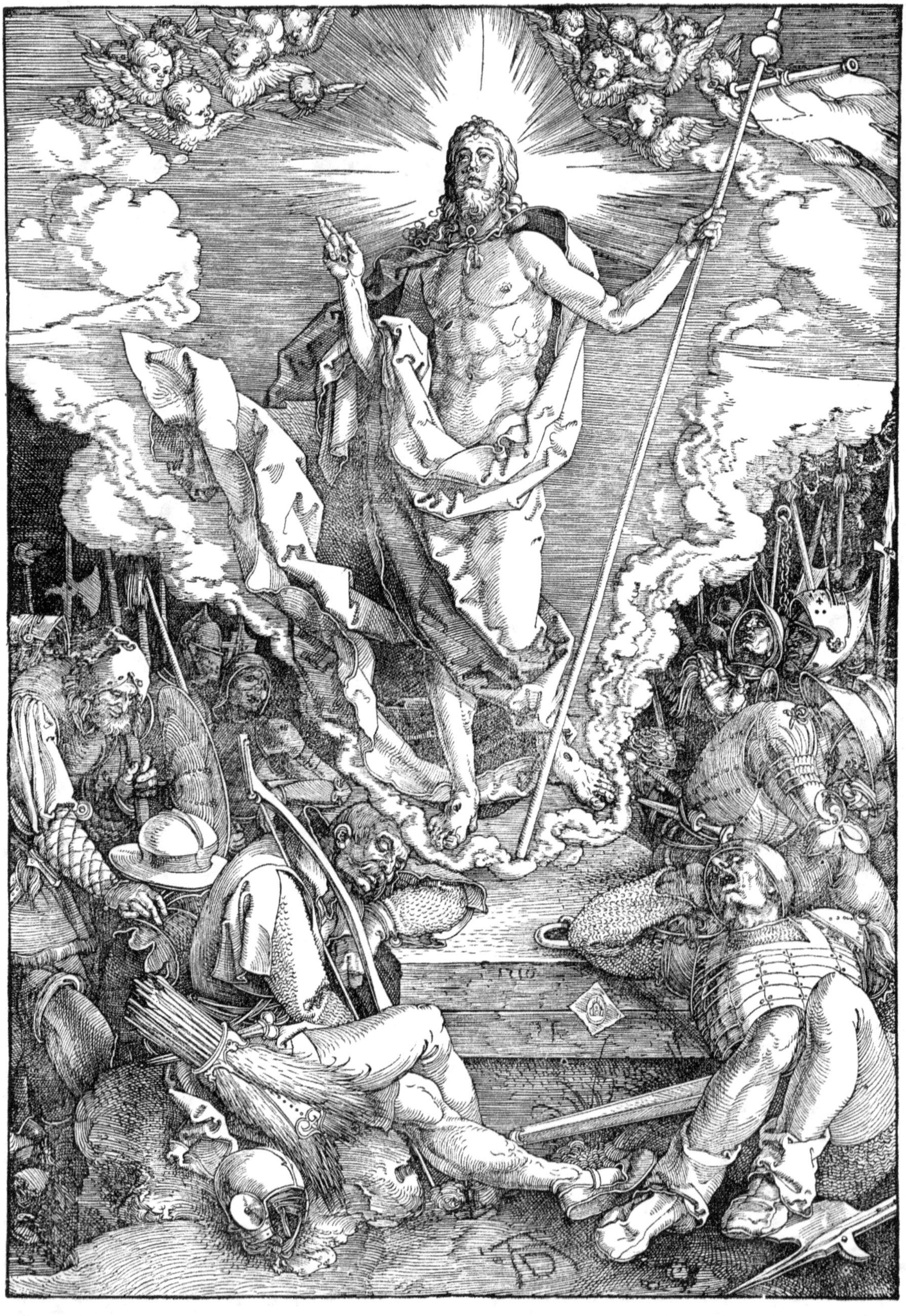

ALBRECHT DÜRER

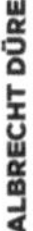

42. Resurrection, Albrecht Dürer. 1565 - 1575

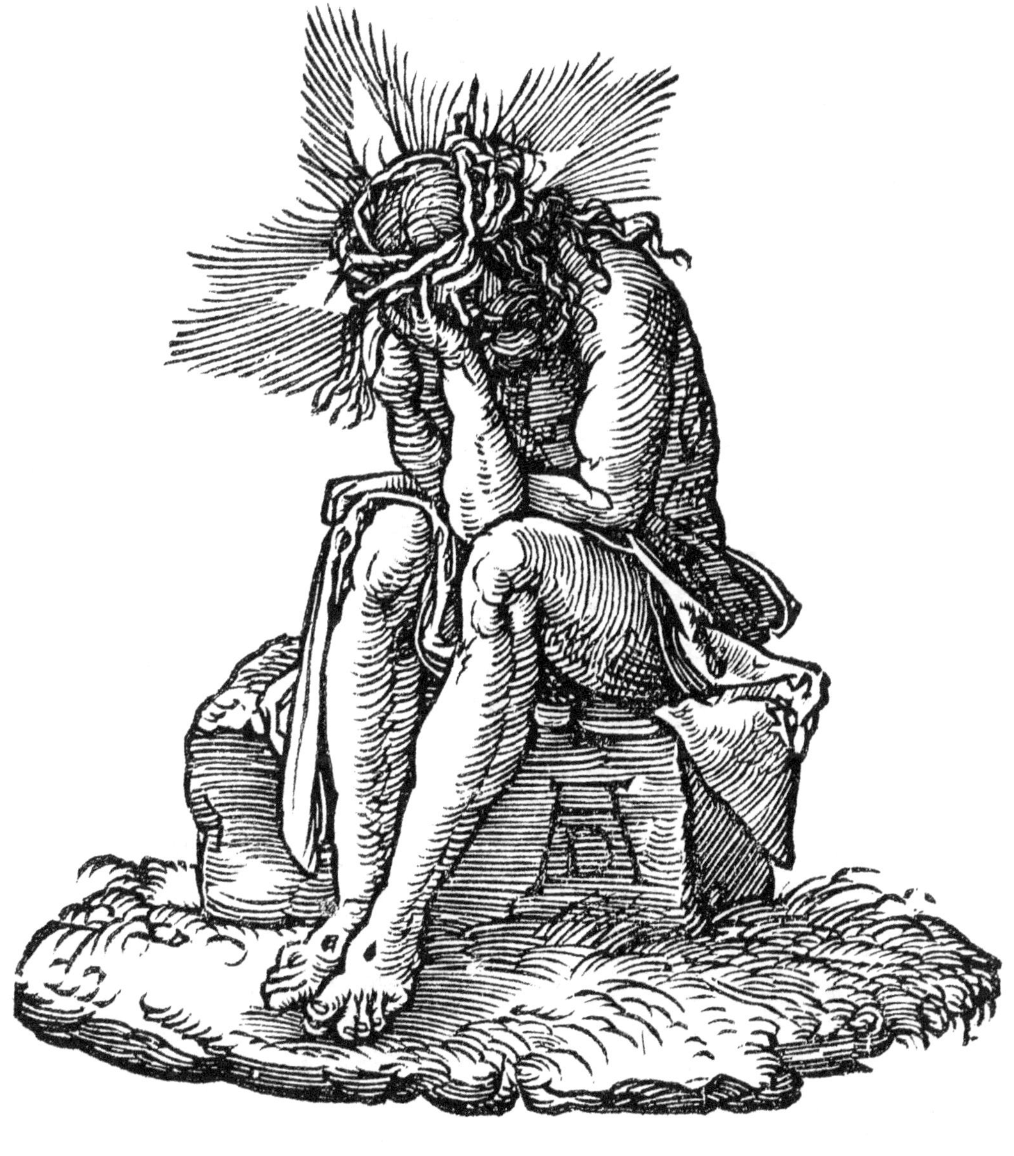

43. The Man of Sorrows Seated, title page of
"The Small Passion" (copy). J. Mommard. After
A. Dürer, 1509-1510.

44

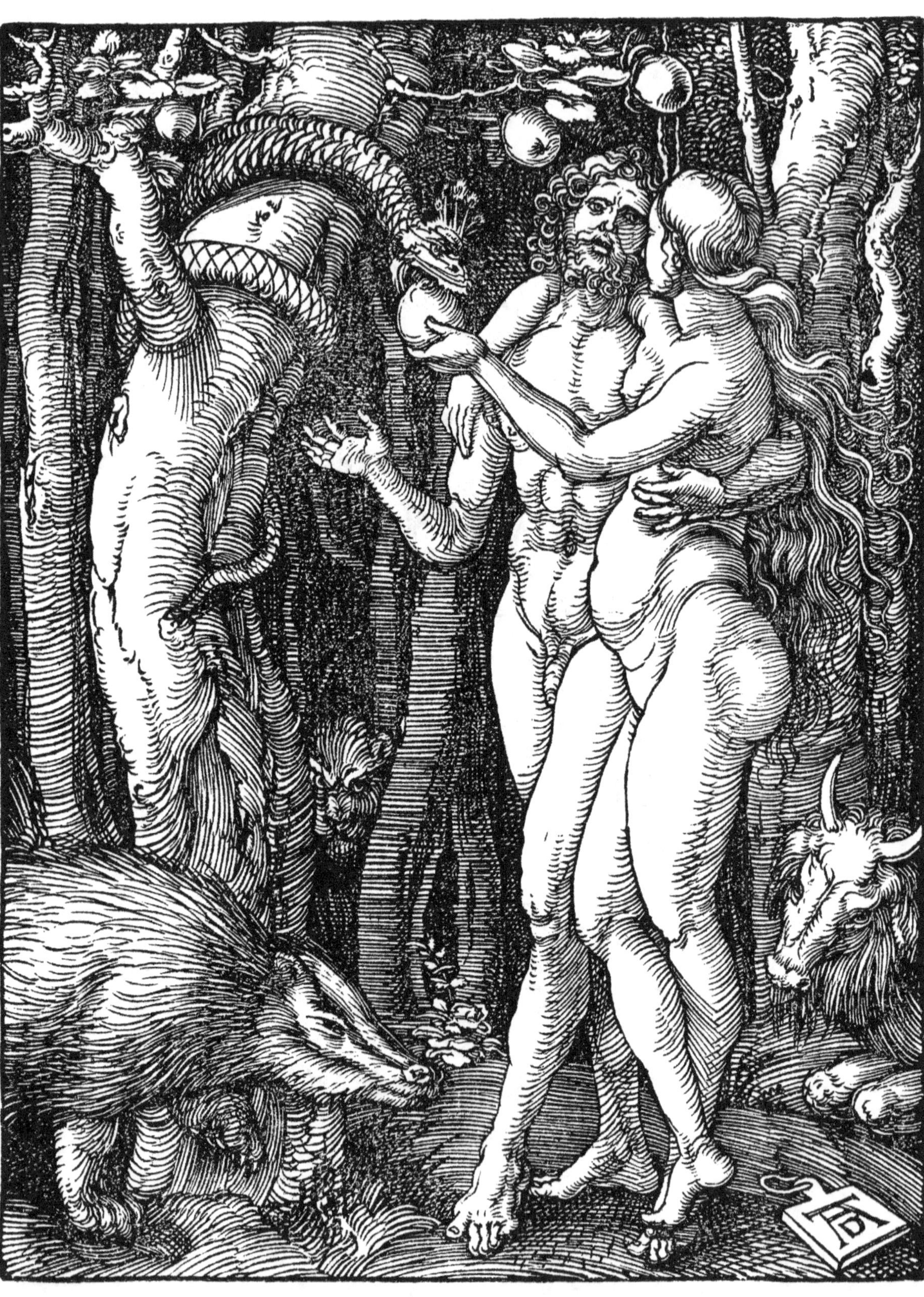

44 *The Fall of Man, Albrecht Dürer, 1509–1511*

45

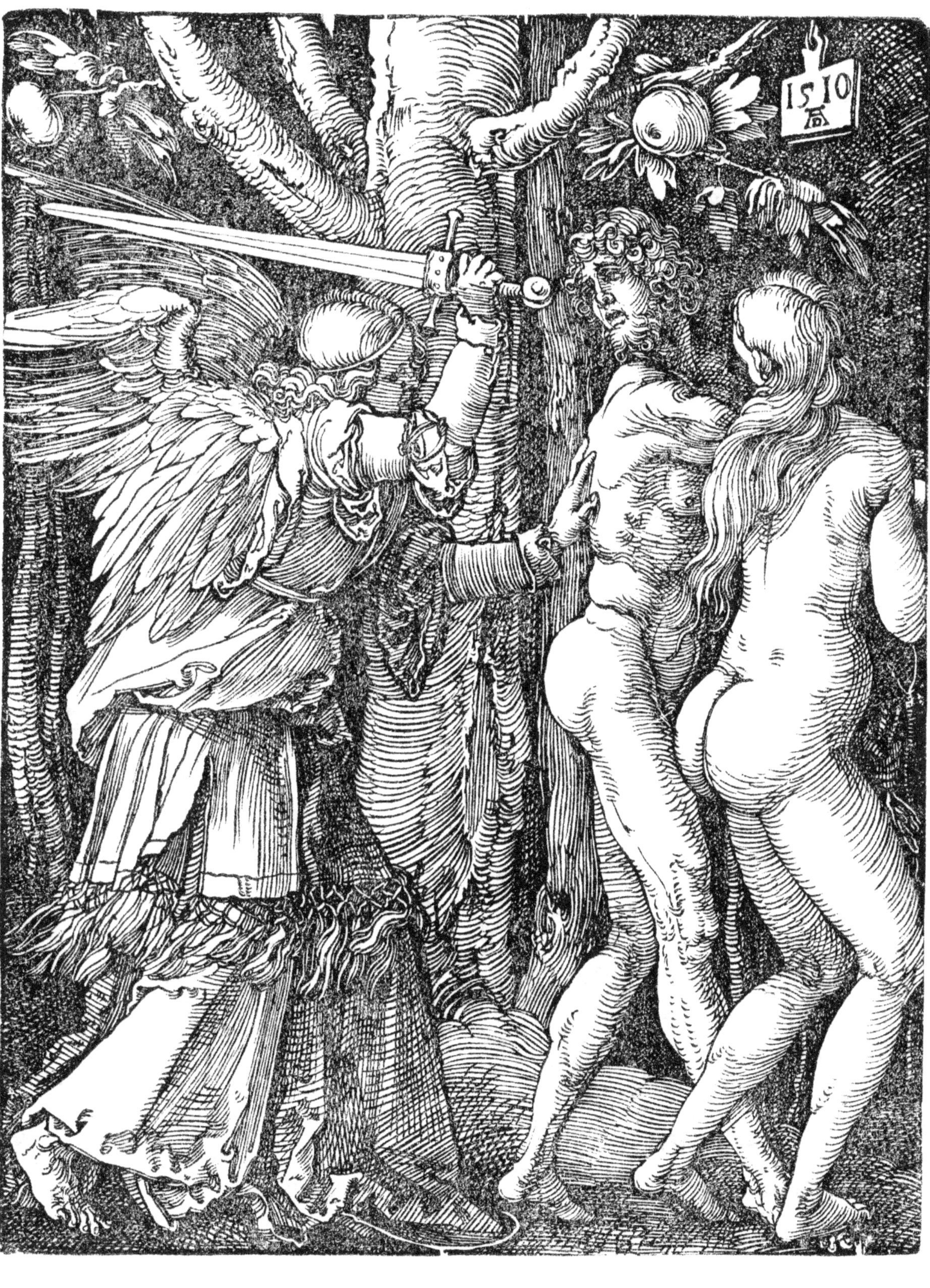

ALBRECHT DÜRER

45. Adam and Eve expelled from Paradise,
Albrecht Dürer, 1510

46

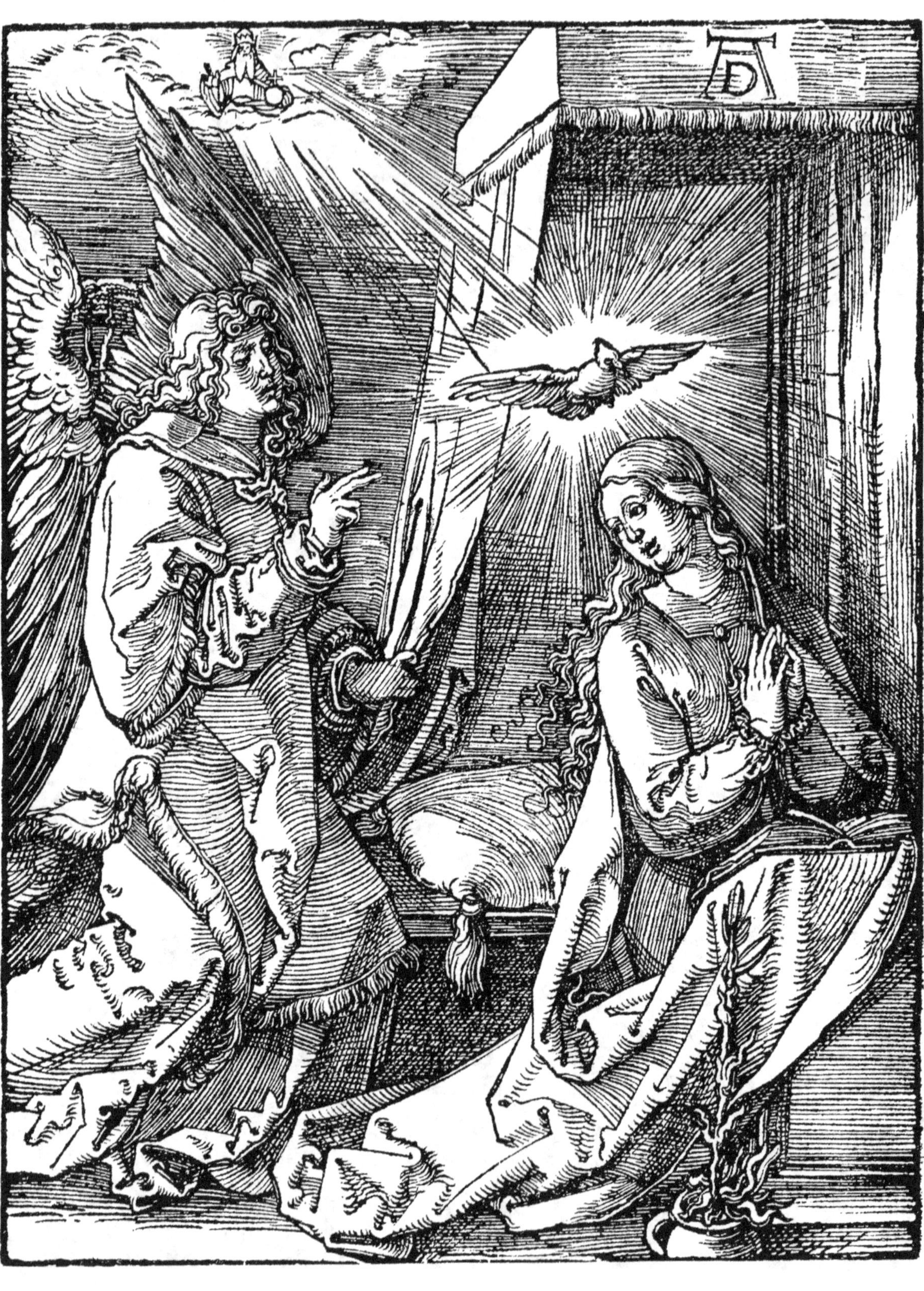

46. The Annunciation, Albrecht Dürer, 1510

47

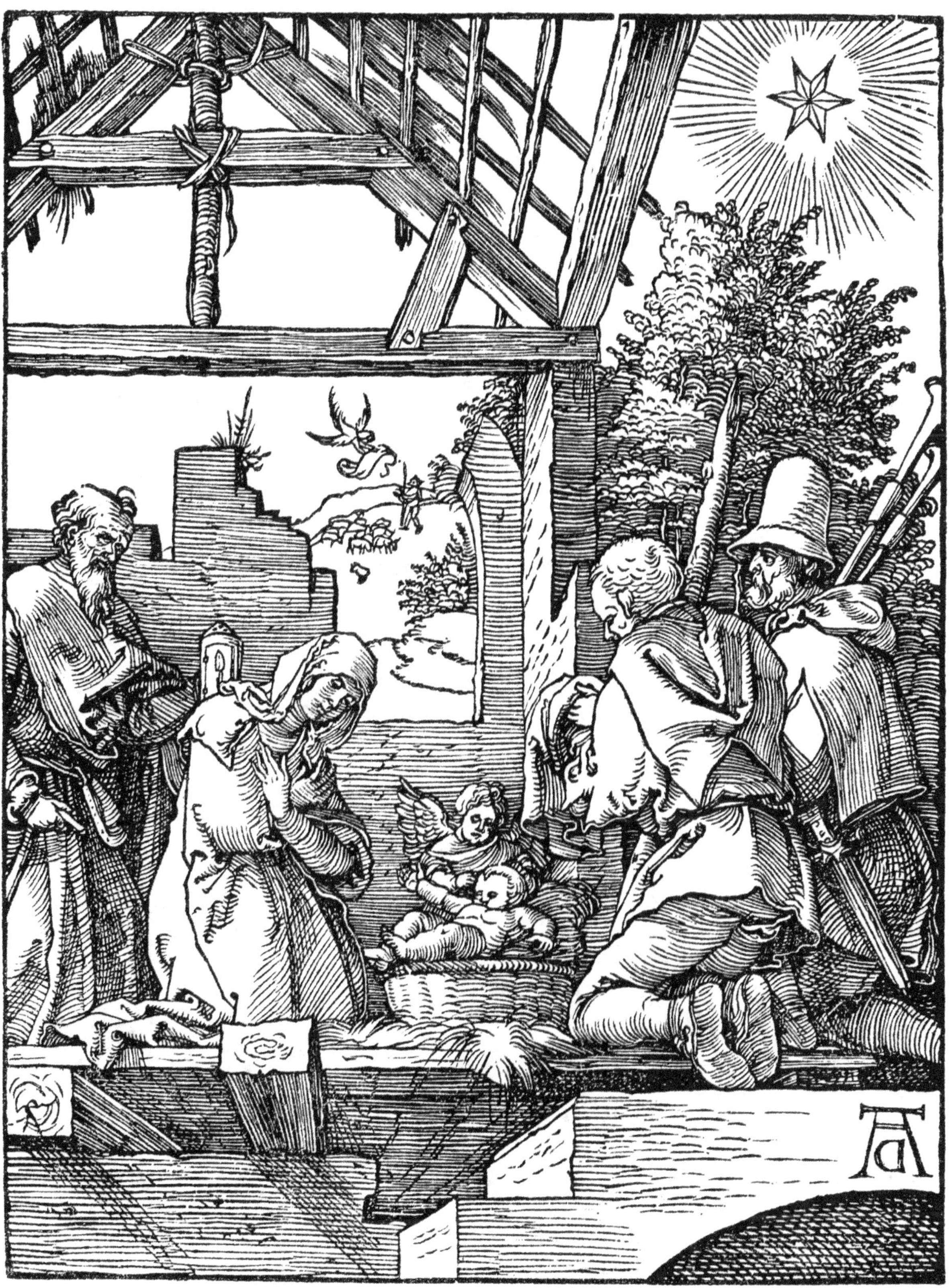

ALBRECHT DÜRER

48

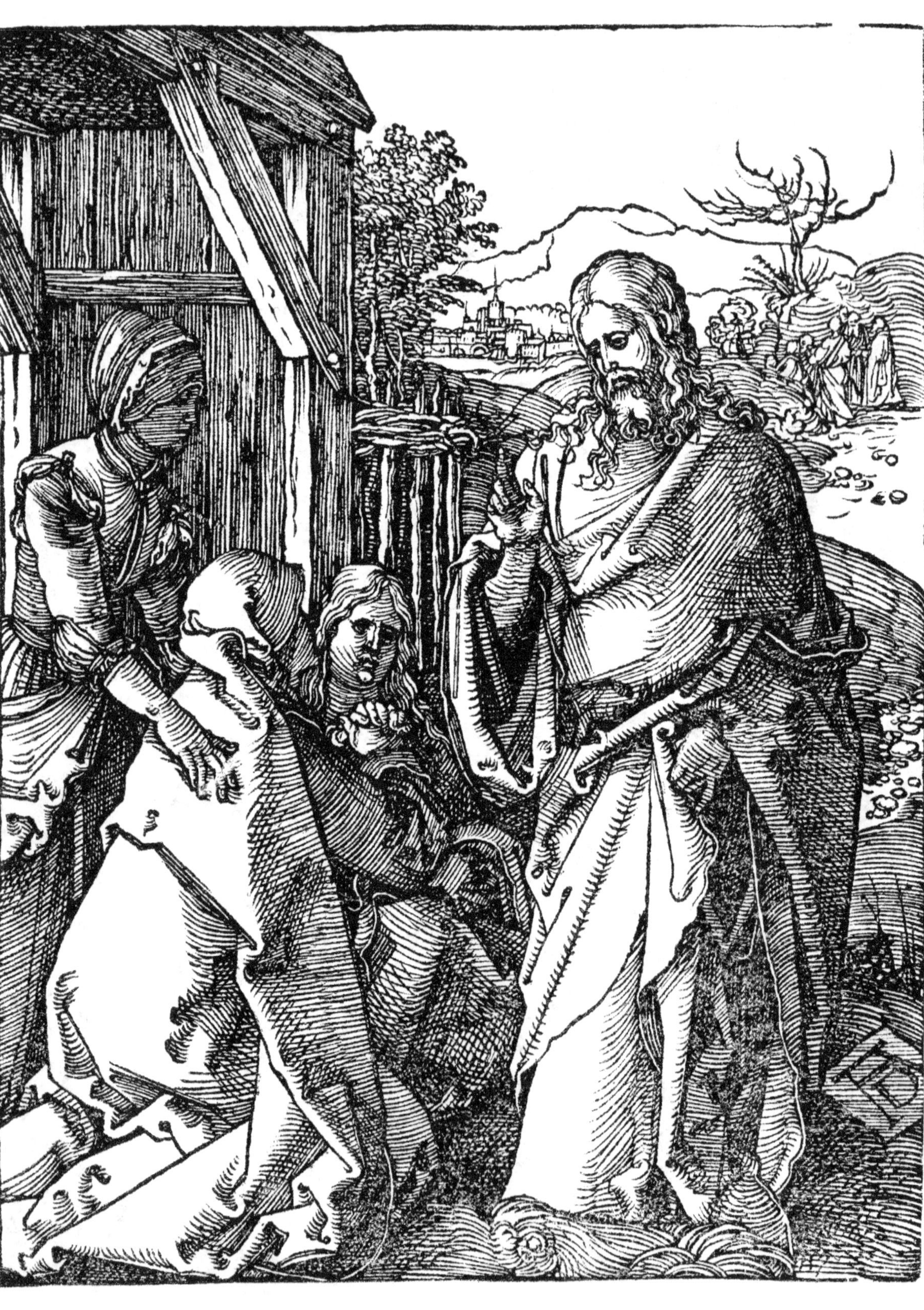

48. Christ says goodbye to his mother, Albrecht
Dürer, 1508 - 1509

49

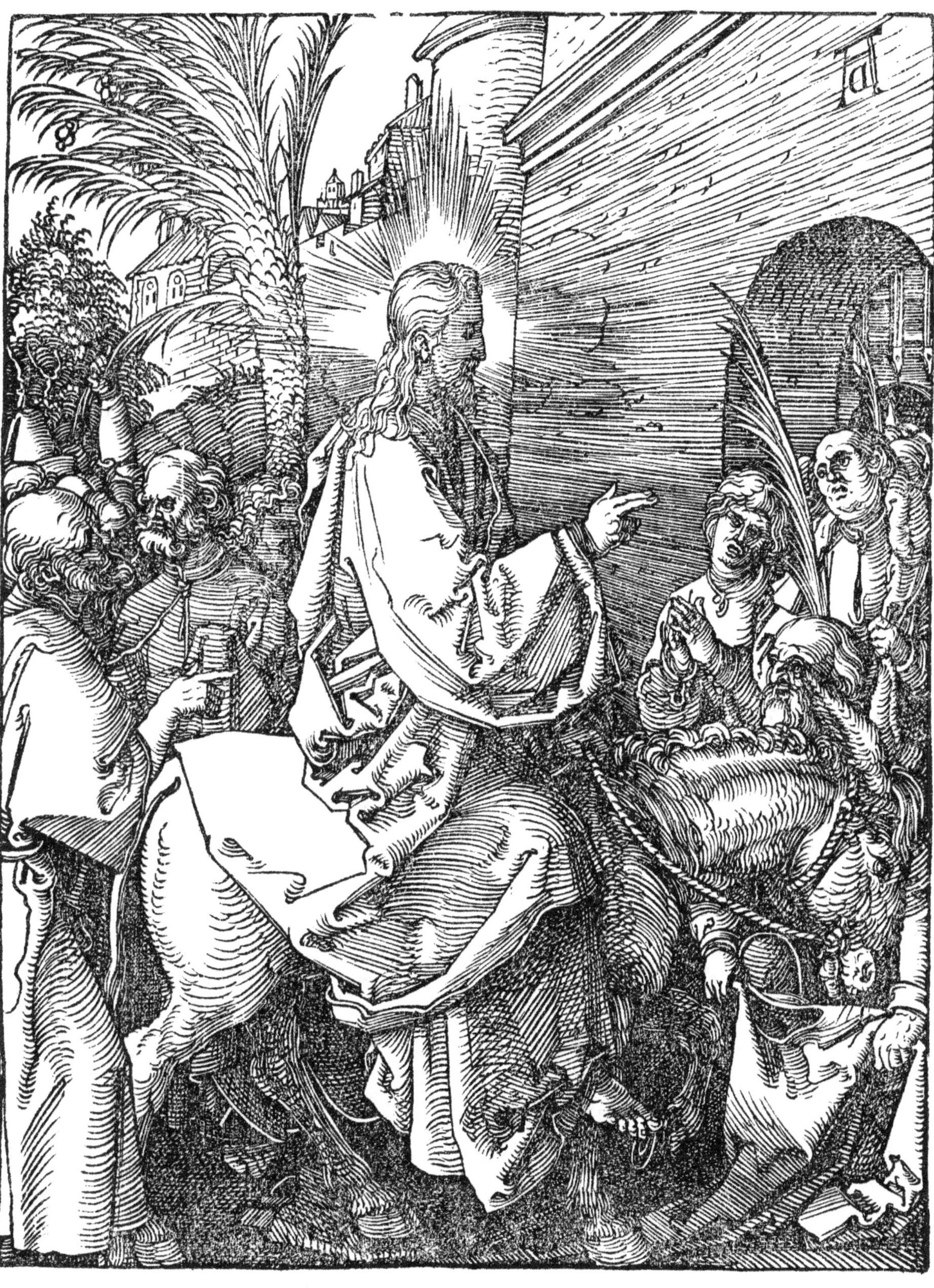

ALBRECHT DÜRER

49. Christ's Entry into Jerusalem, Albrecht
Dürer, 1509 - 1510

50

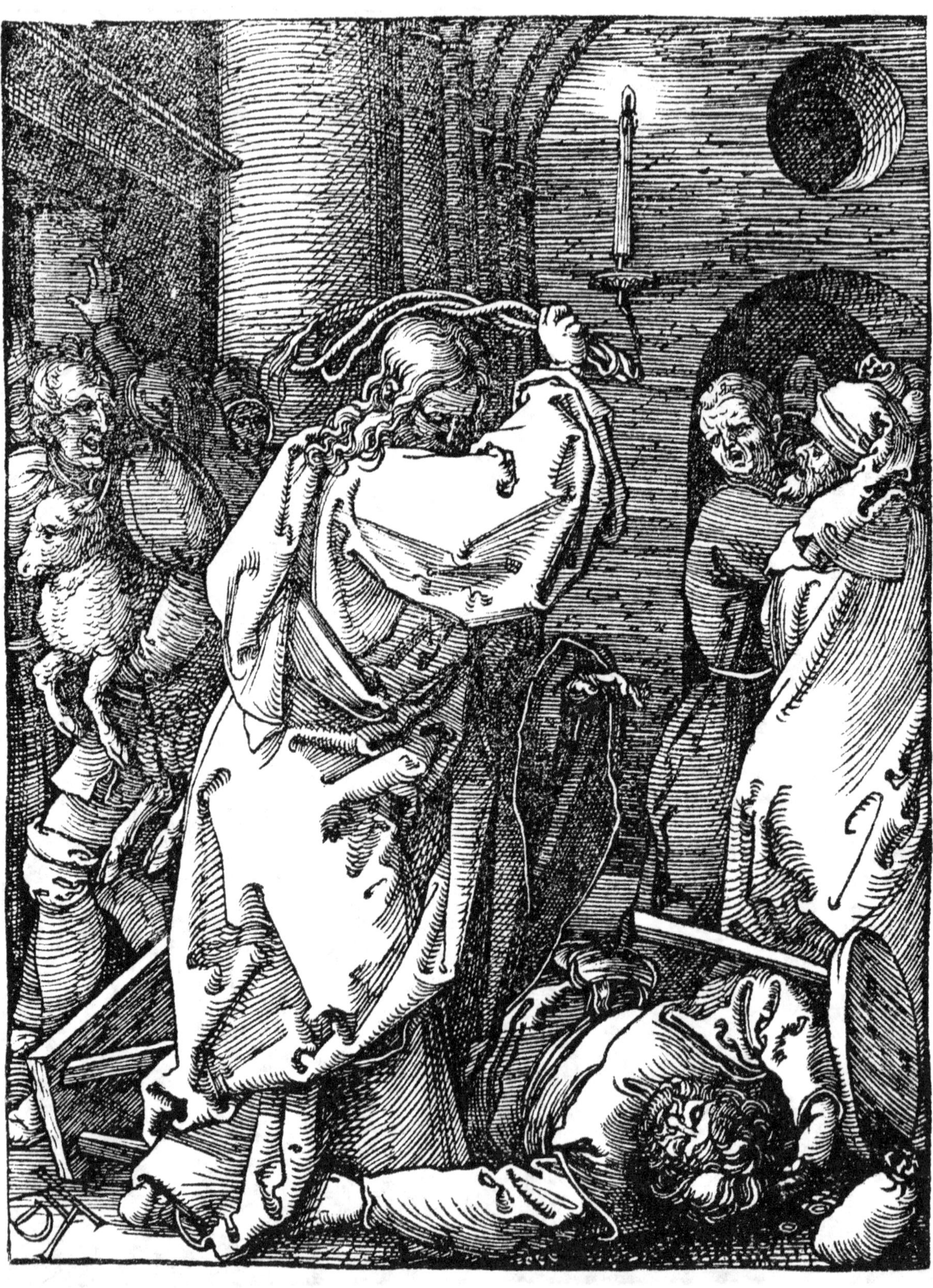

50. Cleansing of the Temple, Albrecht Dürer,
1508 - 1509

51

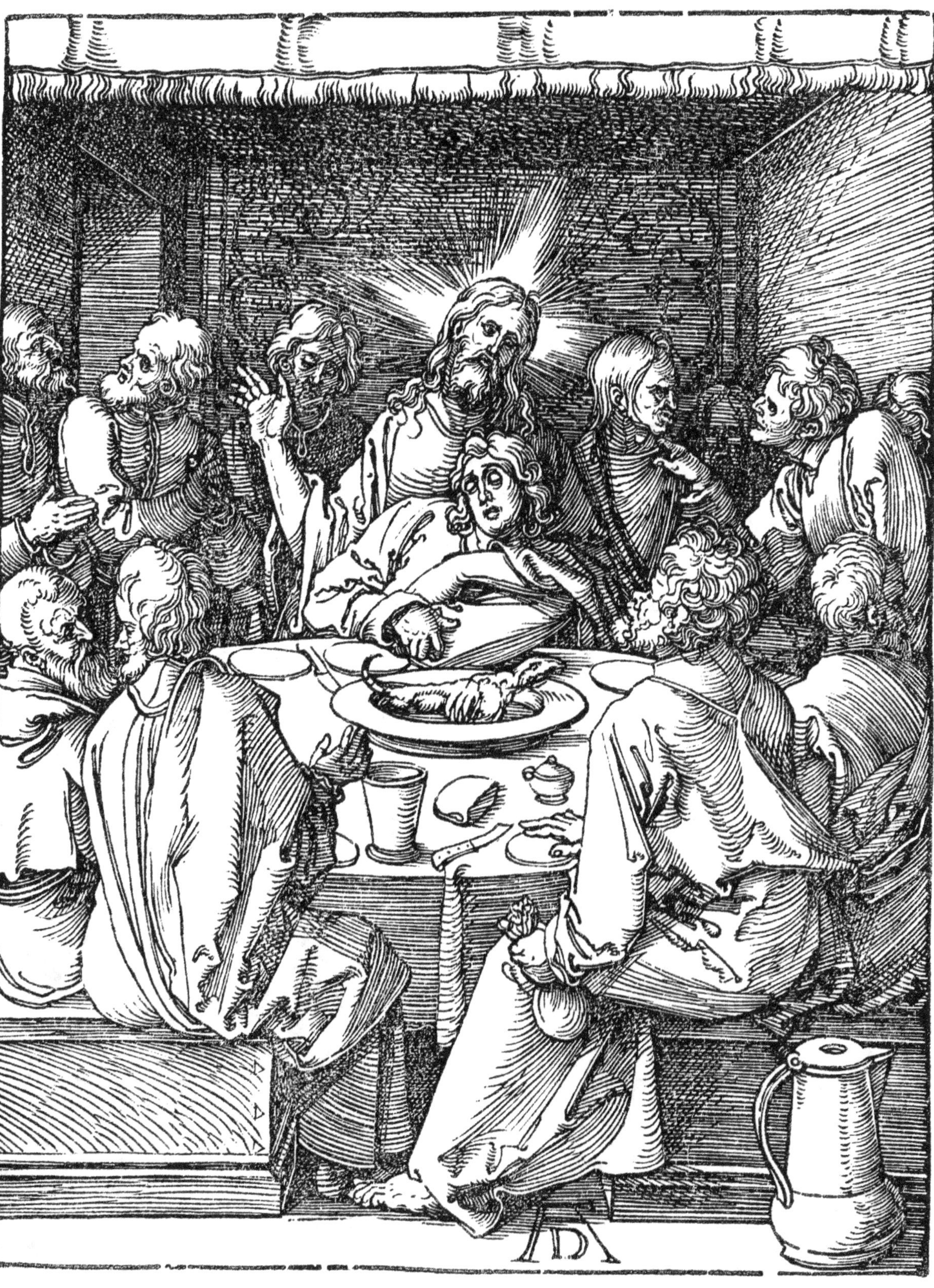

51. The Last Supper, Albrecht Dürer, 1509-1511

52

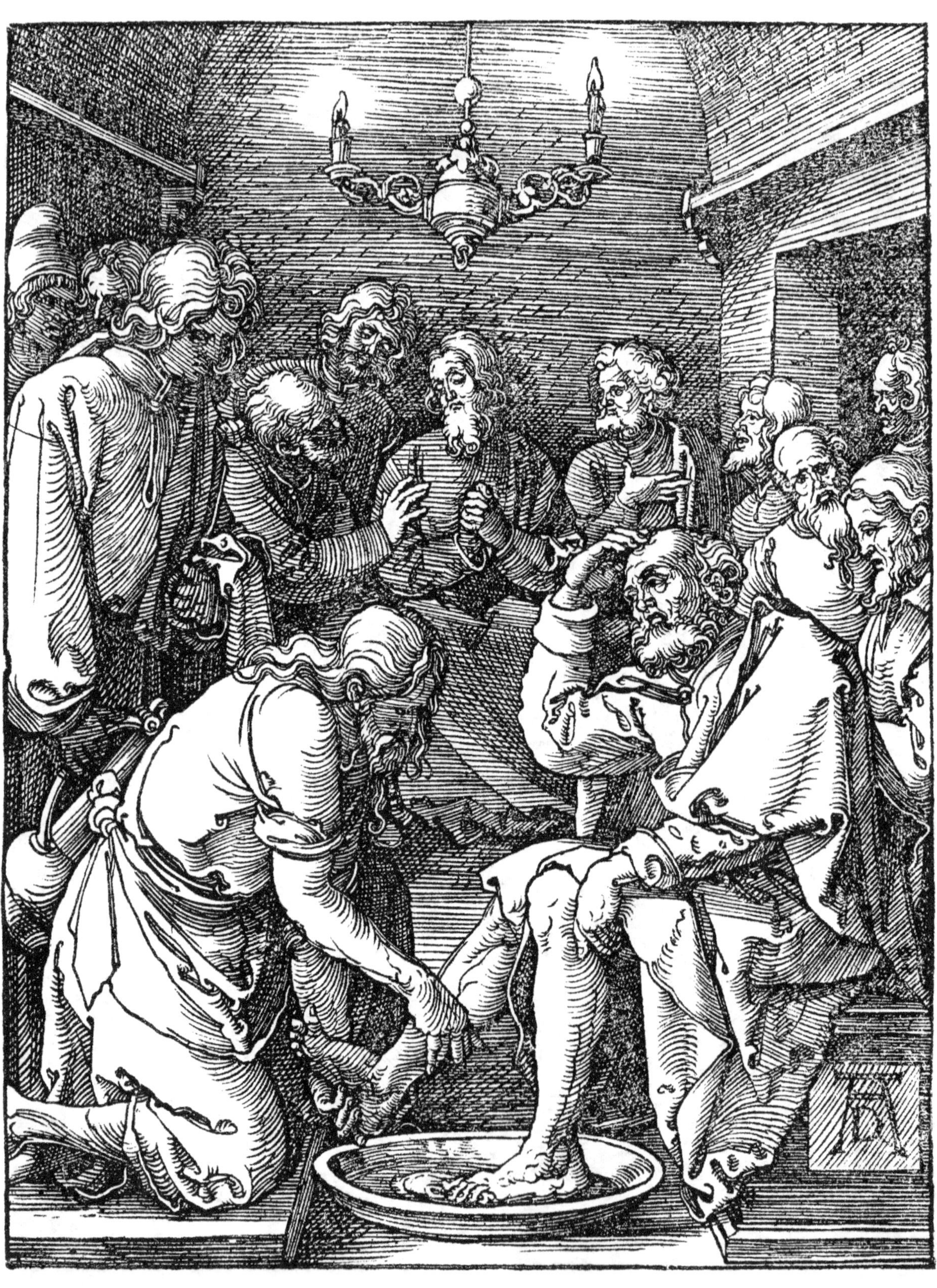

52. *The Washing of the Feet*, Albrecht Dürer.
1509–1511

53

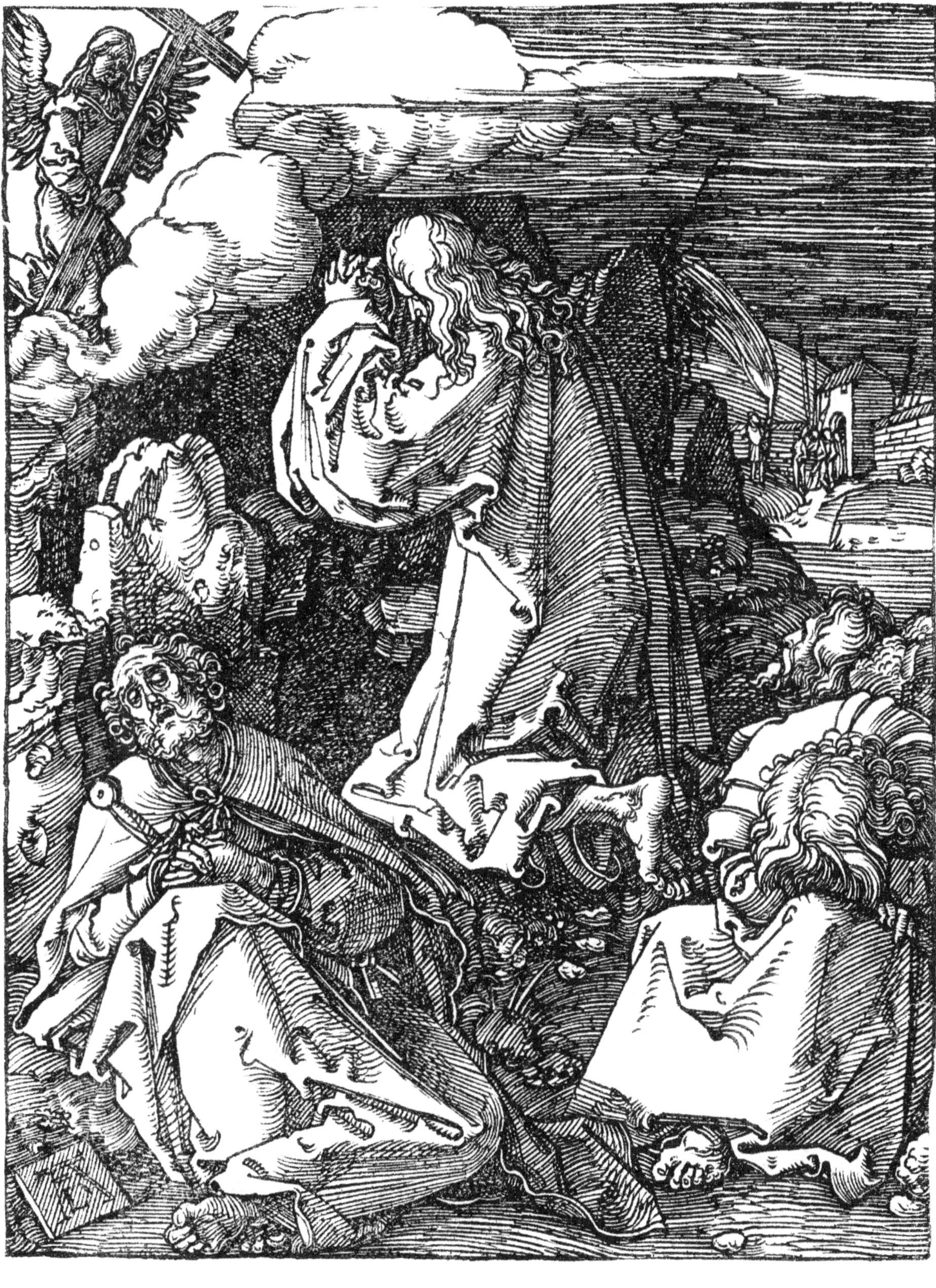

ALBRECHT DÜRER

53. Christ in the Garden of Gethsemane.
Albrecht Dürer, 1510

54

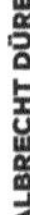

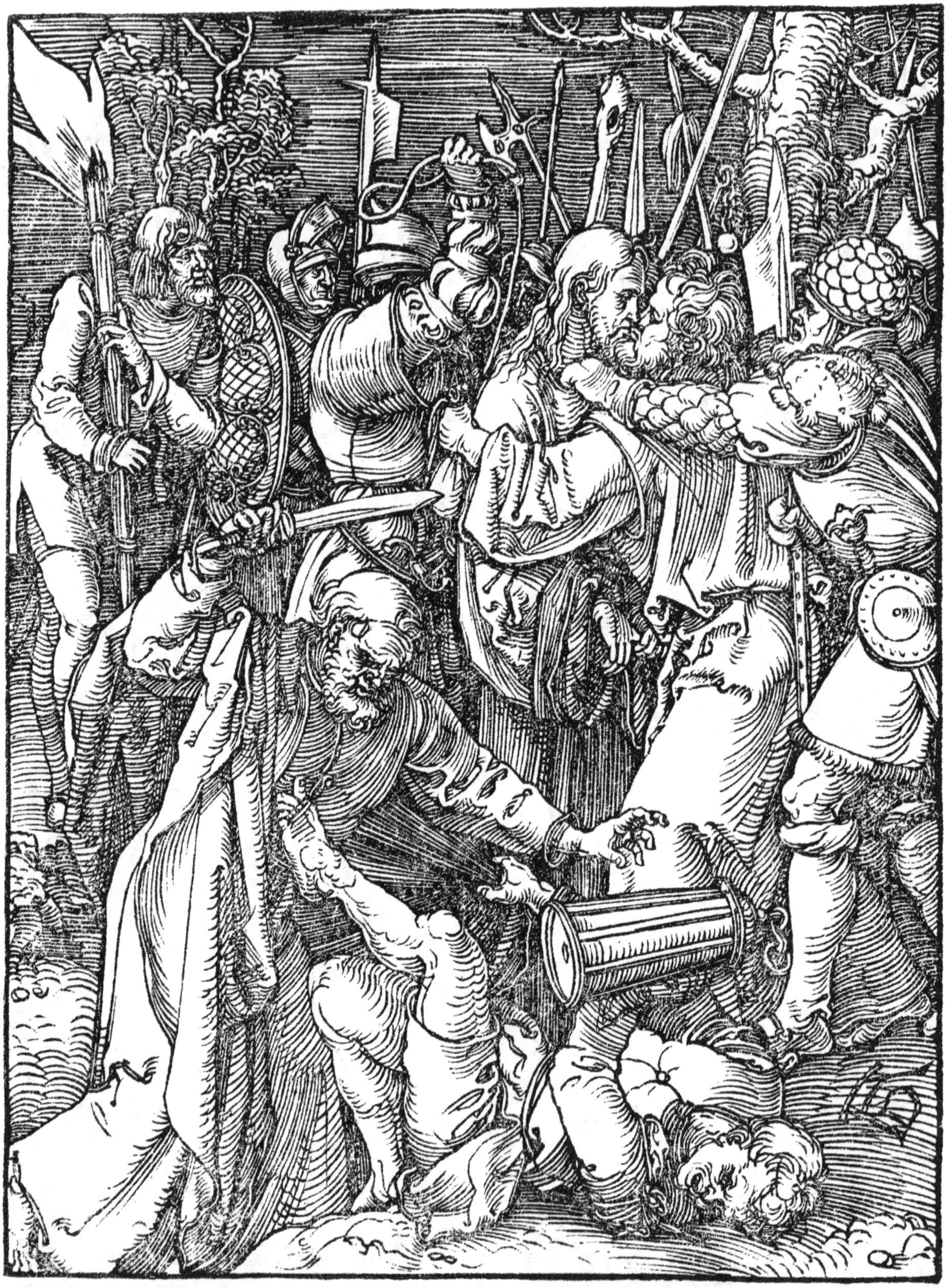

54. *The Arrest of Christ, Albrecht Dürer,*
1509–1511

55

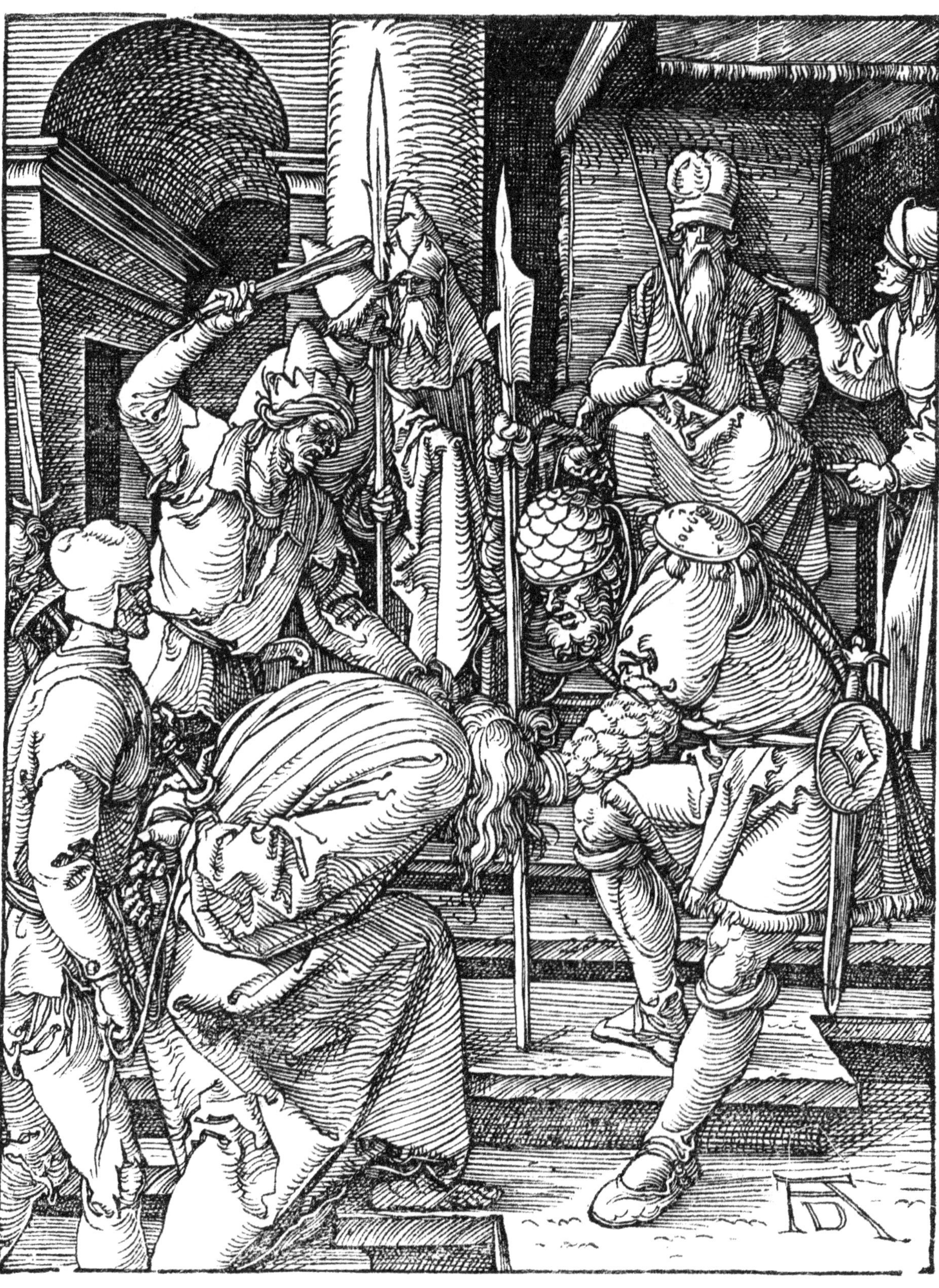

ALBRECHT DÜRER

55. Christ before Ananias. Albrecht Dürer.
1508 - 1509

56

ALBRECHT DÜRER

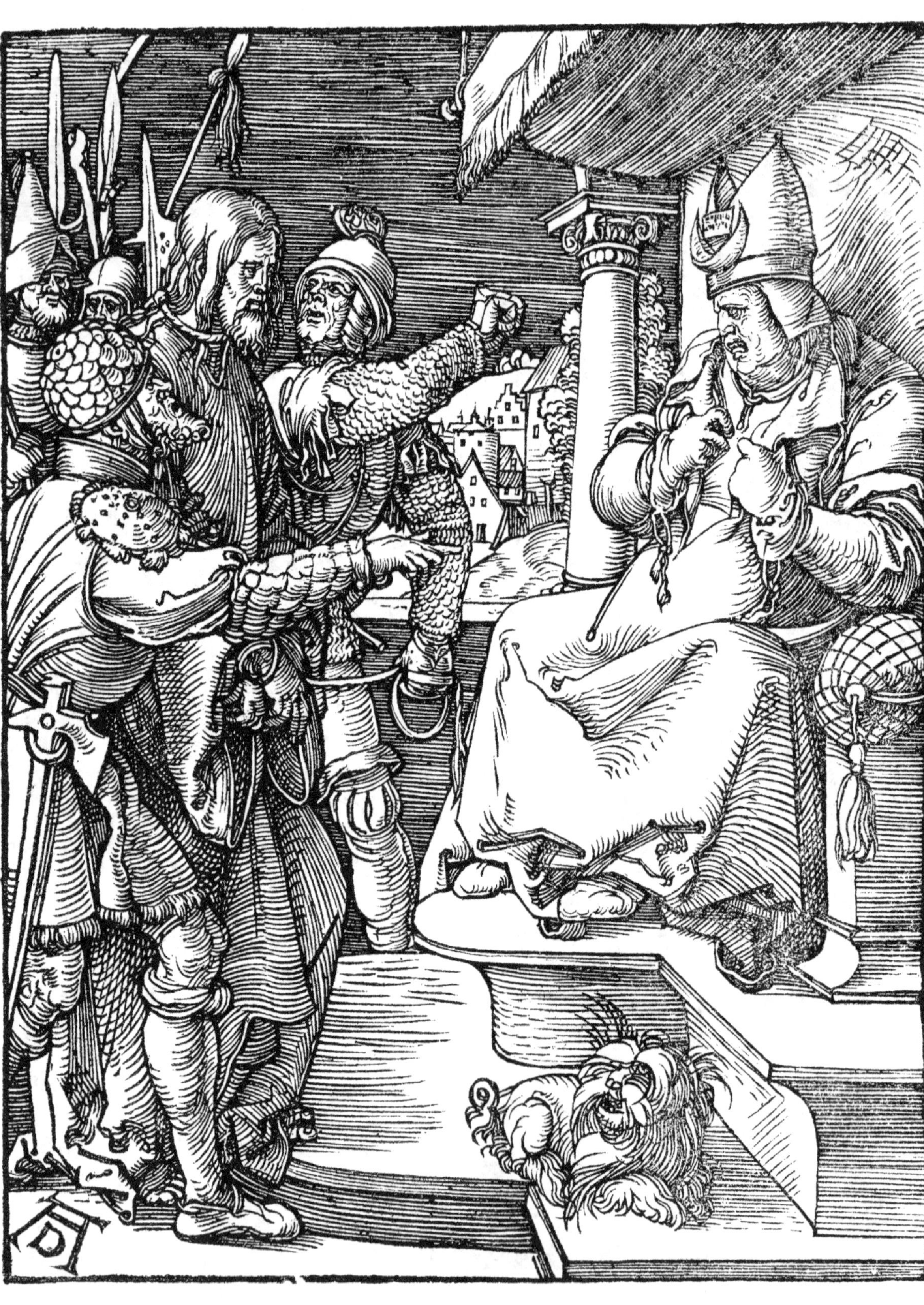

*56. Christ before Caiaphas. Albrecht Dürer.
1509–1511*

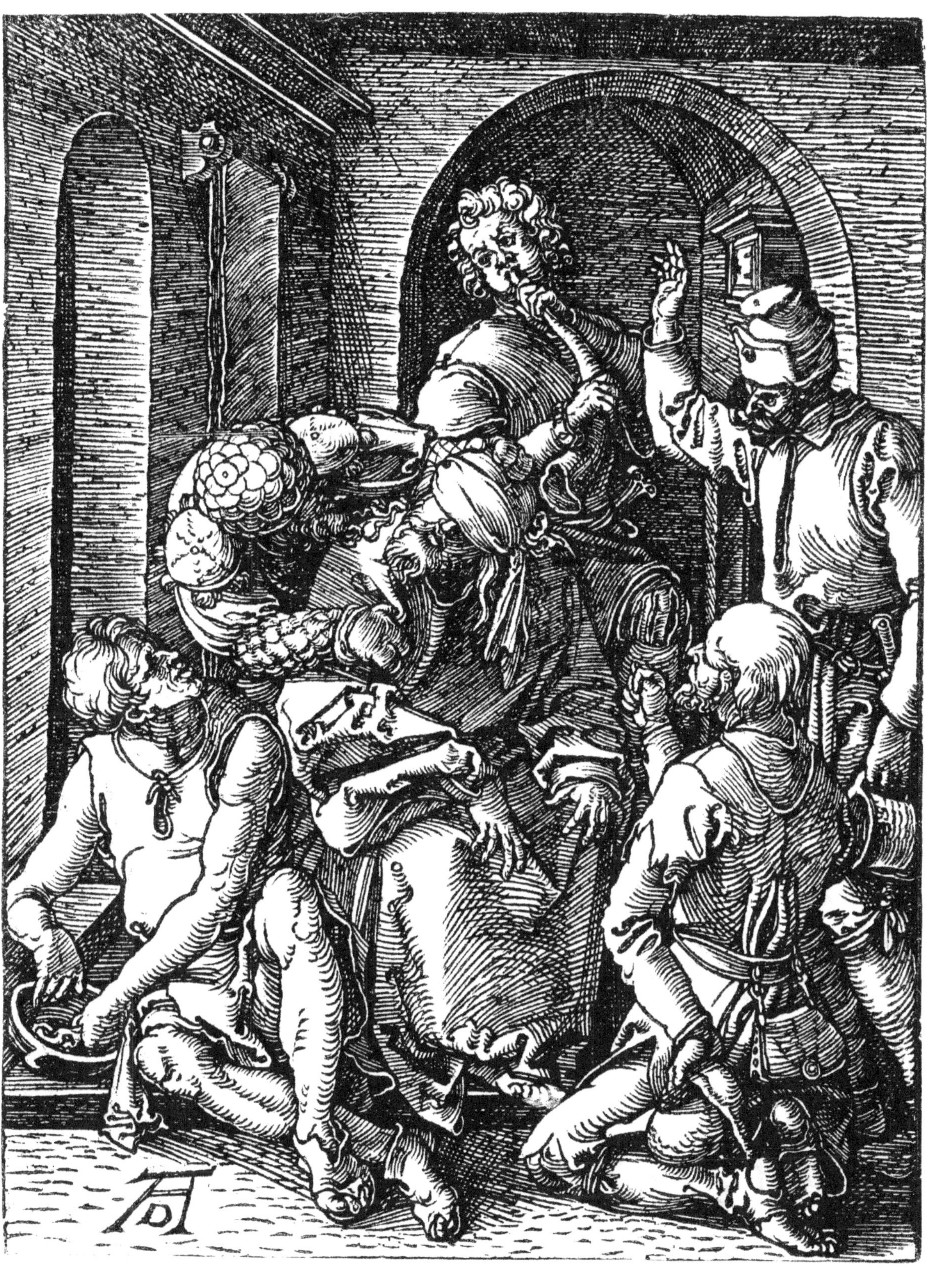

58

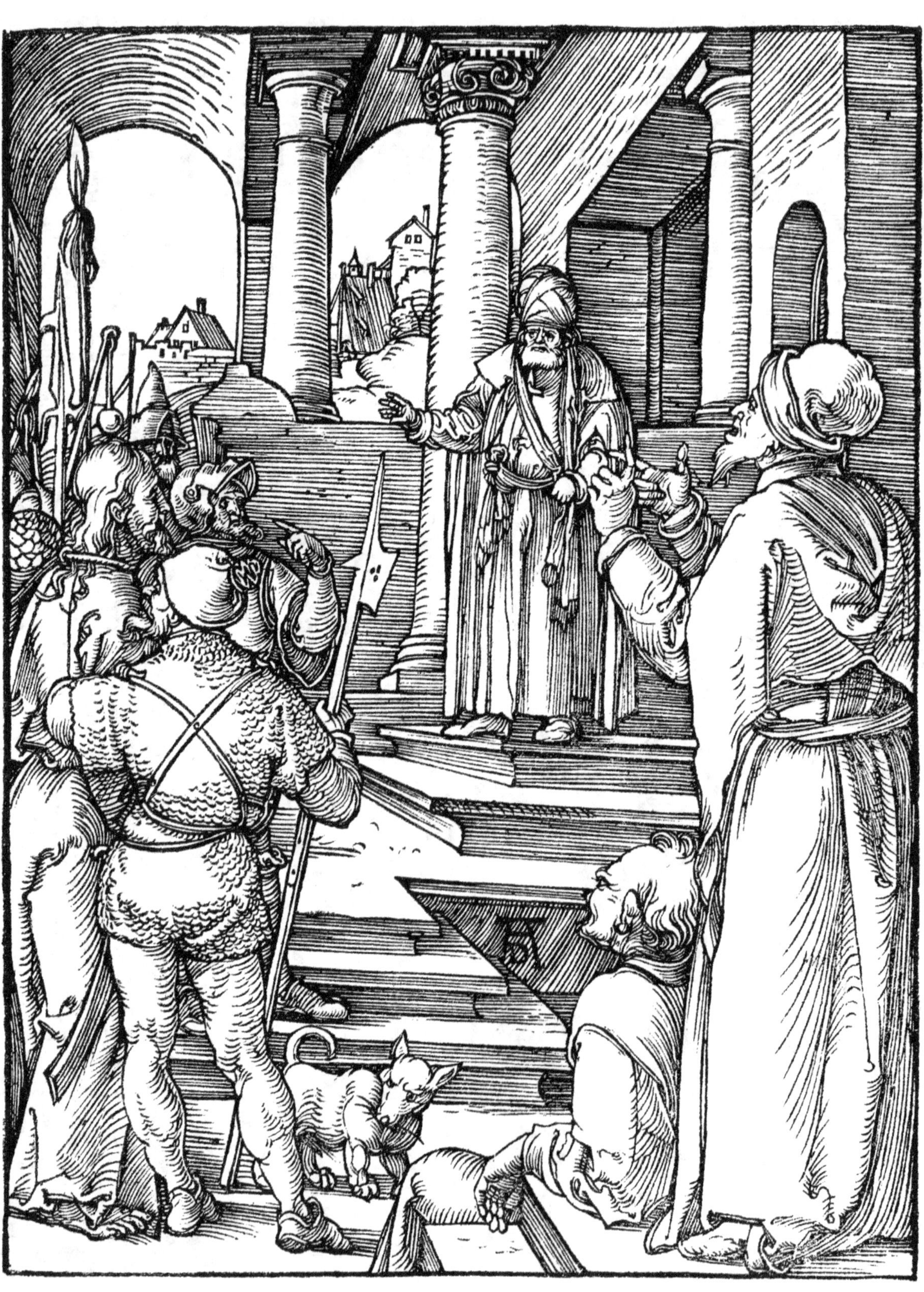

58. Christ before Pilate, Albrecht Dürer, 1509
- 1510

59

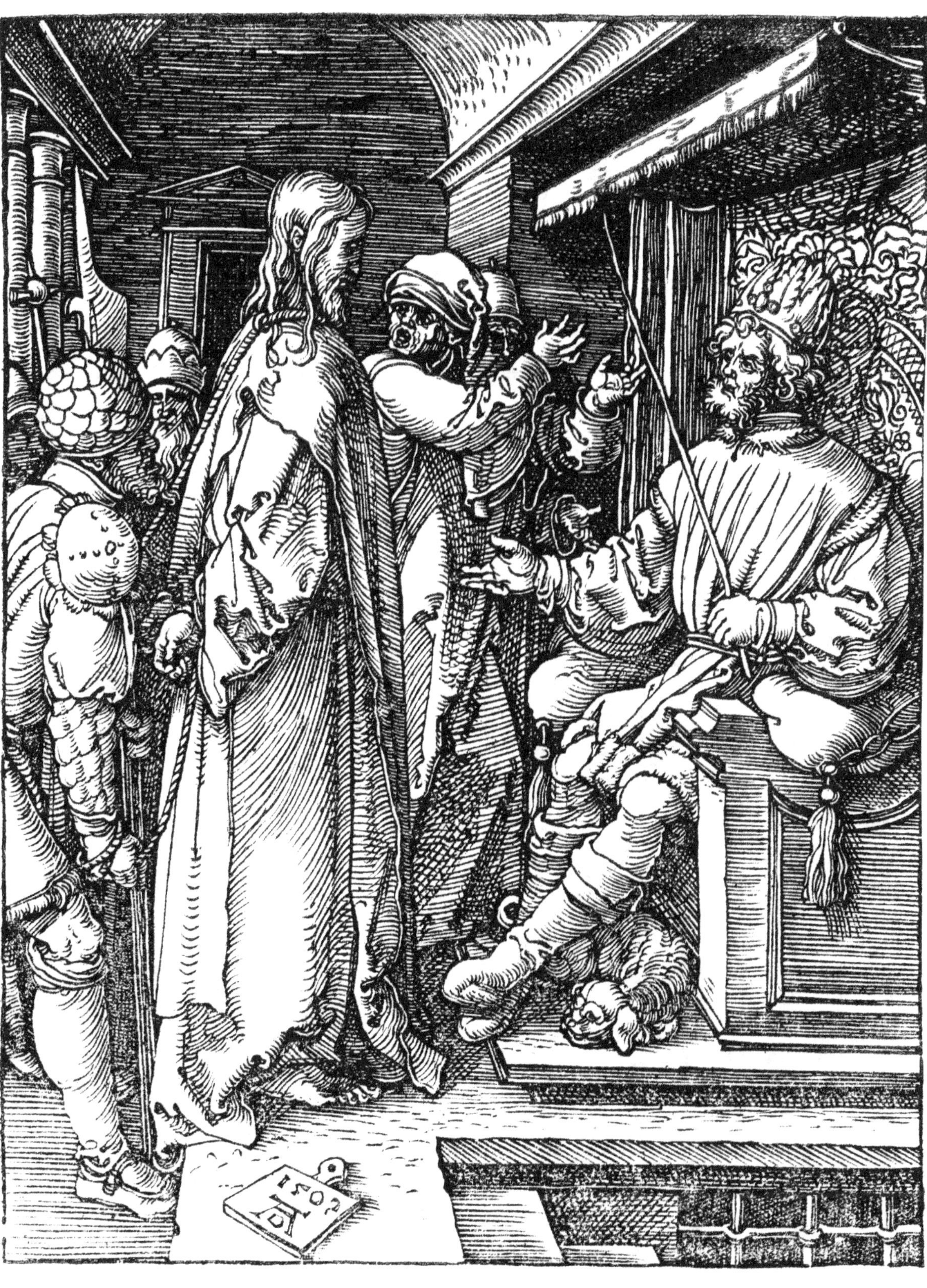

59. Christ before Herod, Albrecht Dürer, 1509

60

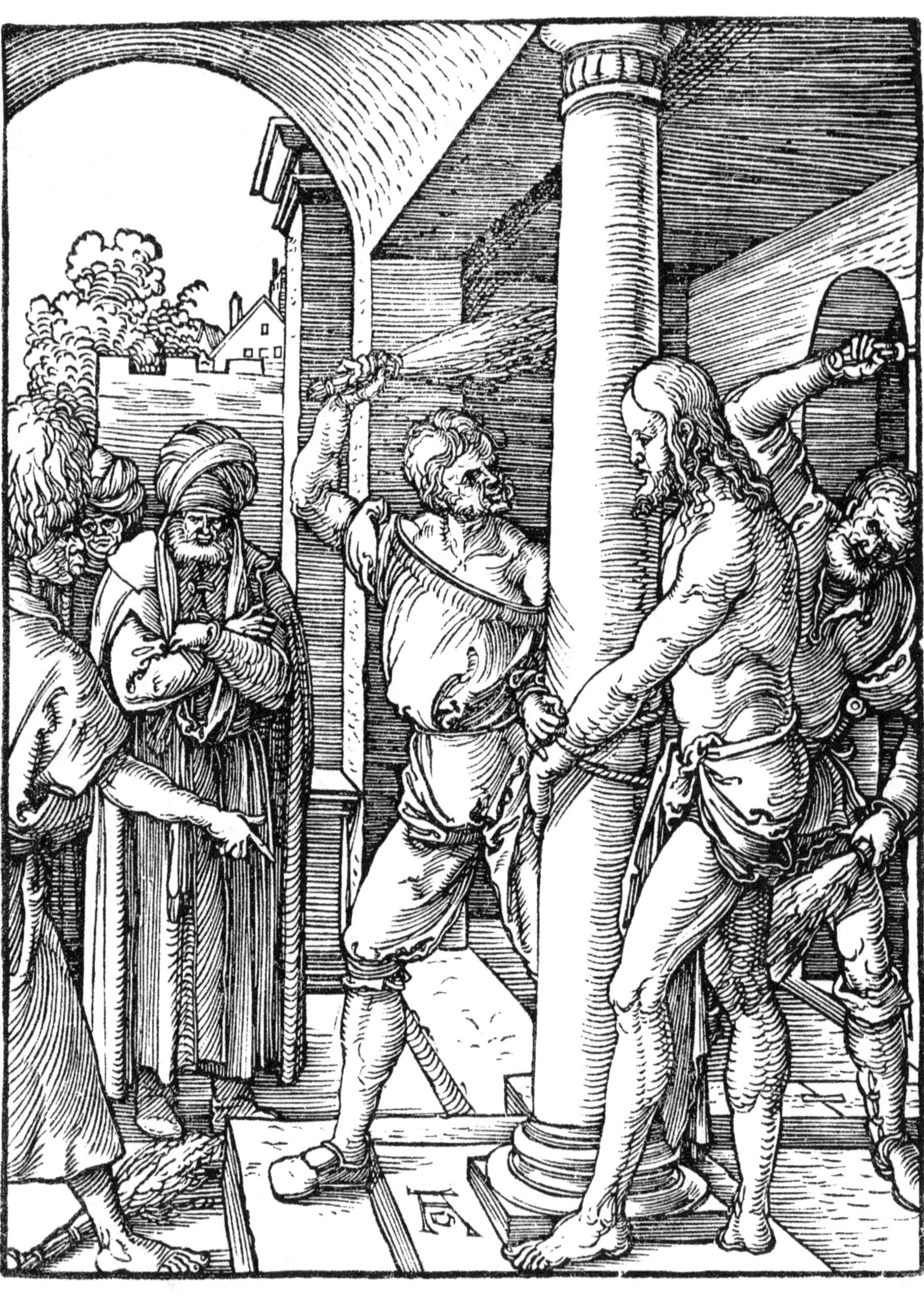

61

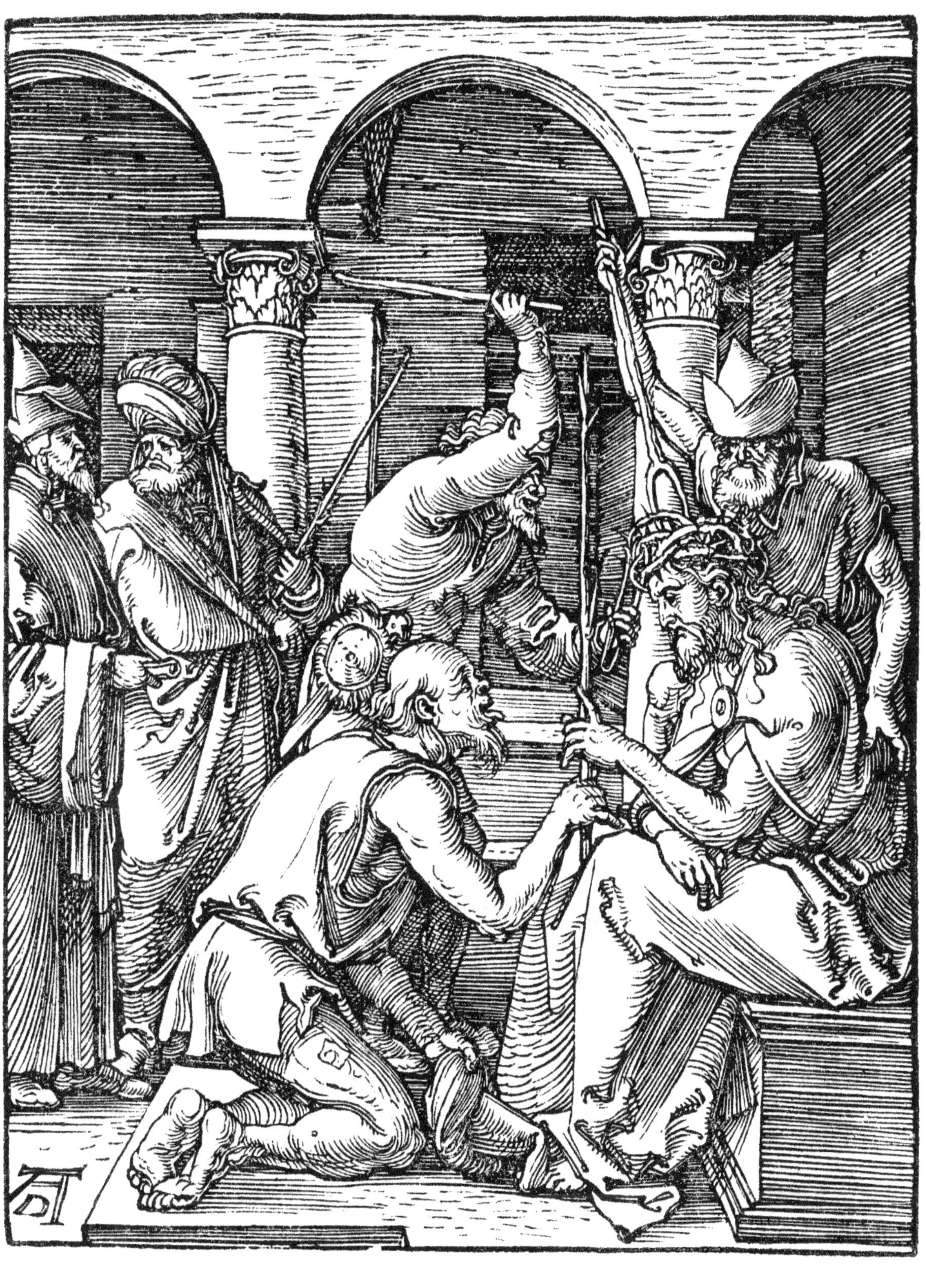

61. Christ Crowned with Thorns, Albrecht Dürer,
1509-1510

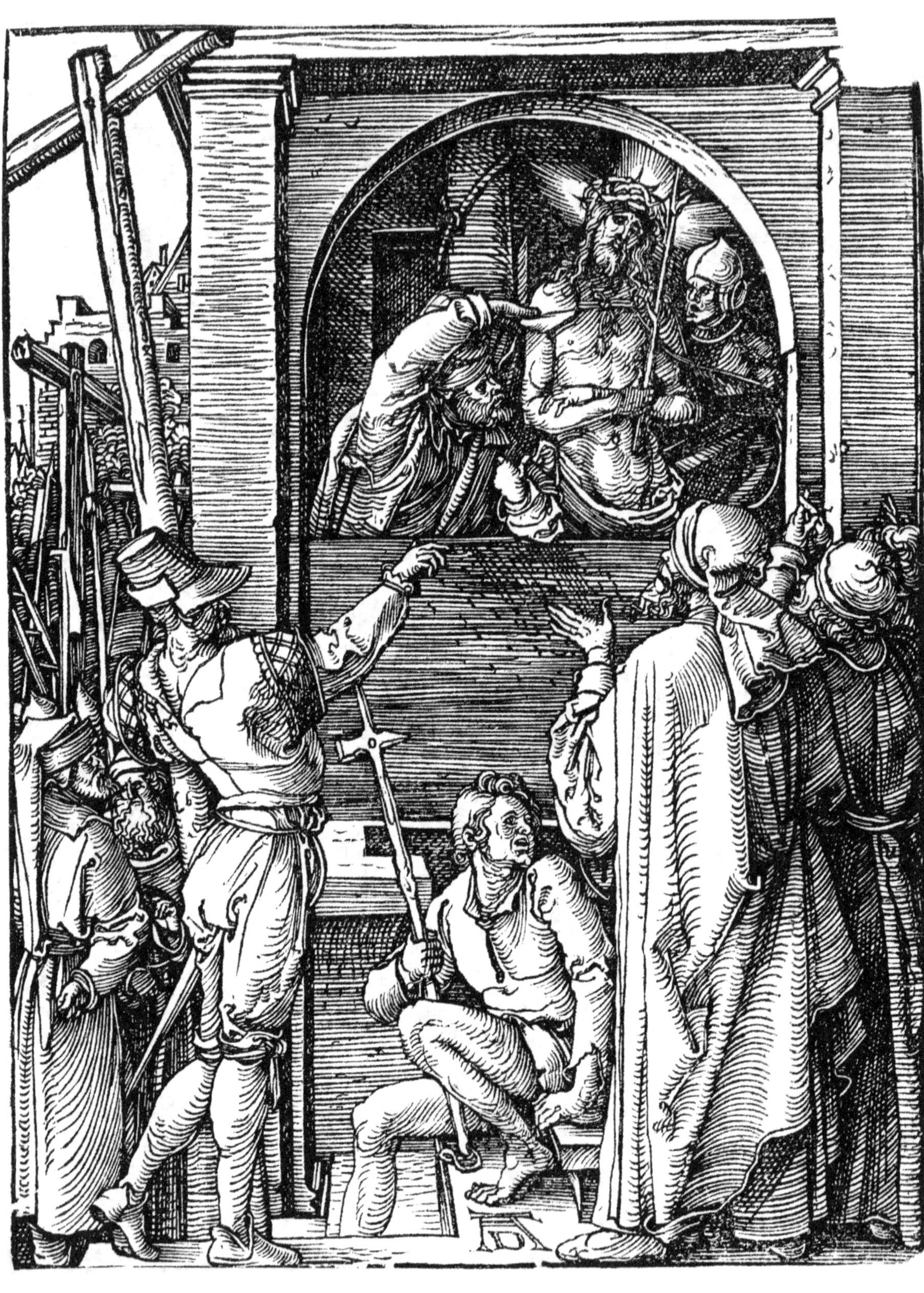

62. Christ shown to the people (Ecce homo),
Albrecht Dürer, 1509

63

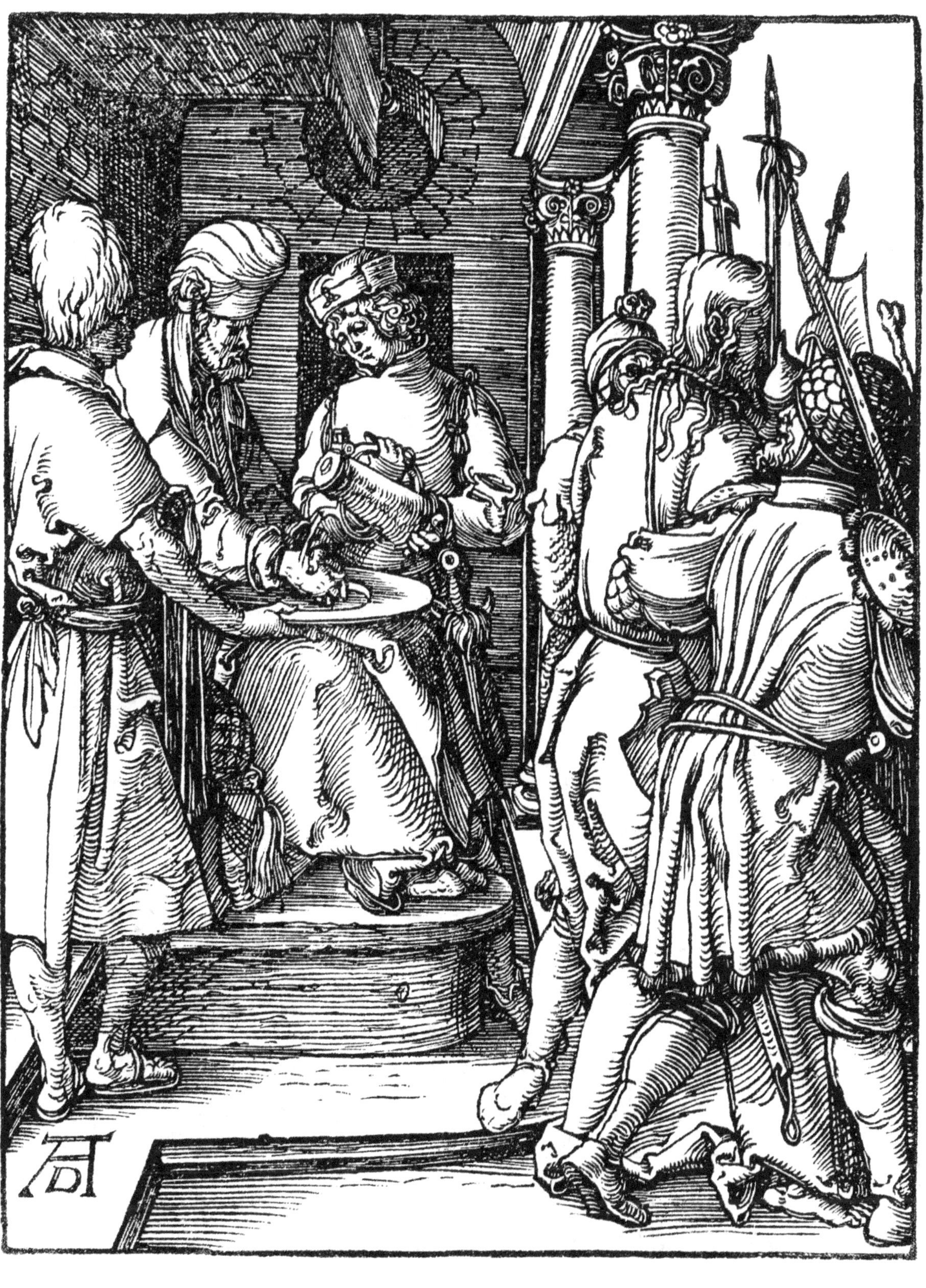

63. *Pilate washing his hands. Albrecht Dürer.*
1509-1510

64

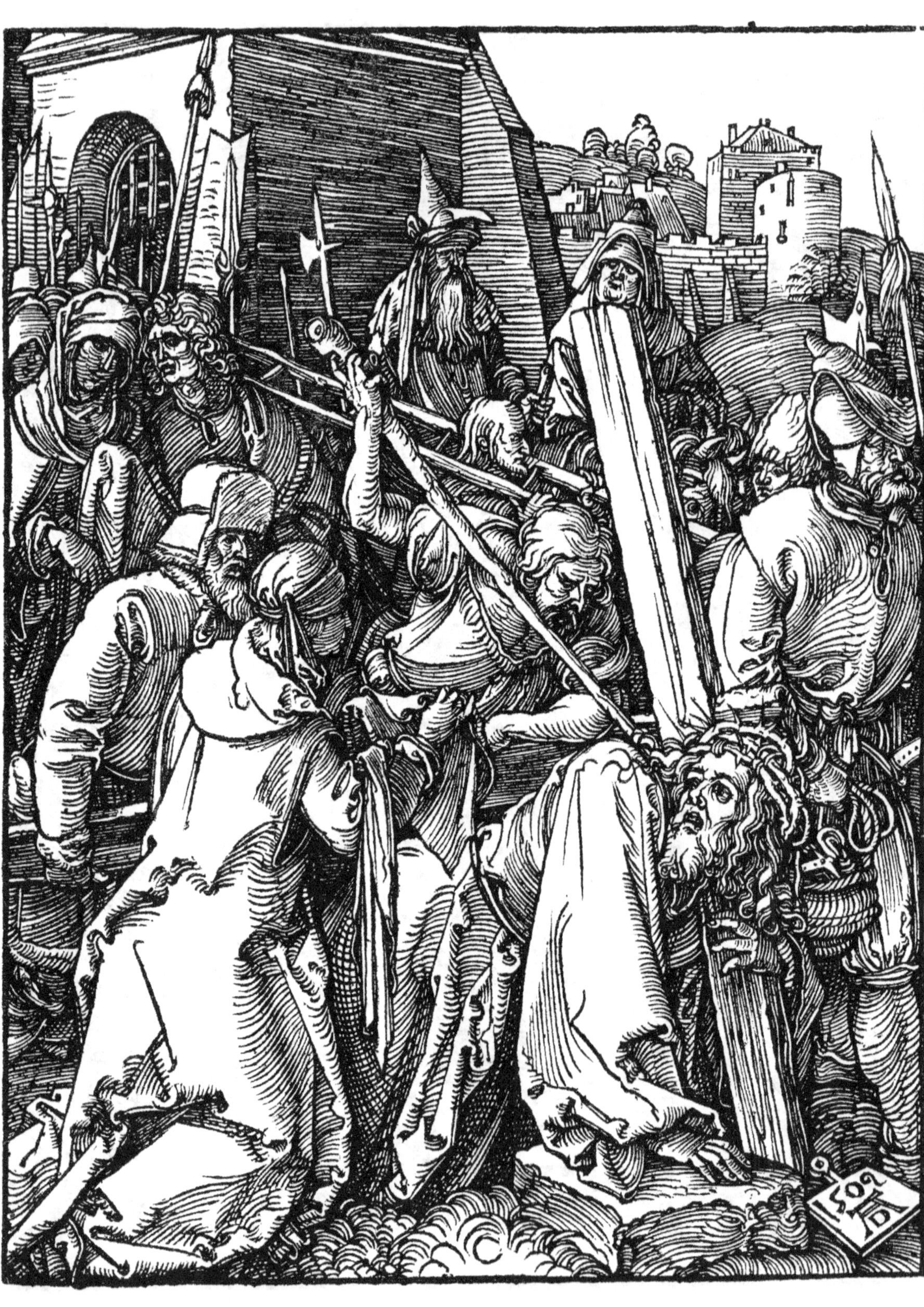

64. Carrying the Cross, Albrecht Dürer, 1509

65

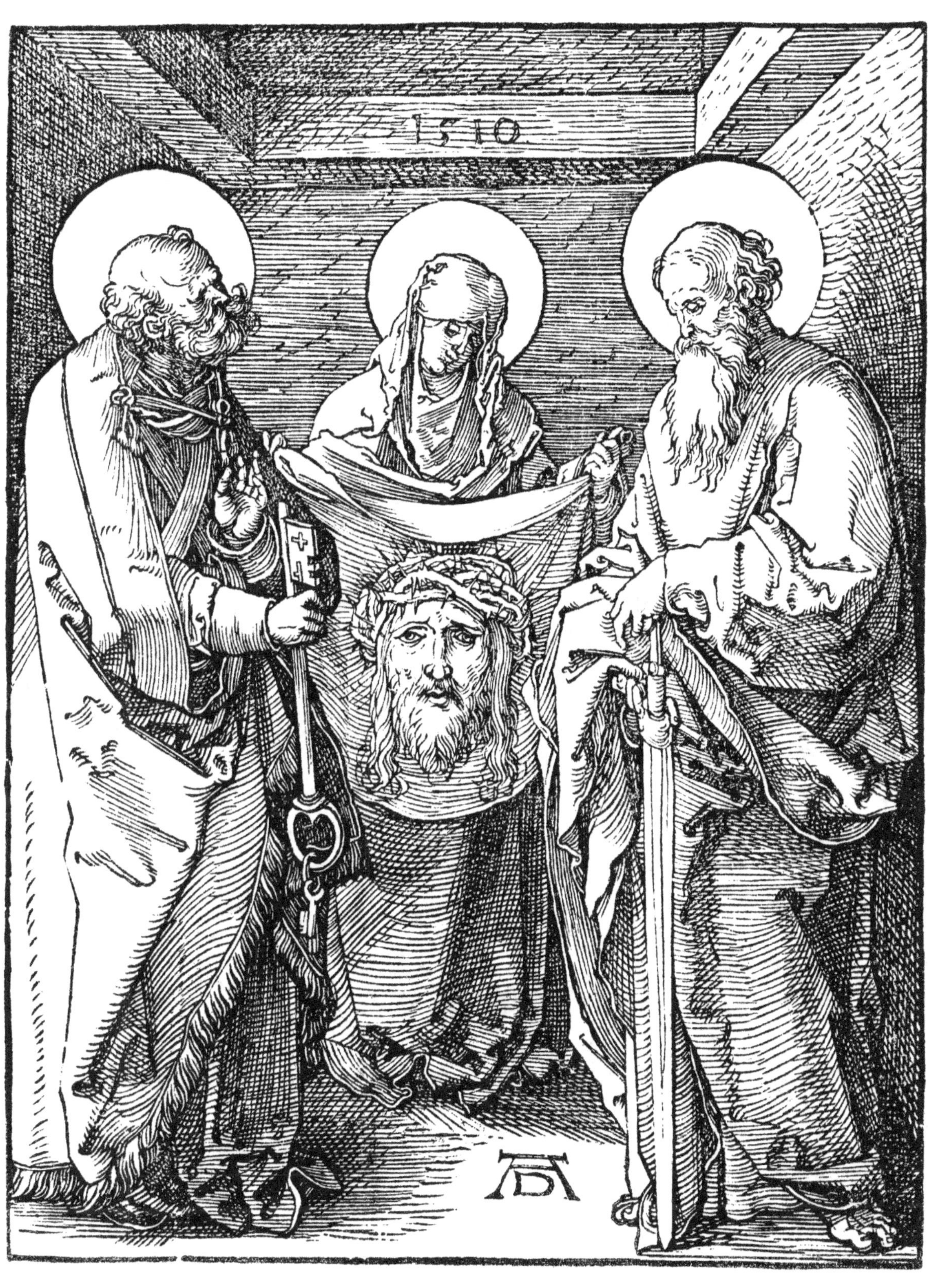

65. Saint Veronica between Saints Peter and
Paul, Albrecht Dürer, 1510

66

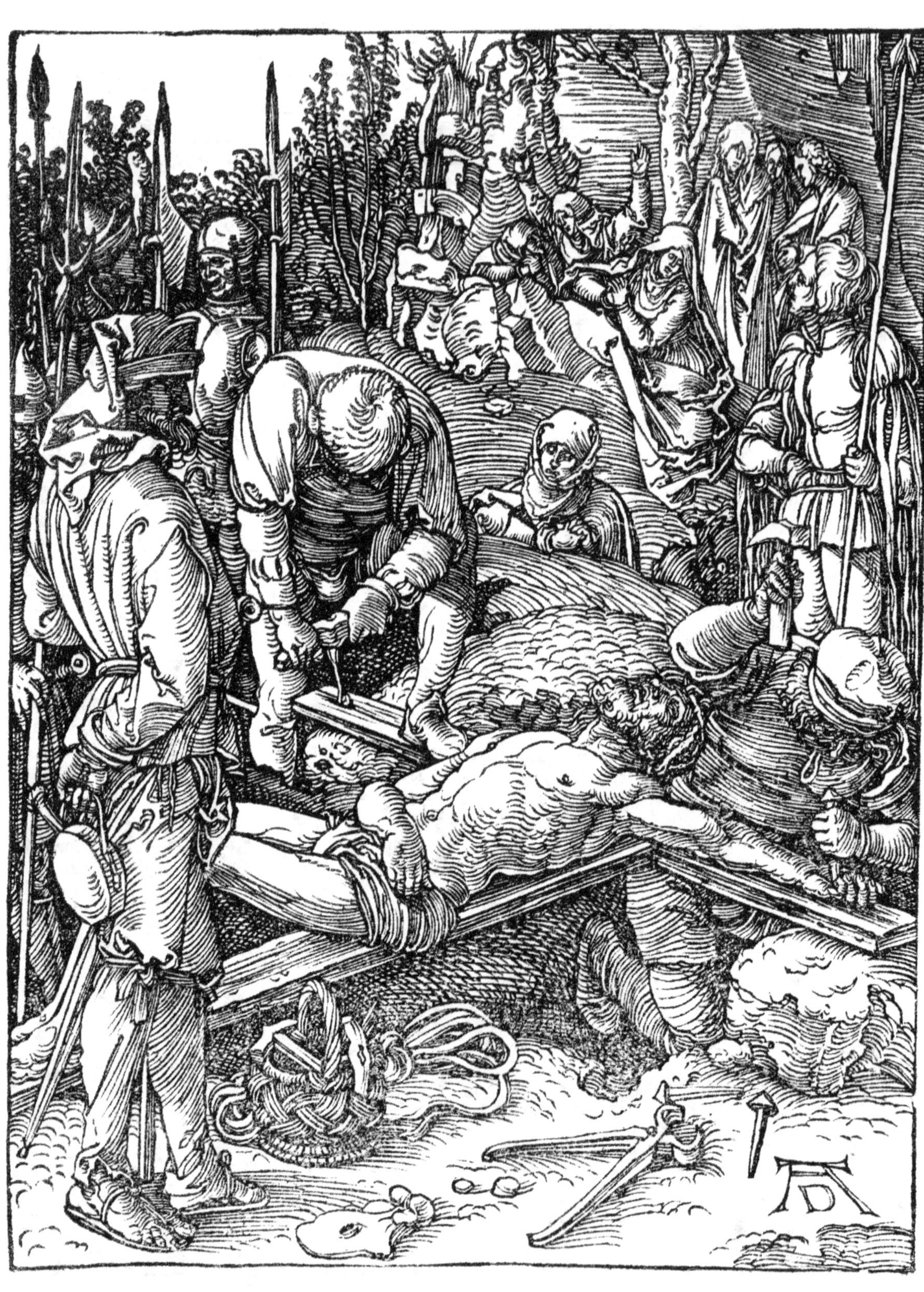

66. Christ nailed to the cross. Albrecht Dürer.
1509

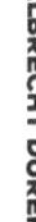

ALBRECHT DÜRER

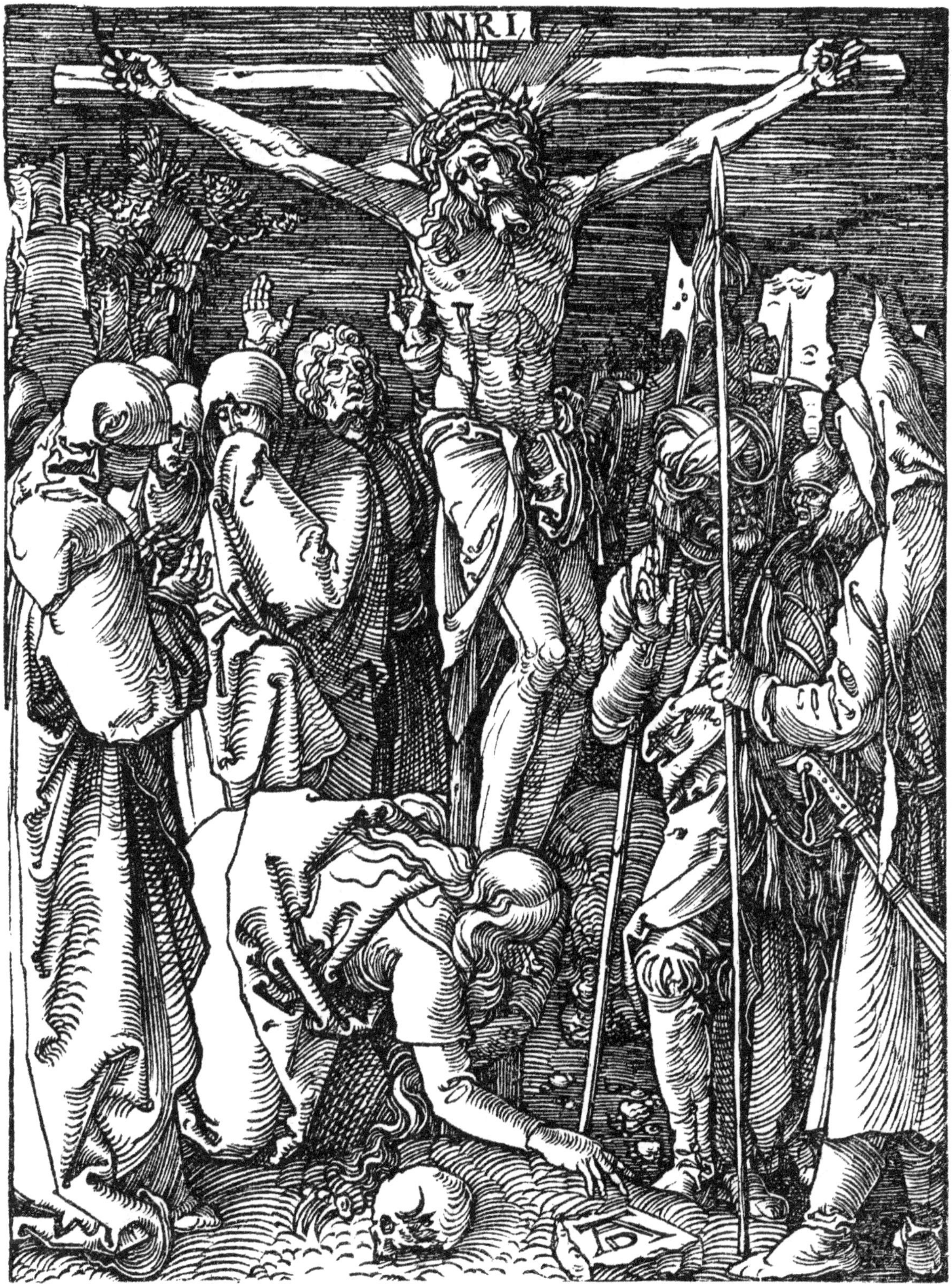

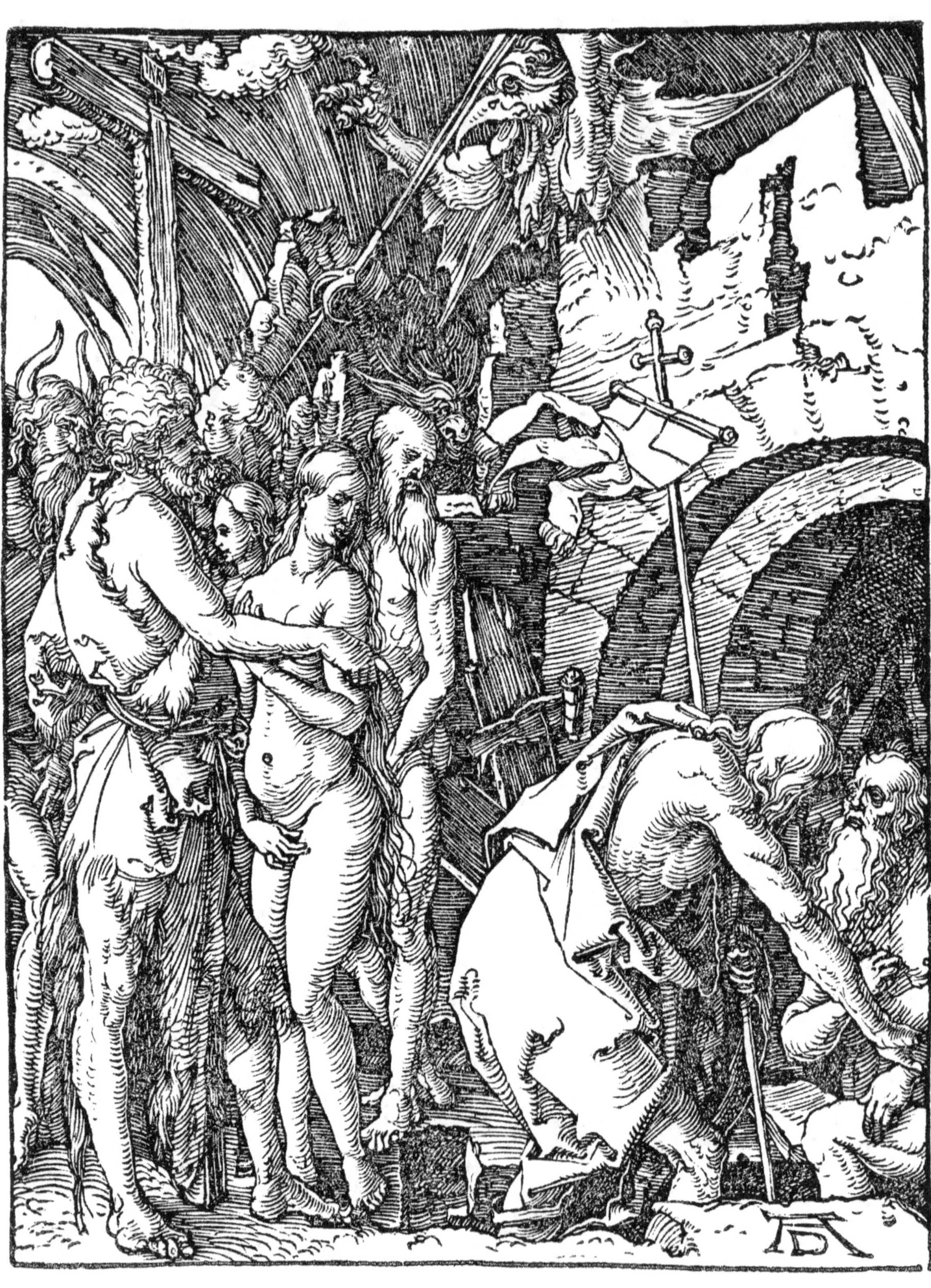

68. Christ in Limbo, Albrecht Dürer, 1509-1510

69

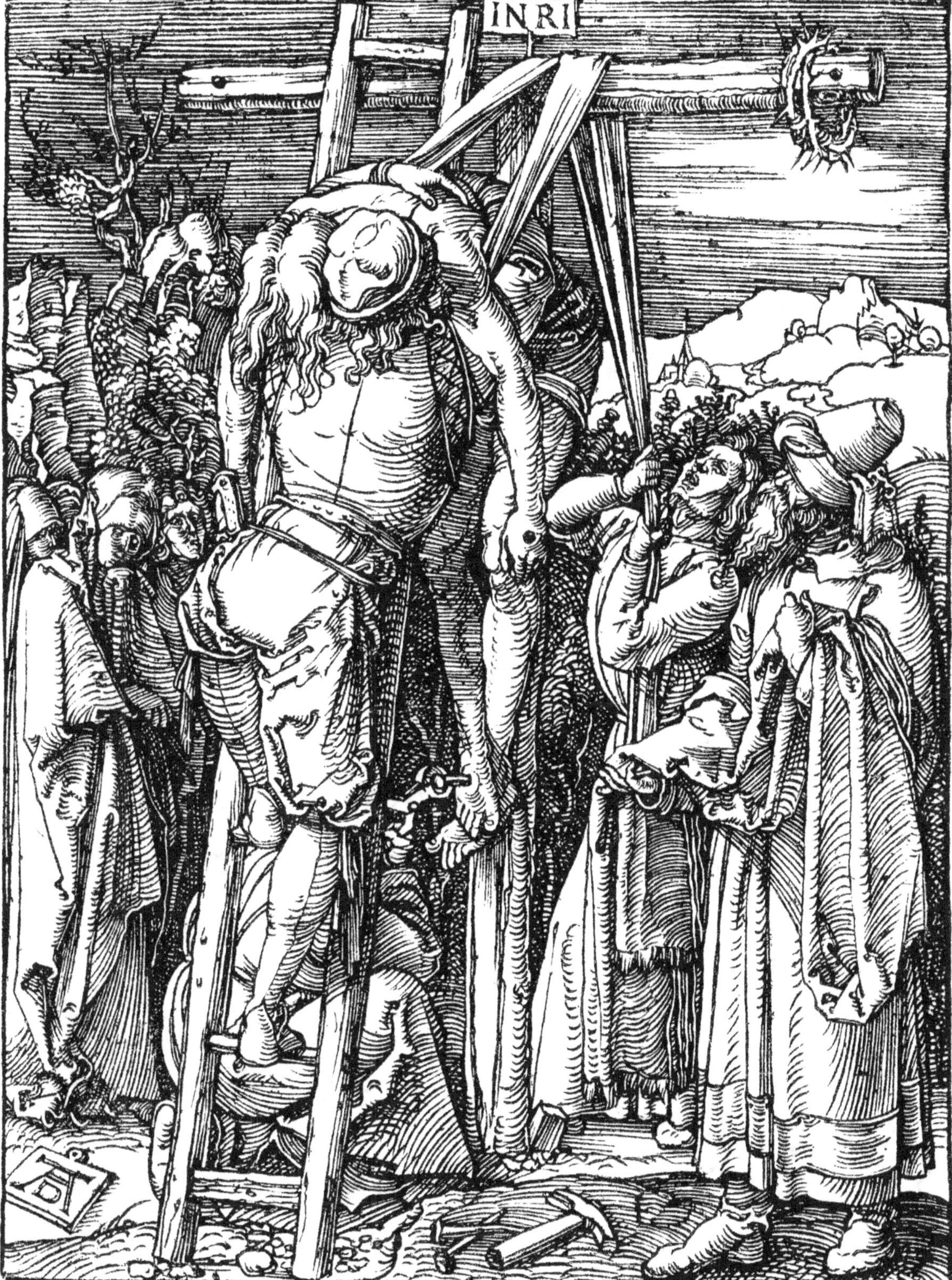

69. The Descent from the Cross, Albrecht Dürer,
1509-1510

70

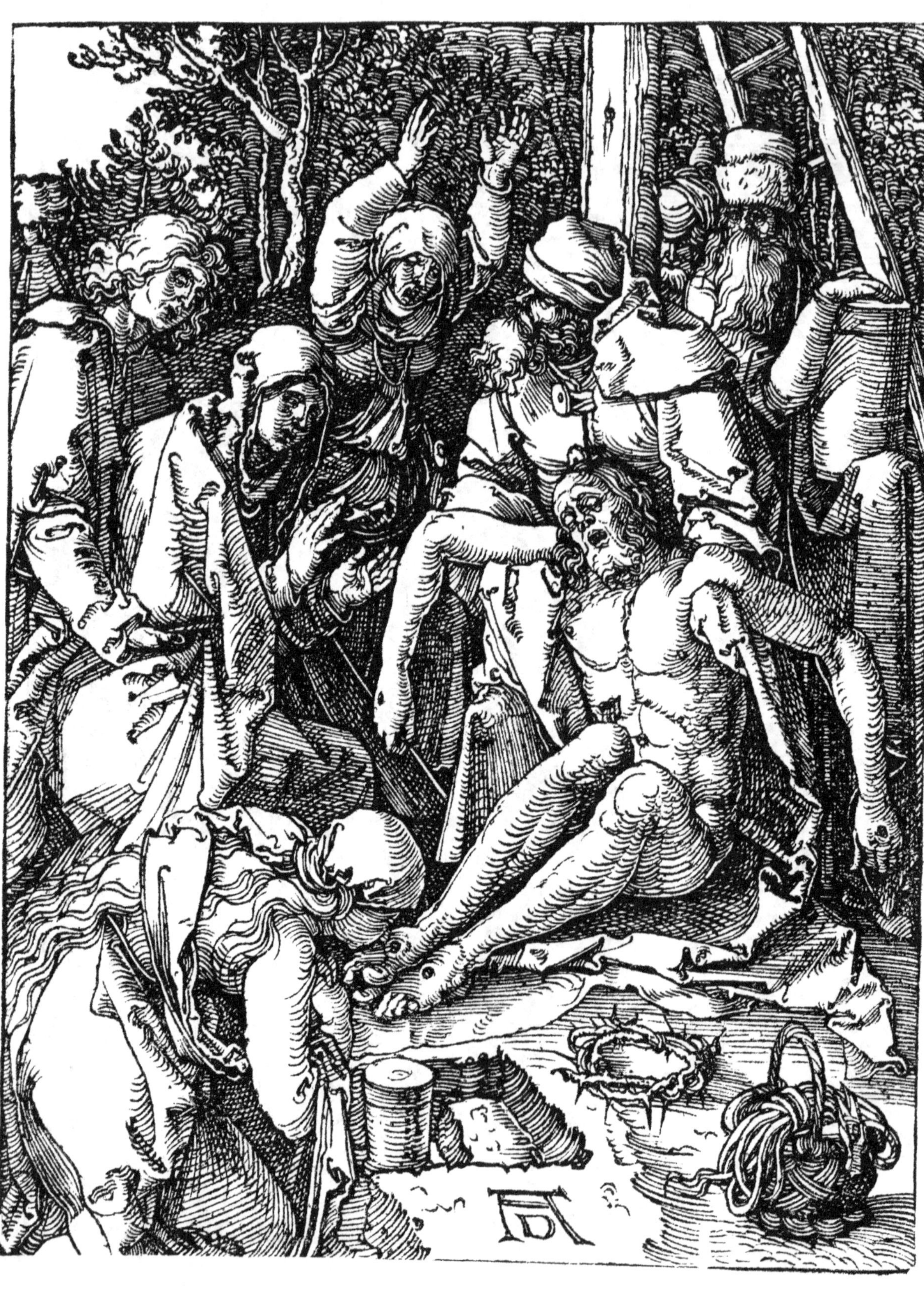

70. Lamentation, Albrecht Dürer, 1509 - 1510

71

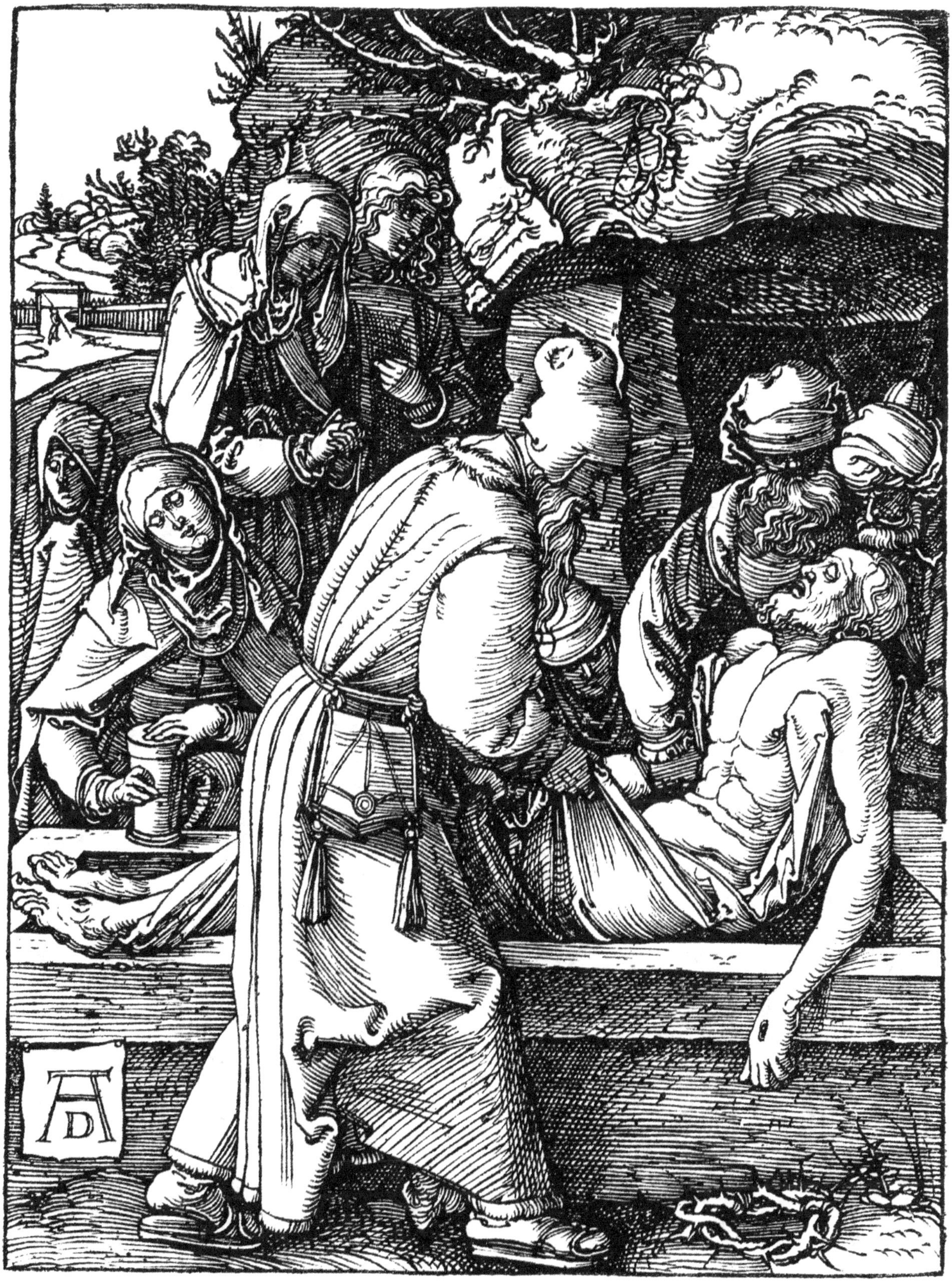

ALBRECHT DÜRER

72

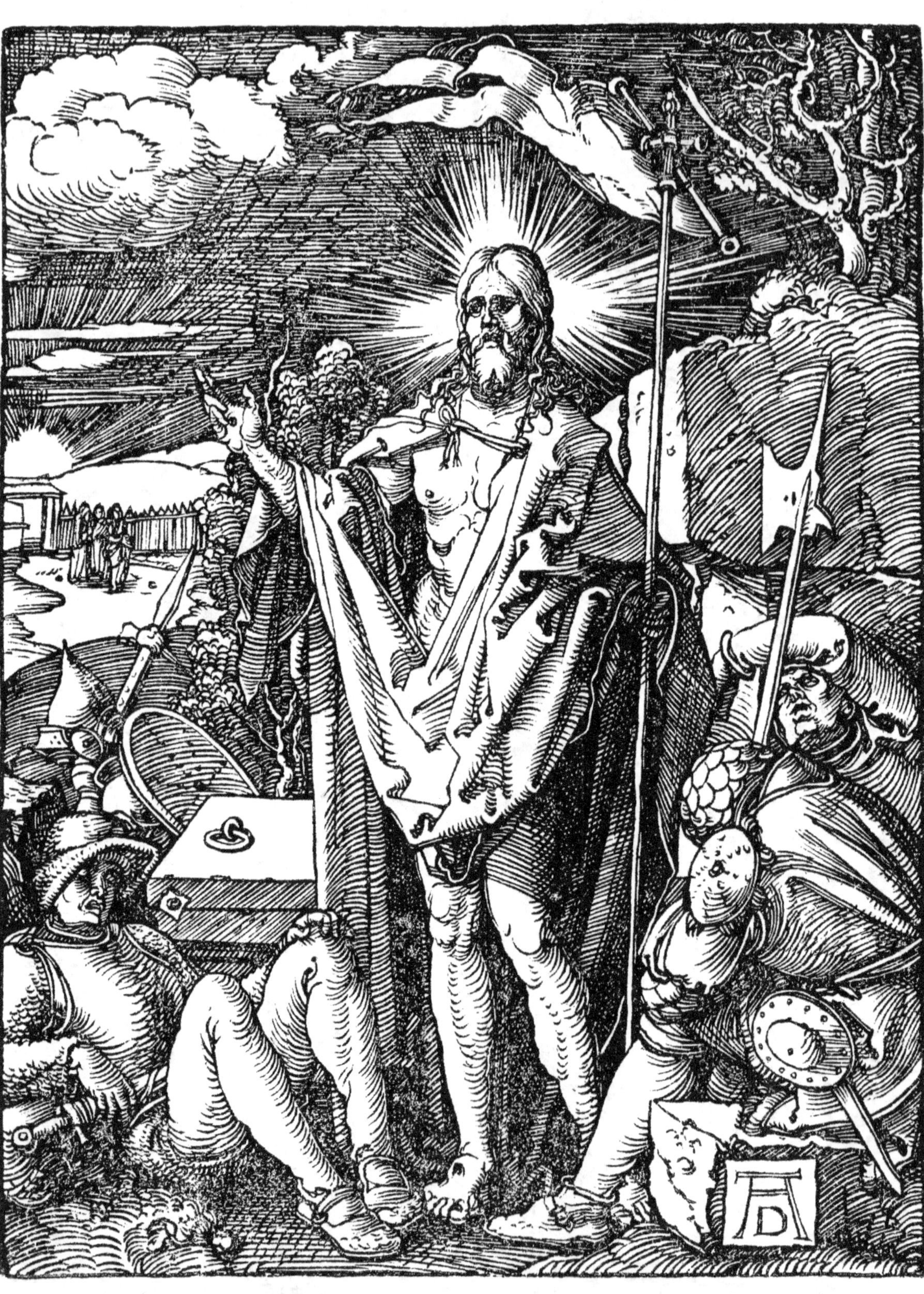

72. *The Resurrection, Albrecht Dürer, 1509-1510*

73

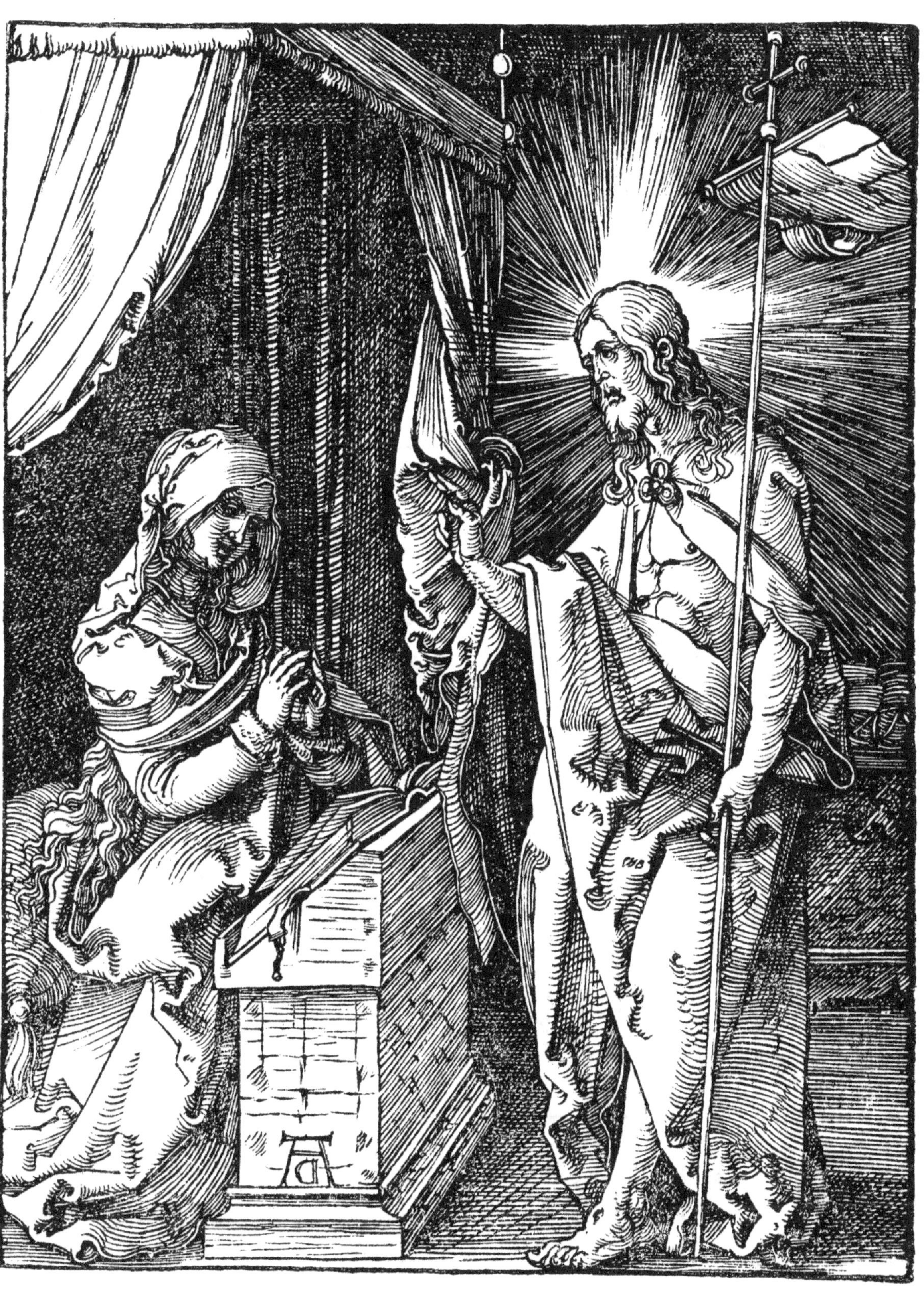

73. Christ Appearing to His Mother, Albrecht
Dürer, 1509-1510

74

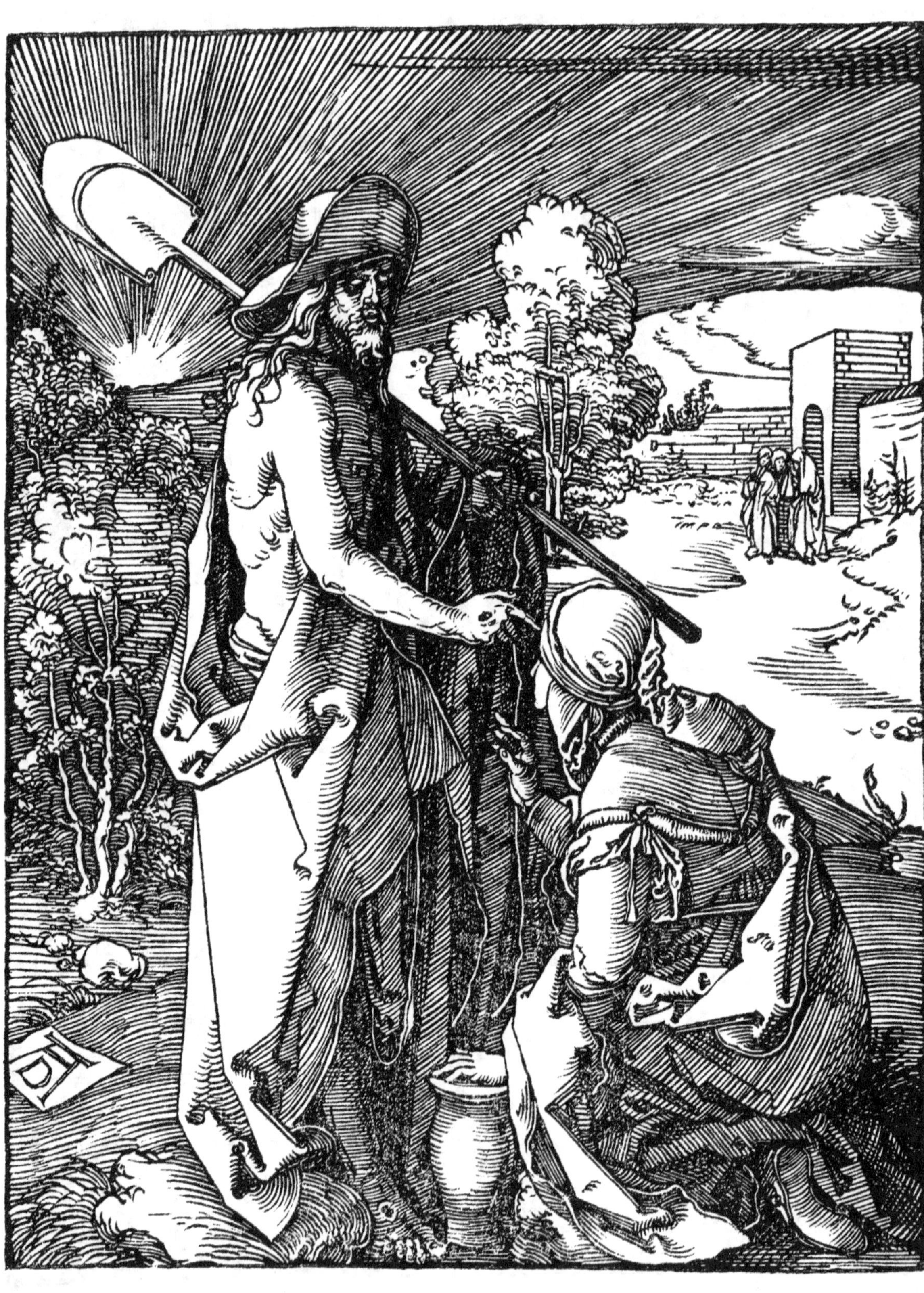

74. Christ Appearing to Mary Magdalene.
Albrecht Dürer, 1509-1510

75

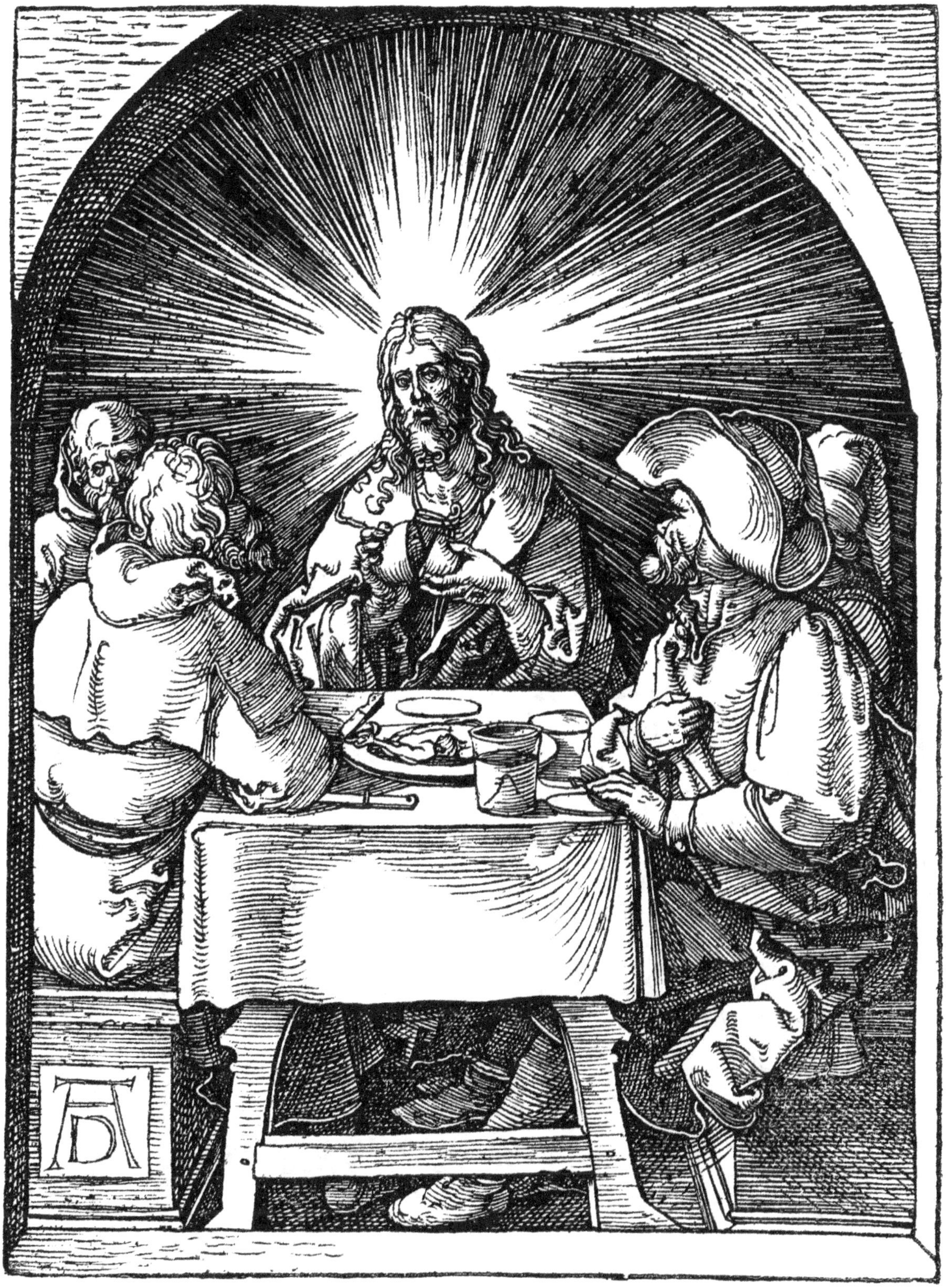

75. Christ at Emmaus. Albrecht Dürer. 1509-1510.

76

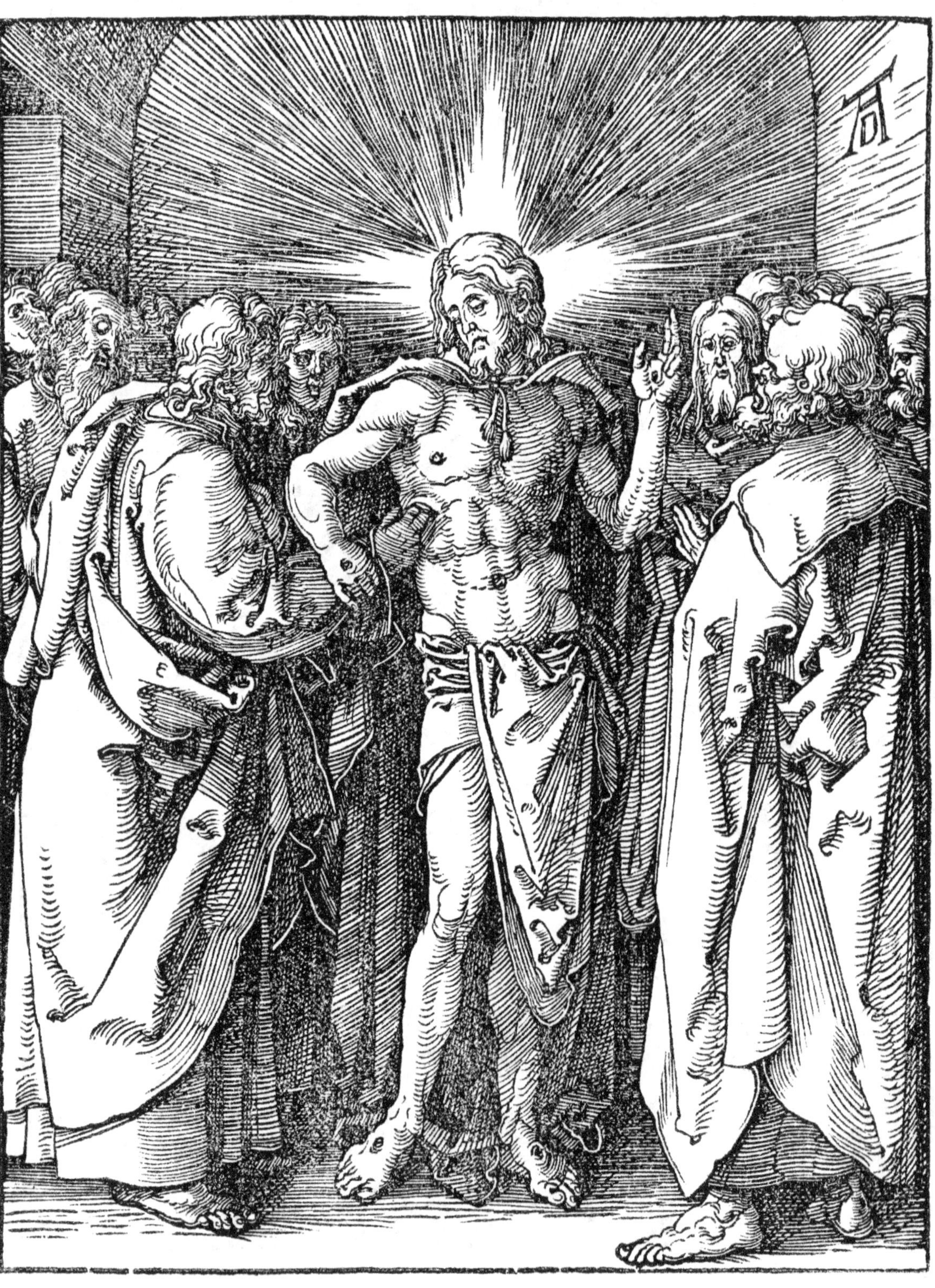

76. Incredulity of Saint Thomas. Albrecht Dürer, 1510

77

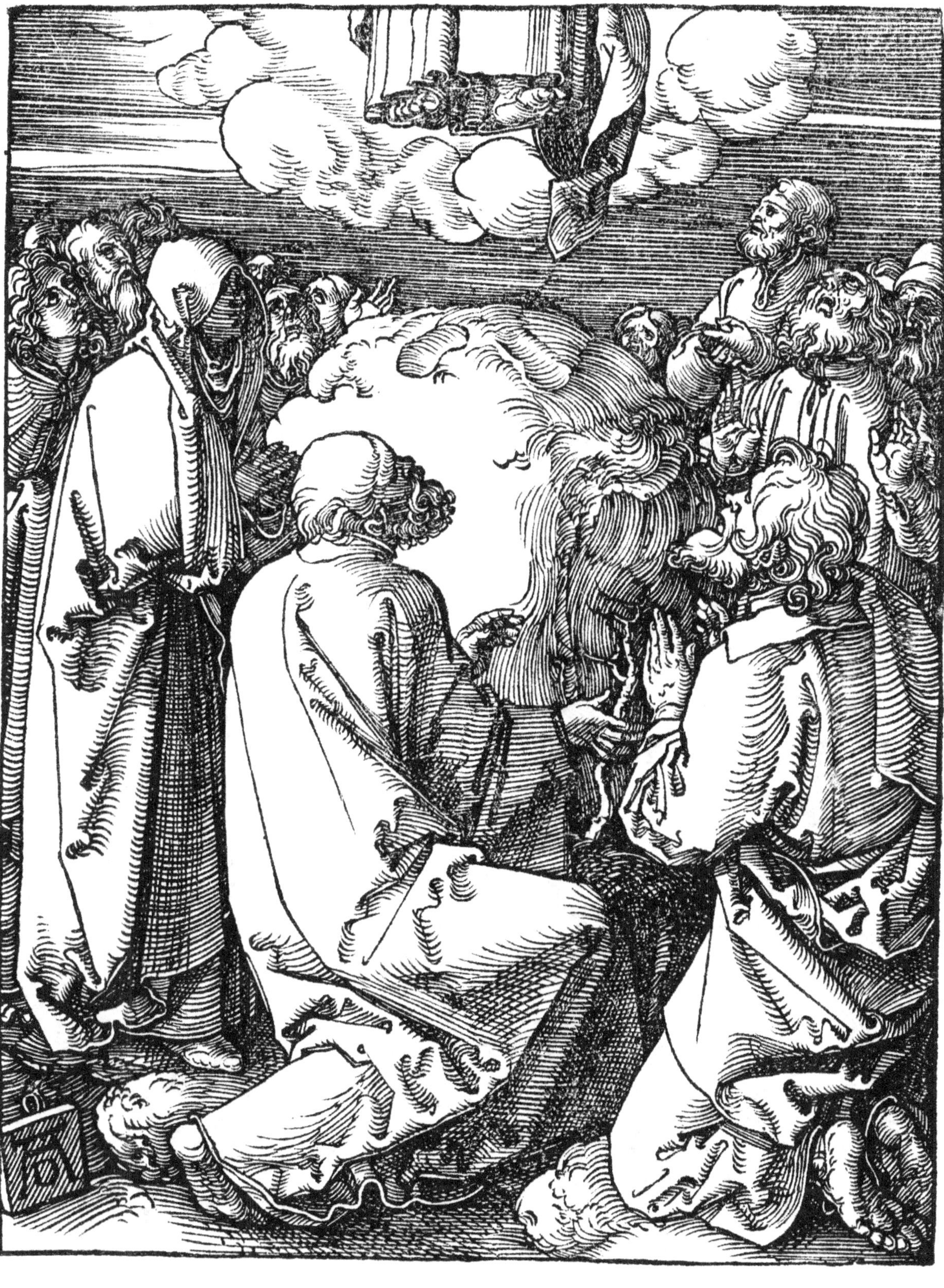

77. Ascension Day, Albrecht Dürer, 1510

78

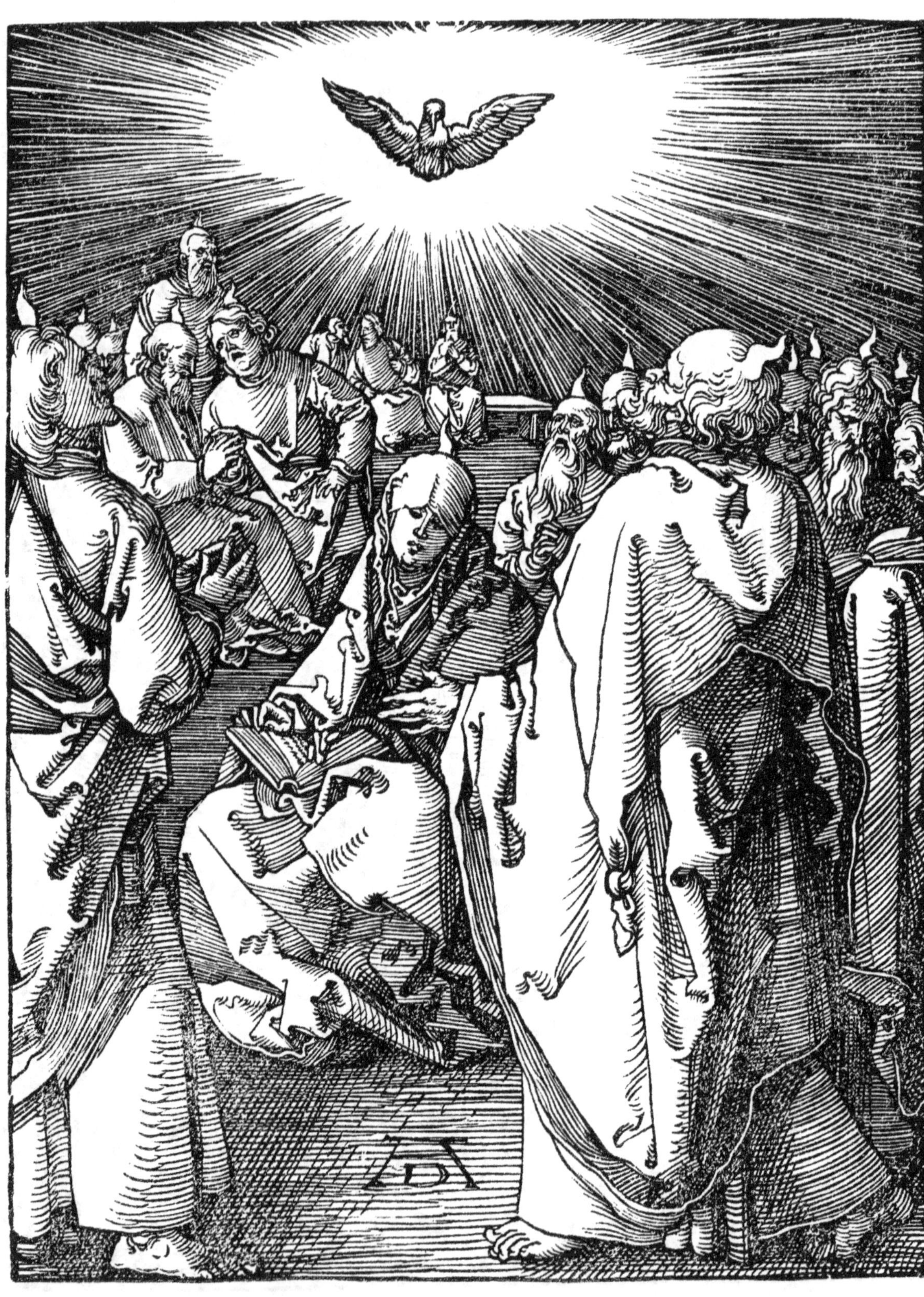

78. Pentecost. Albrecht Dürer. 1509-1510.

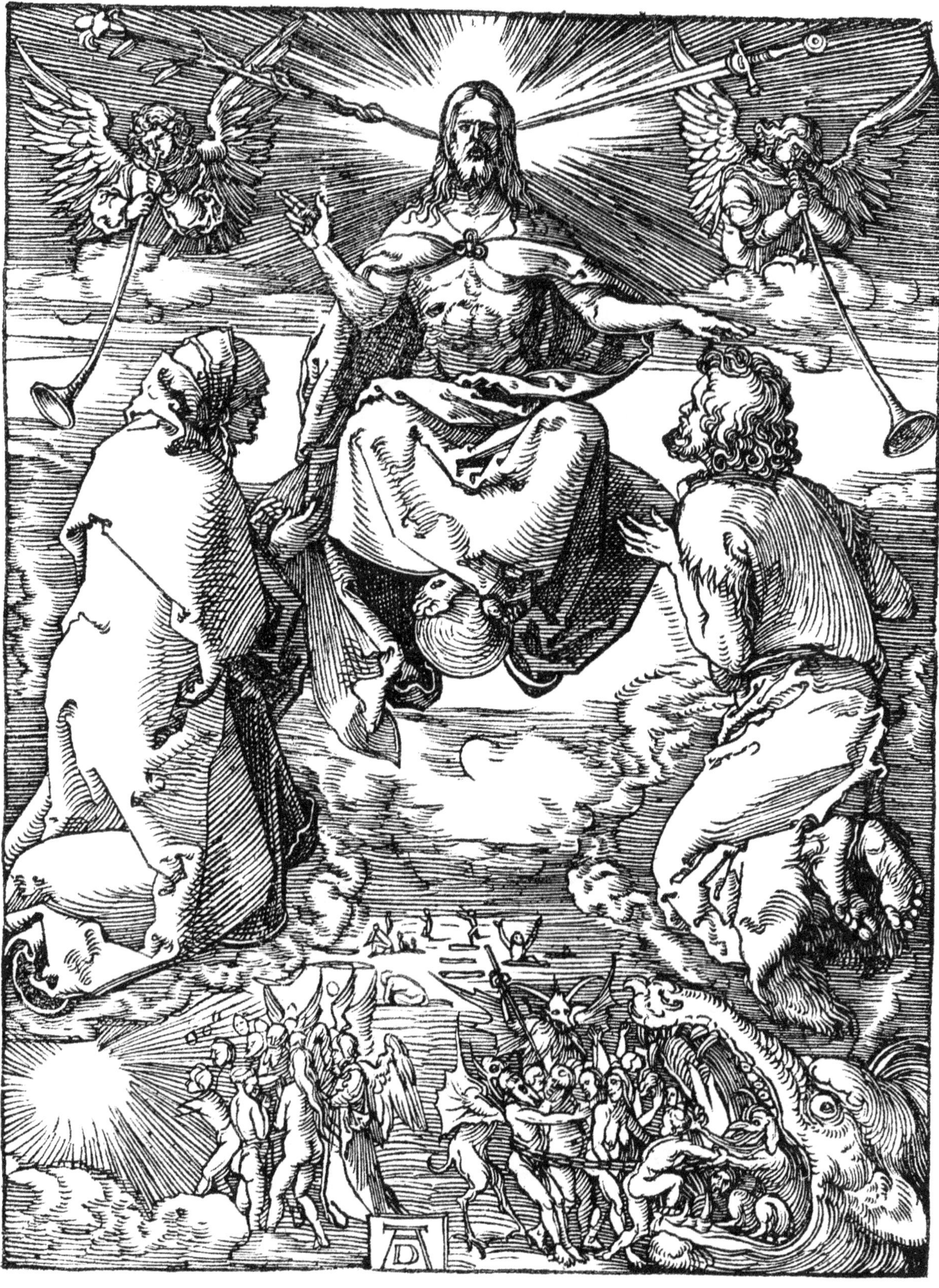

79. Last Judgment, Albrecht Dürer, 1510

80

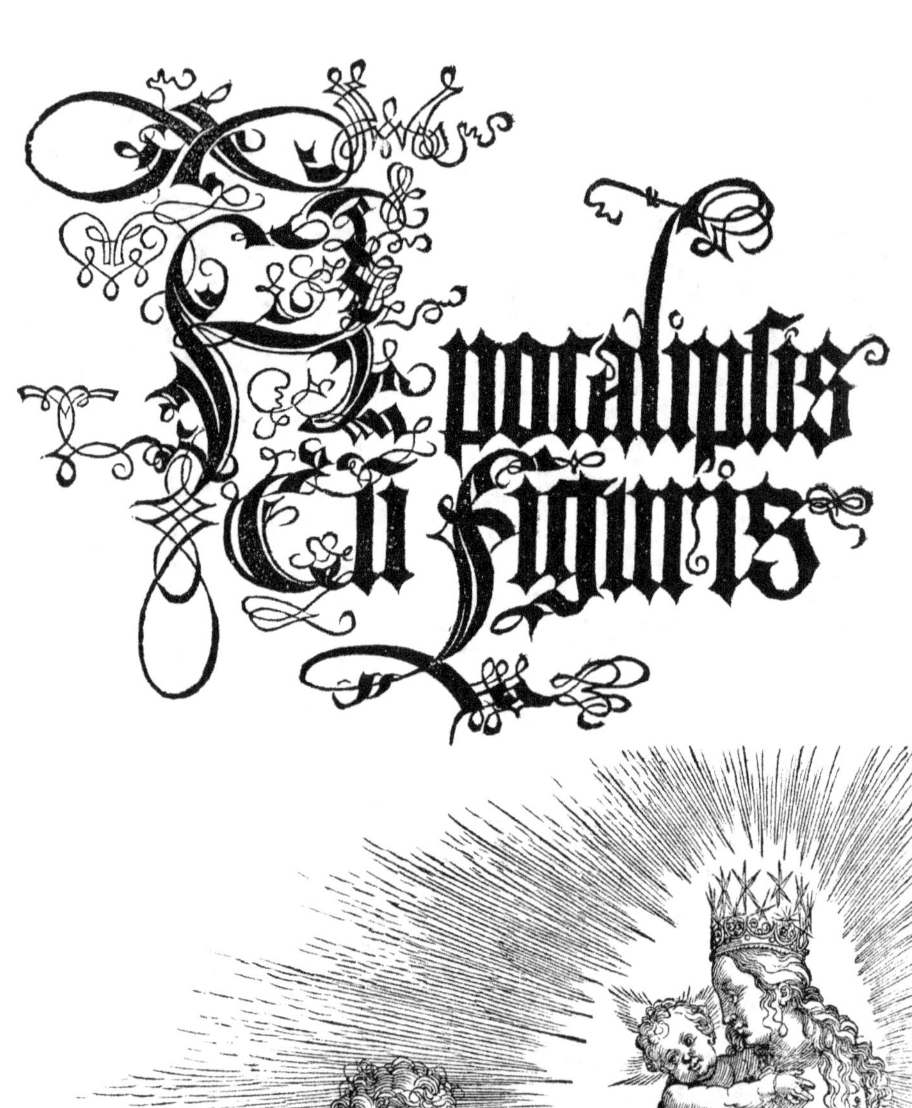

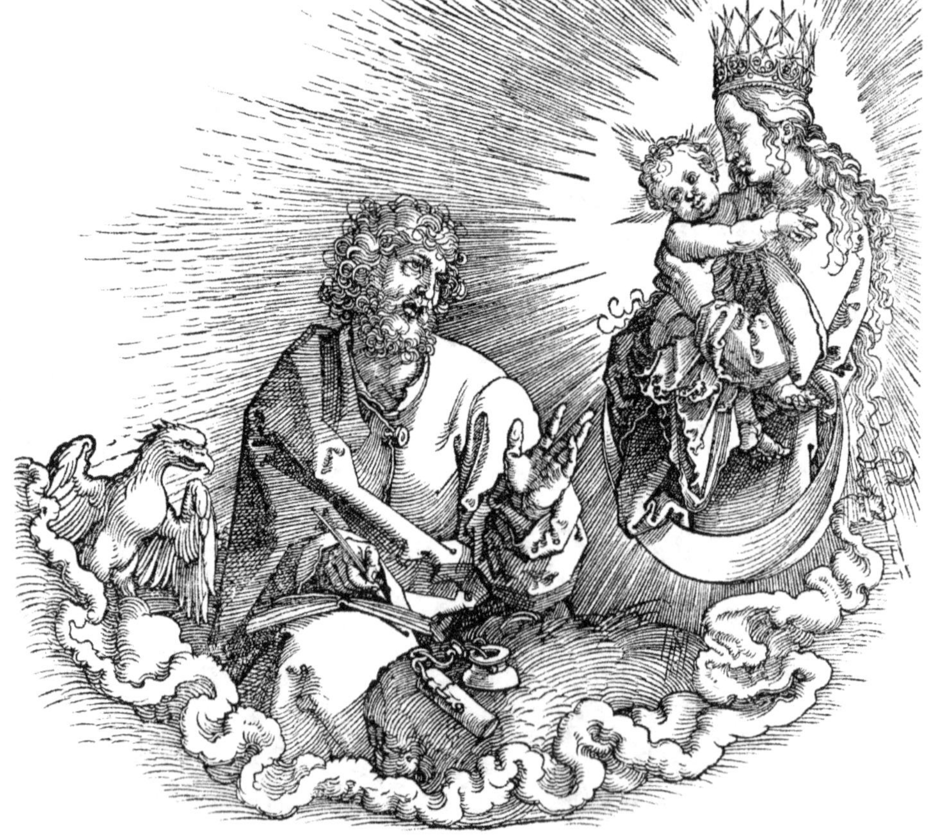

*80. Title page of the second Latin edition of the
Apocalypse series. Albrecht Dürer, 1511*

81

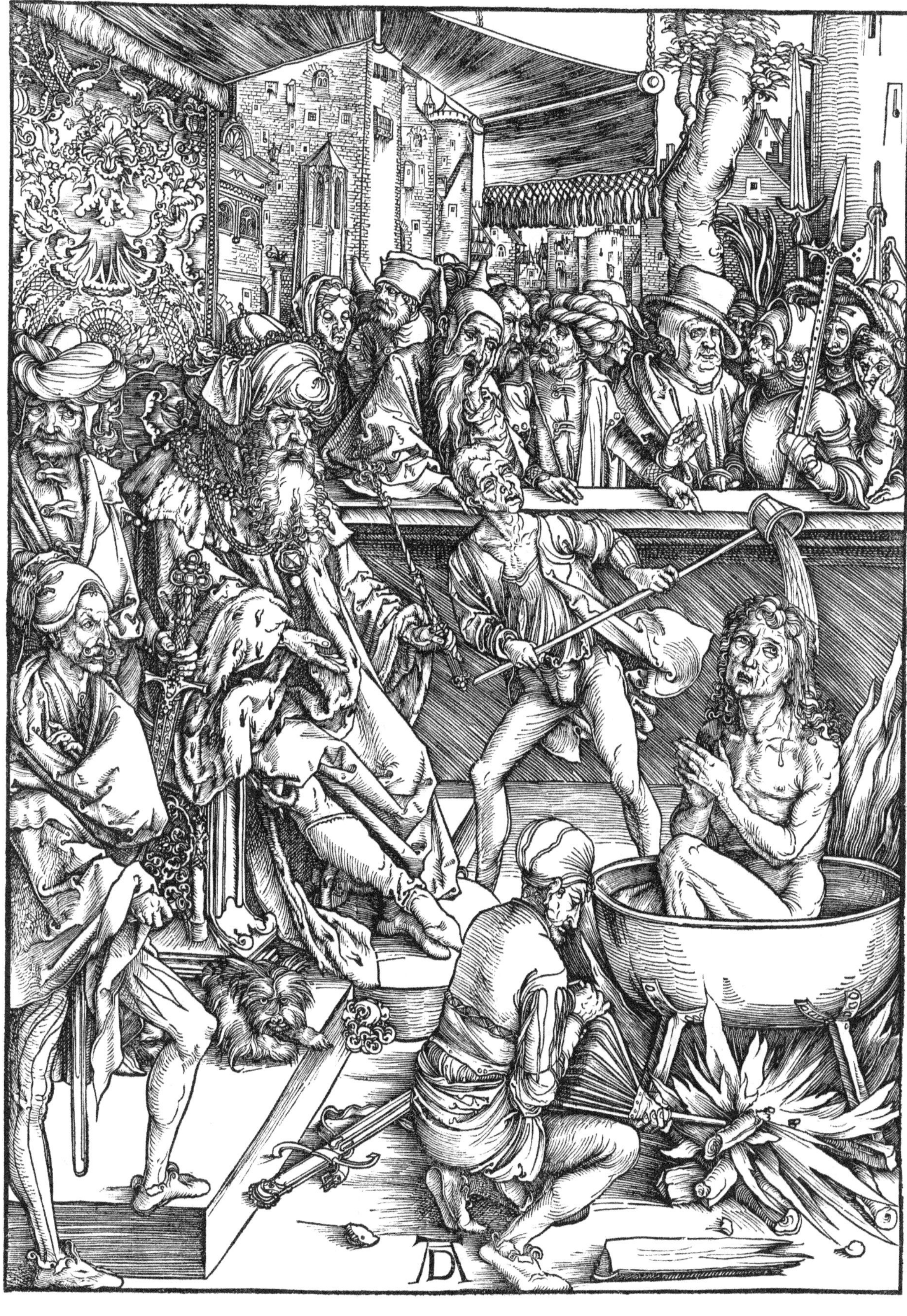

ALBRECHT DÜRER

82

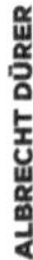

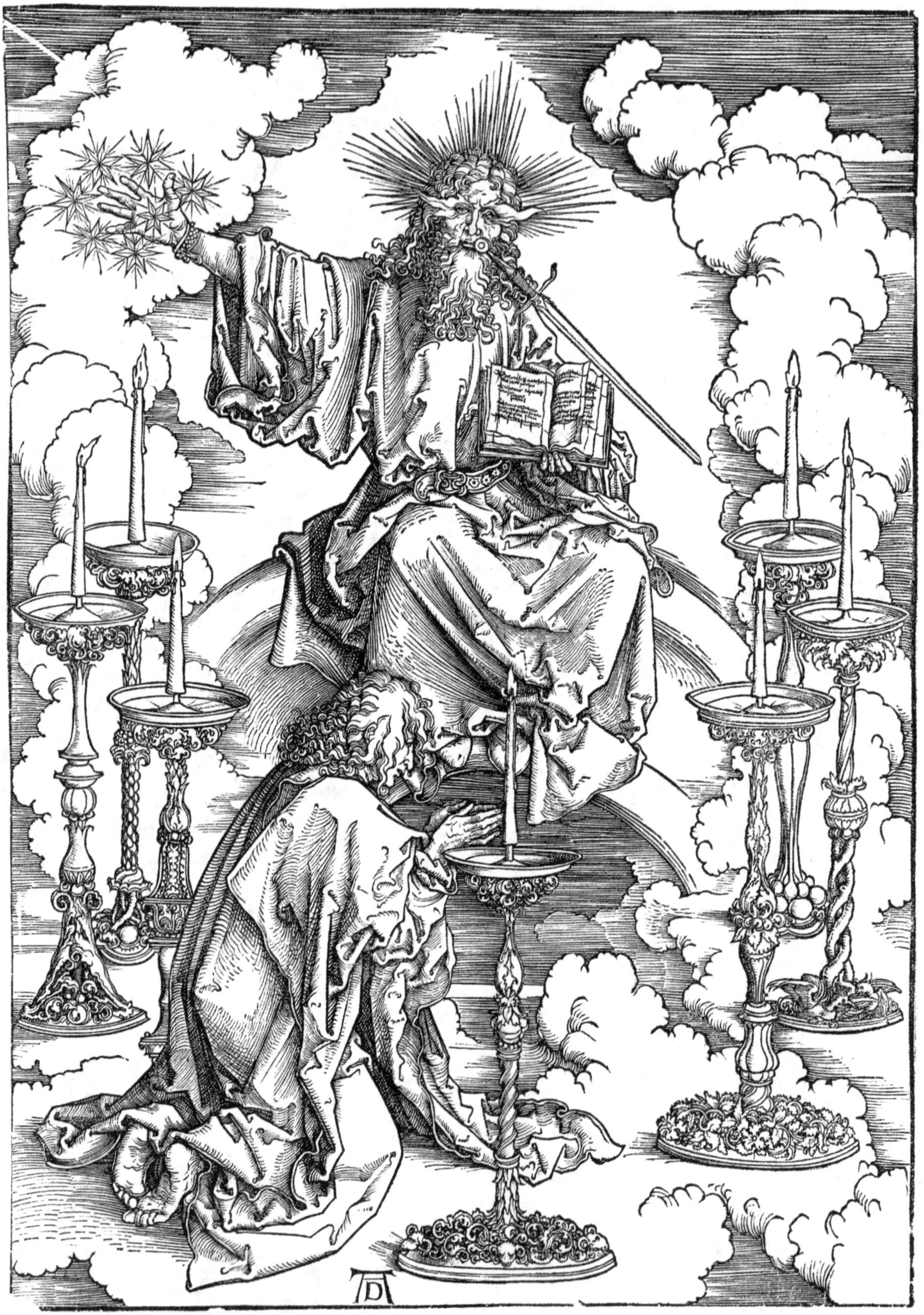

82. John the Evangelist kneels before Christ
amid seven candlesticks, Albrecht Dürer, 1498

83

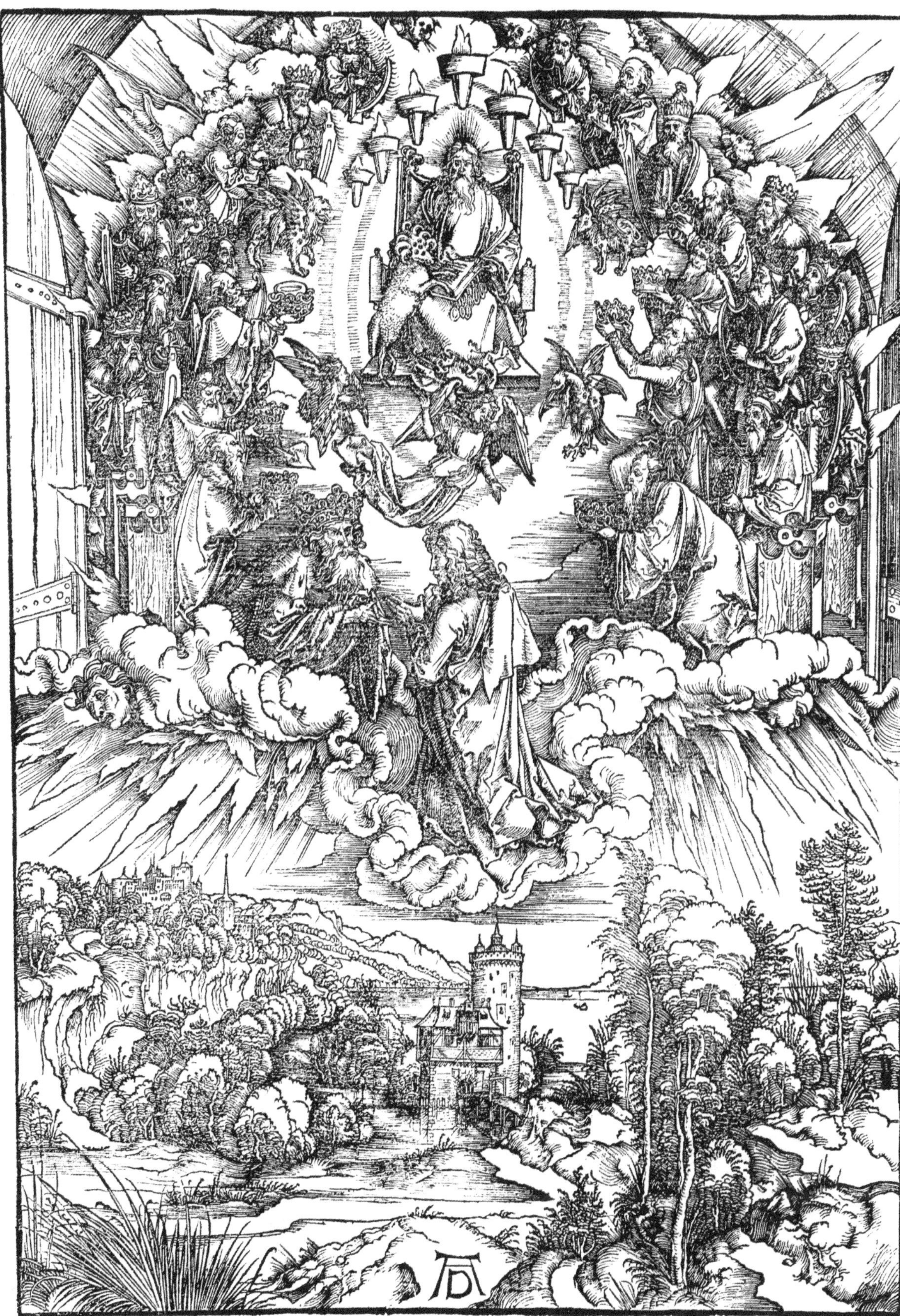

83. St John kneeling before Christ and the
twenty-four elders

84

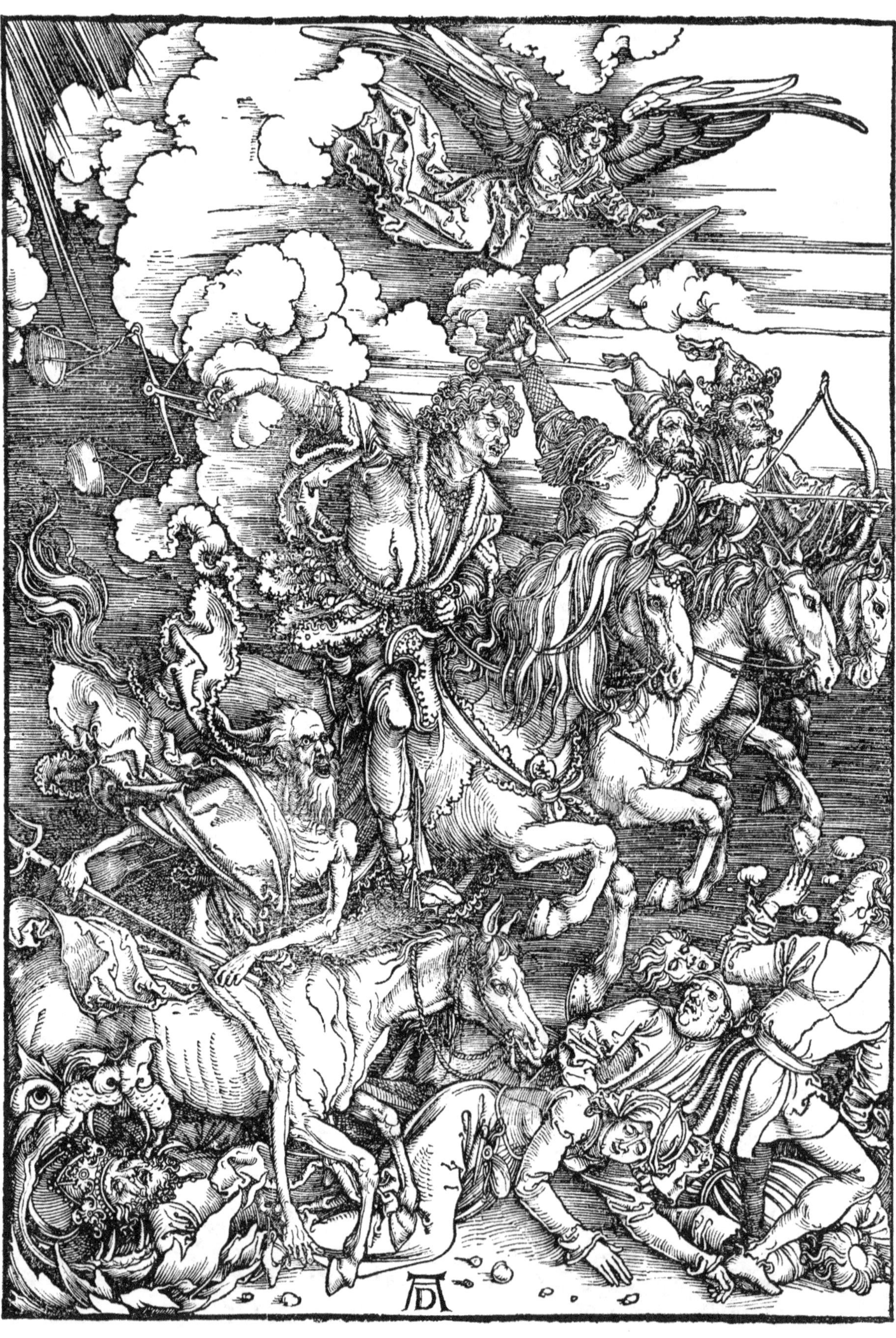

84. *The Four Horsemen of the Apocalypse,*
Albrecht Dürer, 1511

85

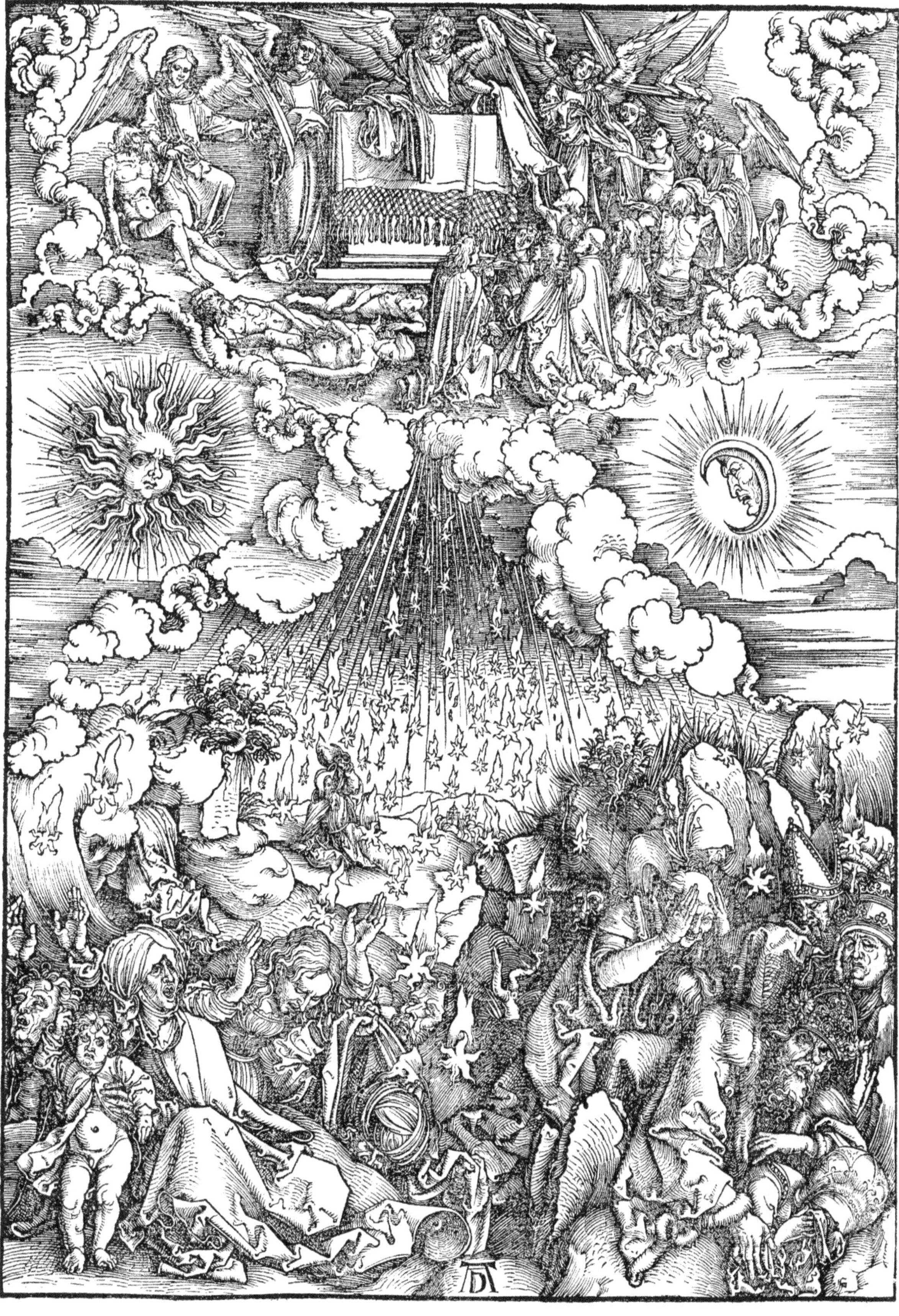

ALBRECHT DÜRER

85. Opening the fifth and sixth seals. Albrecht
Dürer, 1511.

86

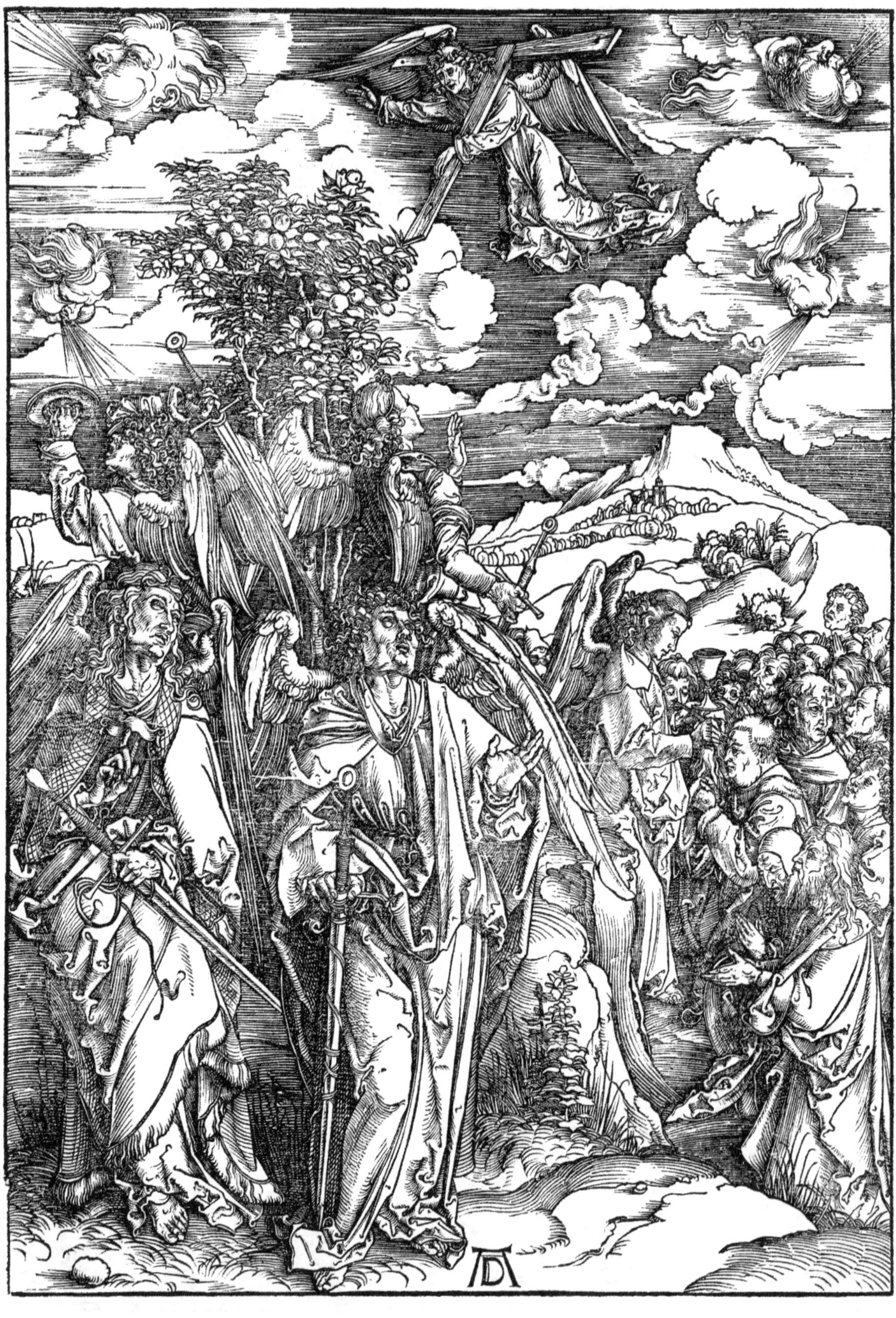

86. Angels hold back the four winds, Albrecht
Dürer, 1511

87

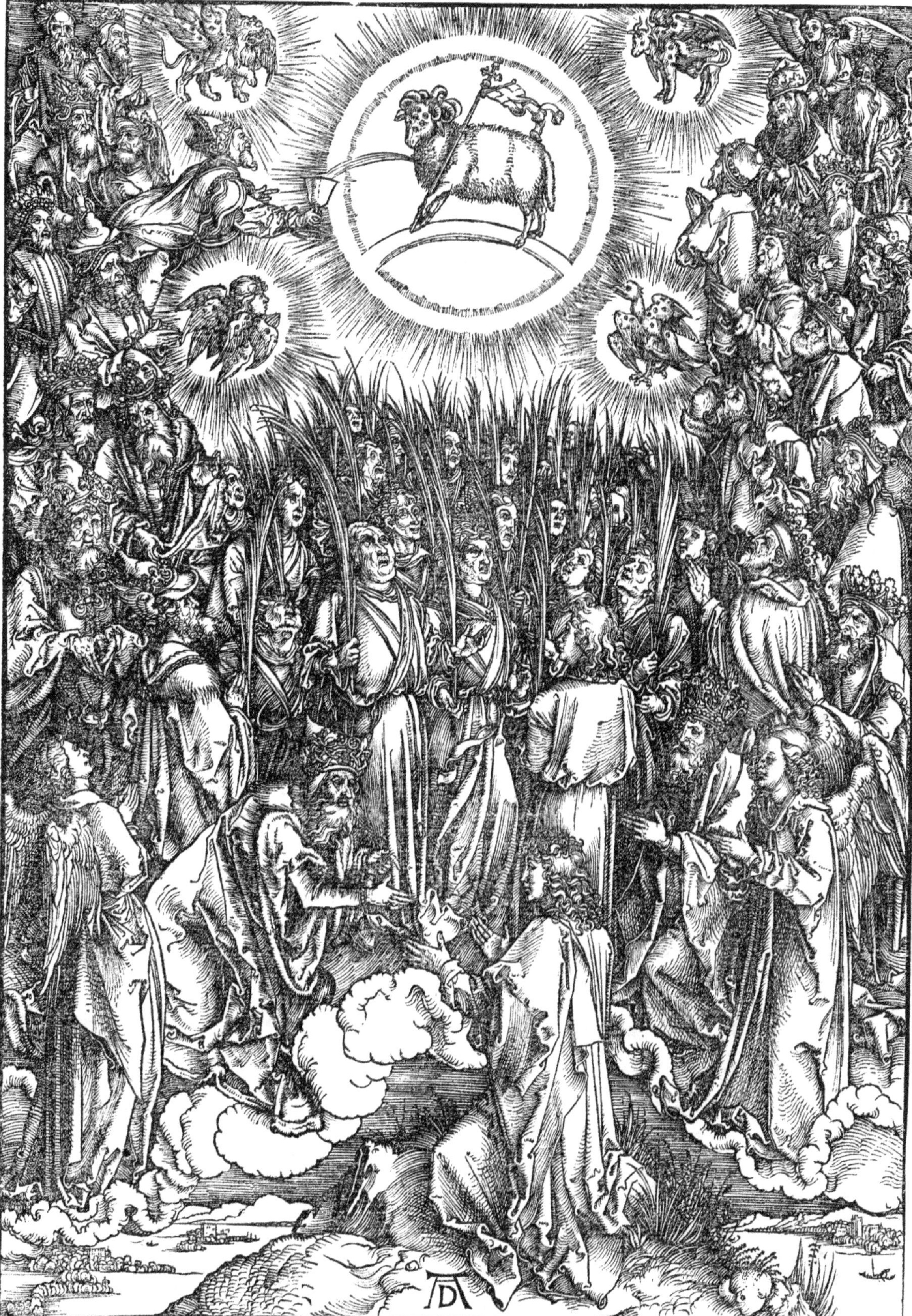

ALBRECHT DÜRER

87. *John the Evangelist Beholds the Adoration
of the Lamb, Albrecht Dürer, 1511*

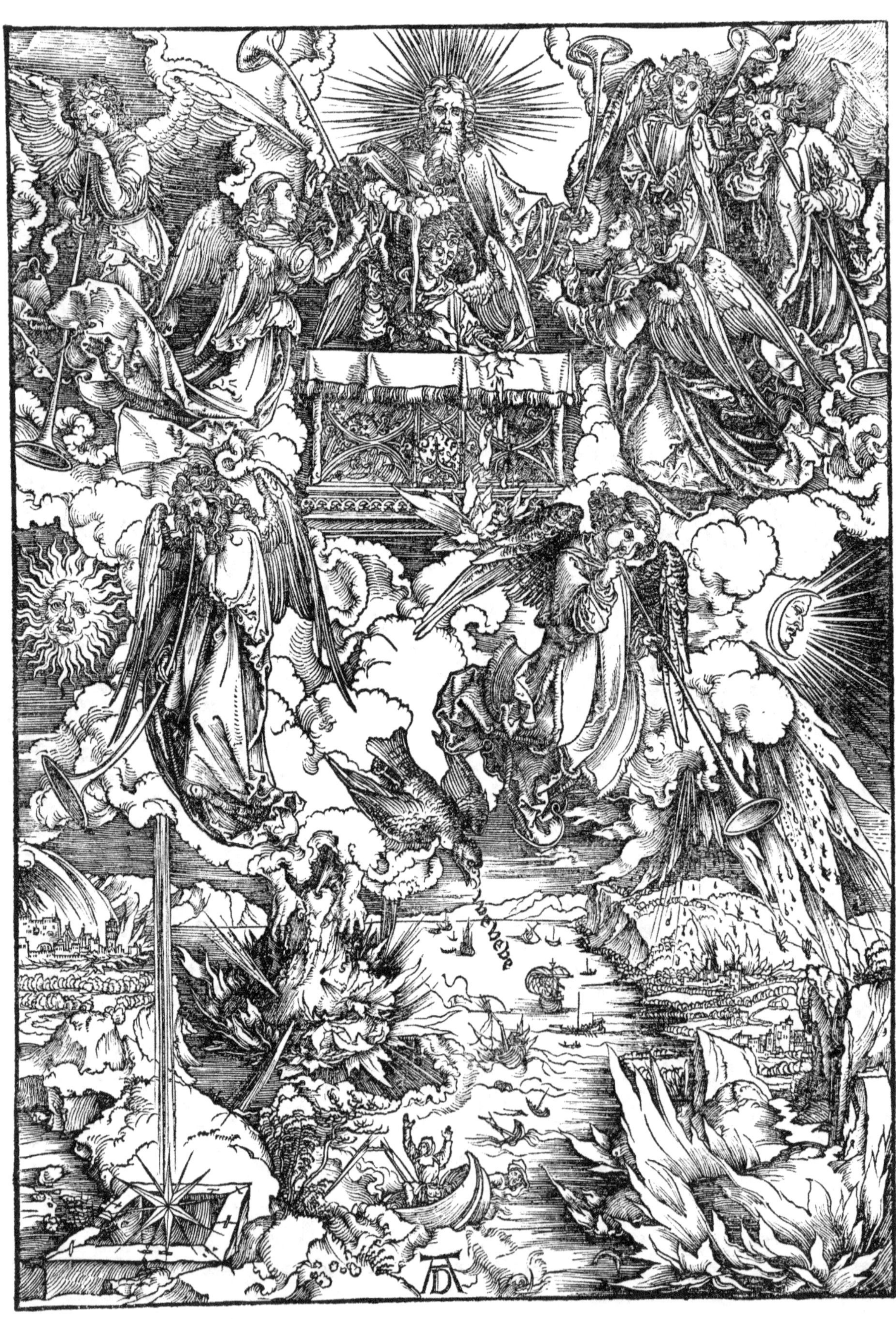

88. *The Seven Angels with the Trumpets.*
Albrecht Dürer, 1511.

89

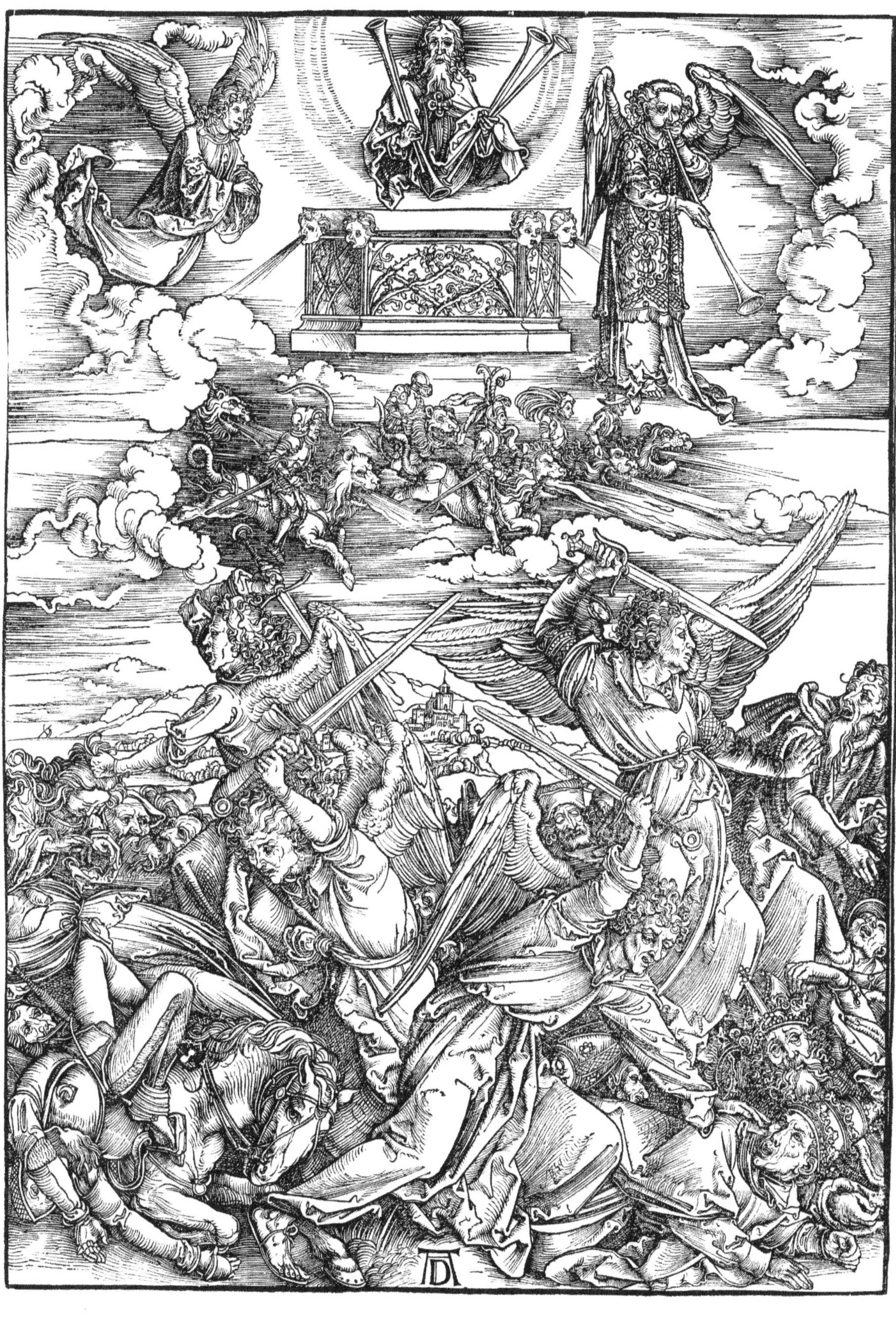

89. The Four Destroying Angels, Albrecht
Dürer, 1511.

90

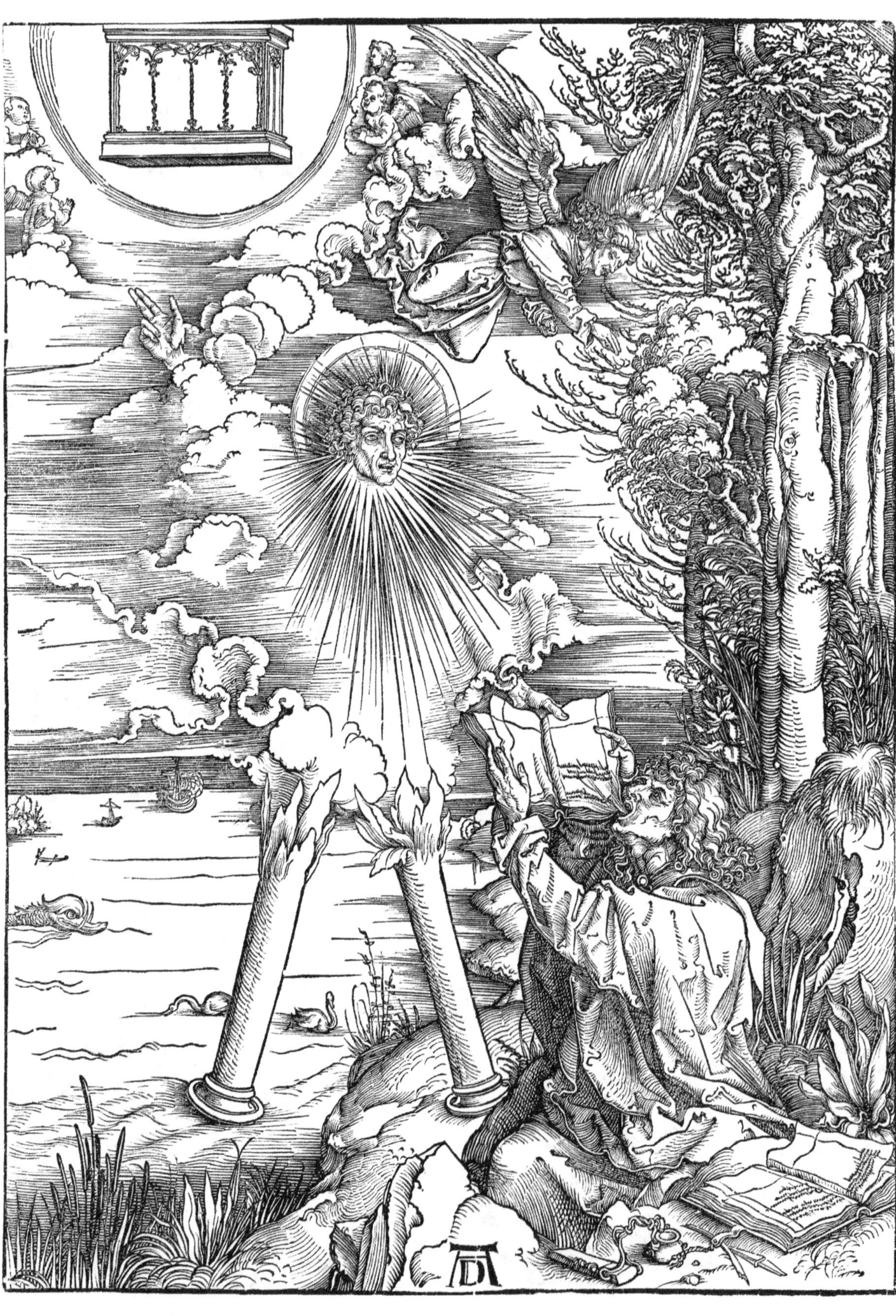

90. John the Evangelist devours the book,
Albrecht Dürer, 1498

91

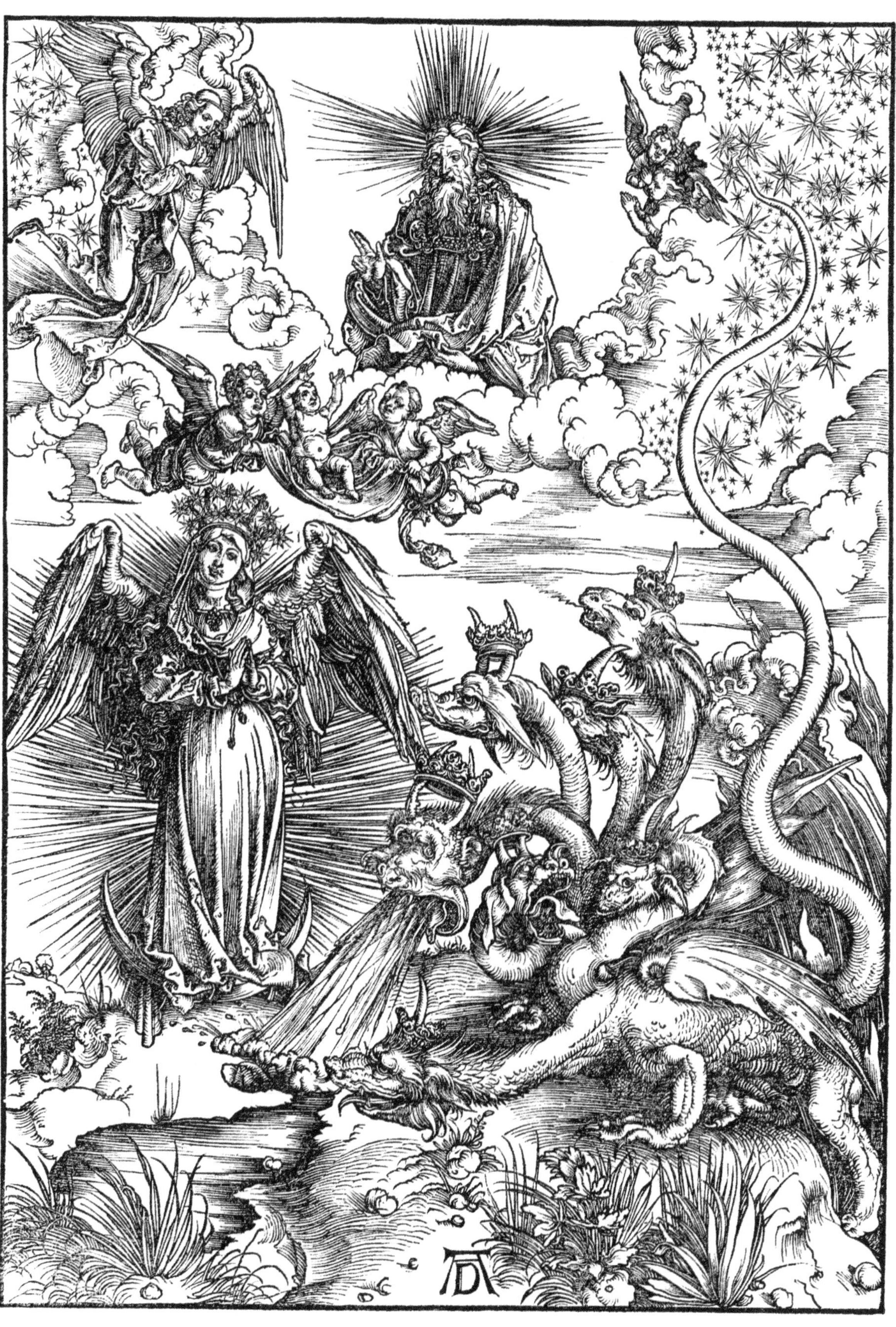

*91. The Apocalyptic Woman and the Seven-
Headed Dragon, Albrecht Dürer, 1511*

92

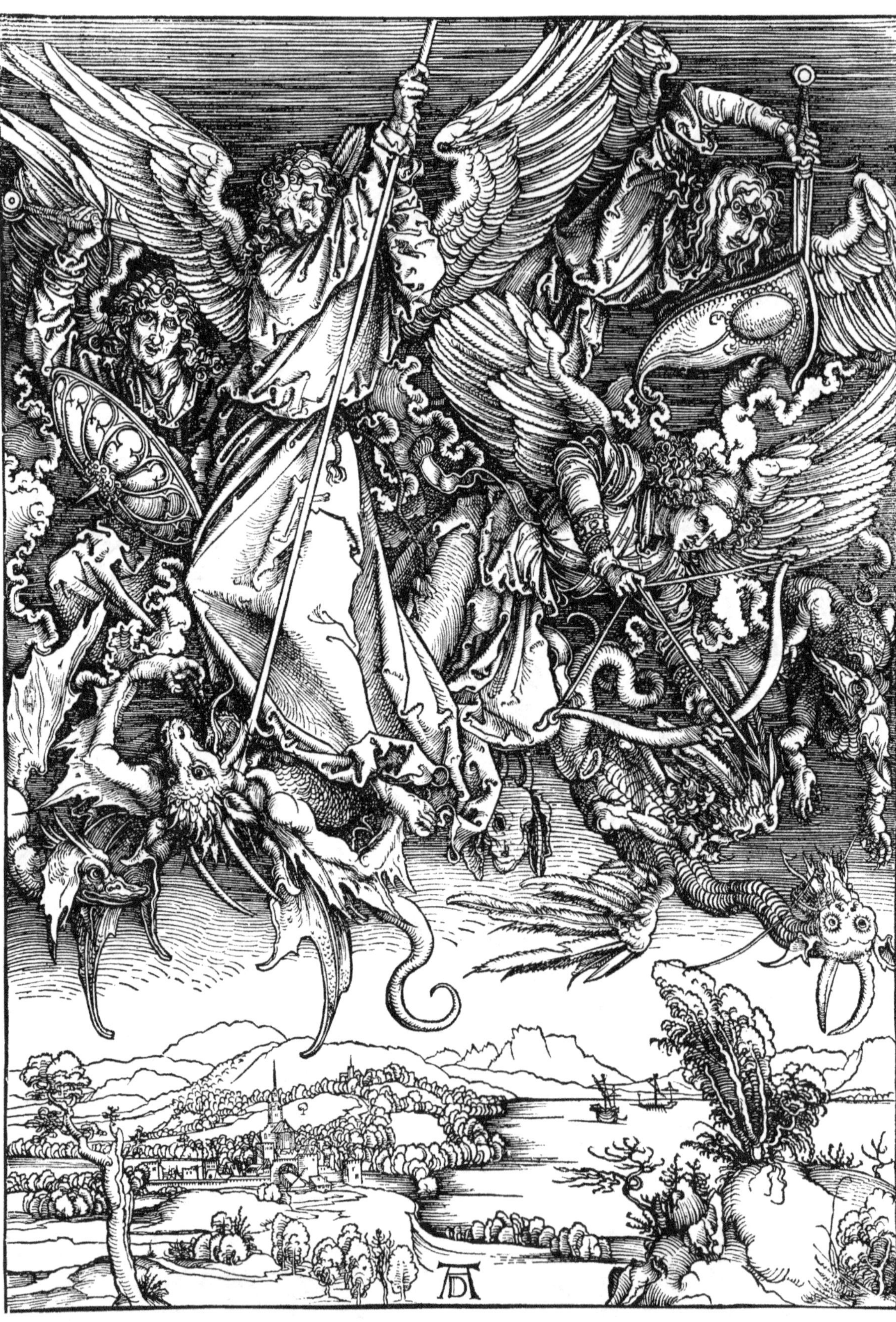

92. *Saint Michael Fighting the Dragon, Albrecht Dürer, 1511.*

93

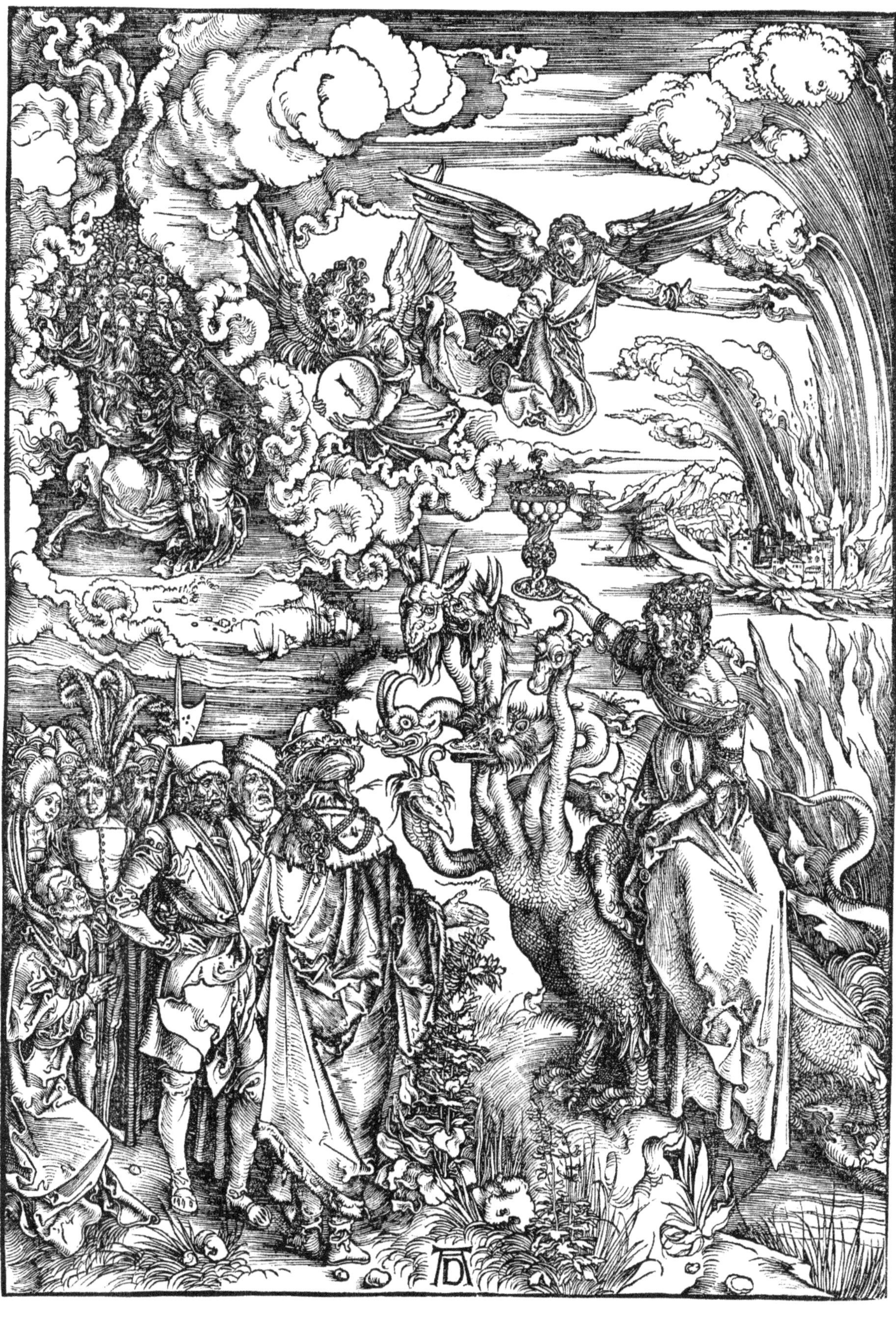

ALBRECHT DÜRER

94

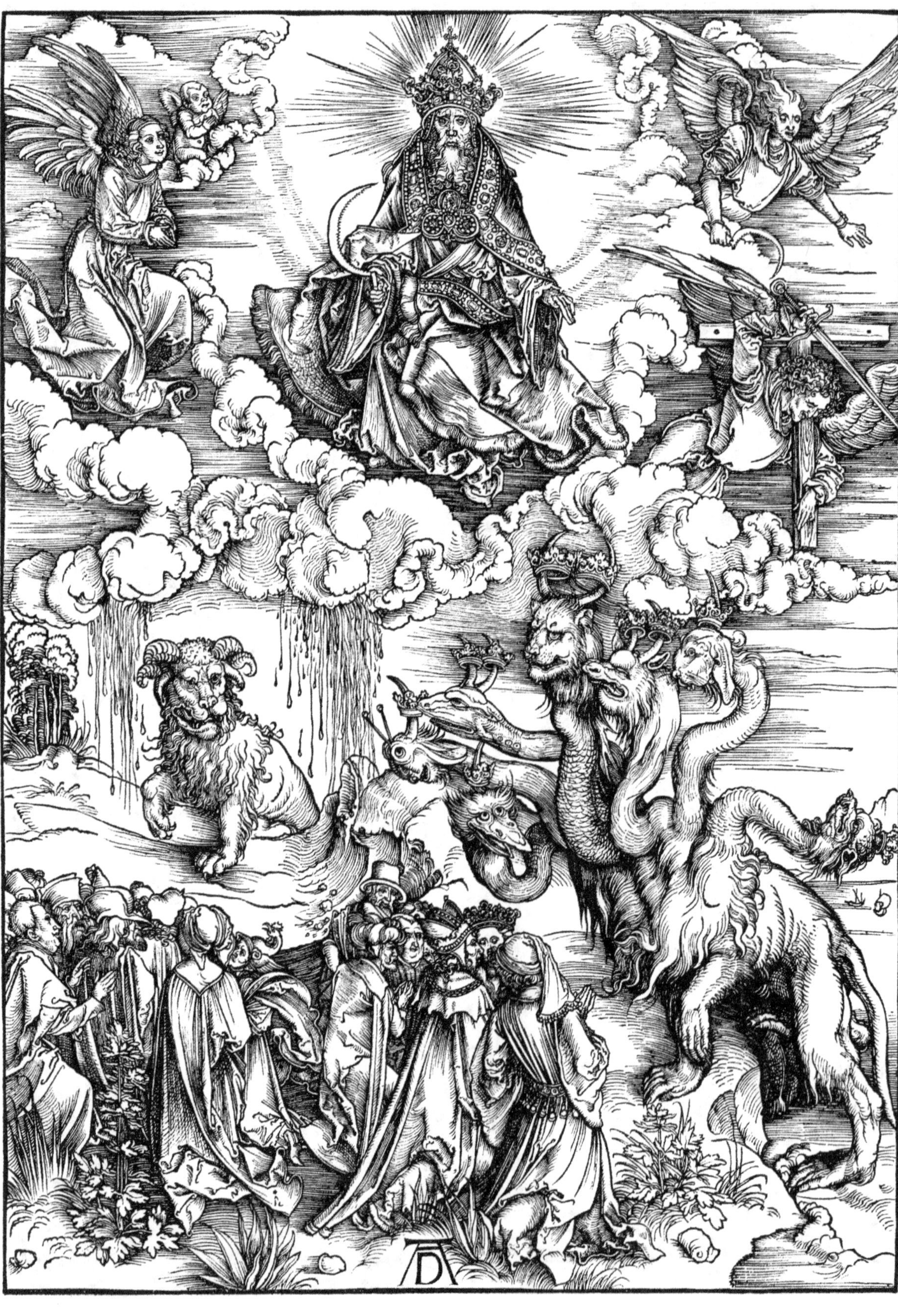

94 The Beast with Seven Heads and the Beast
with Lamb's Horns

95

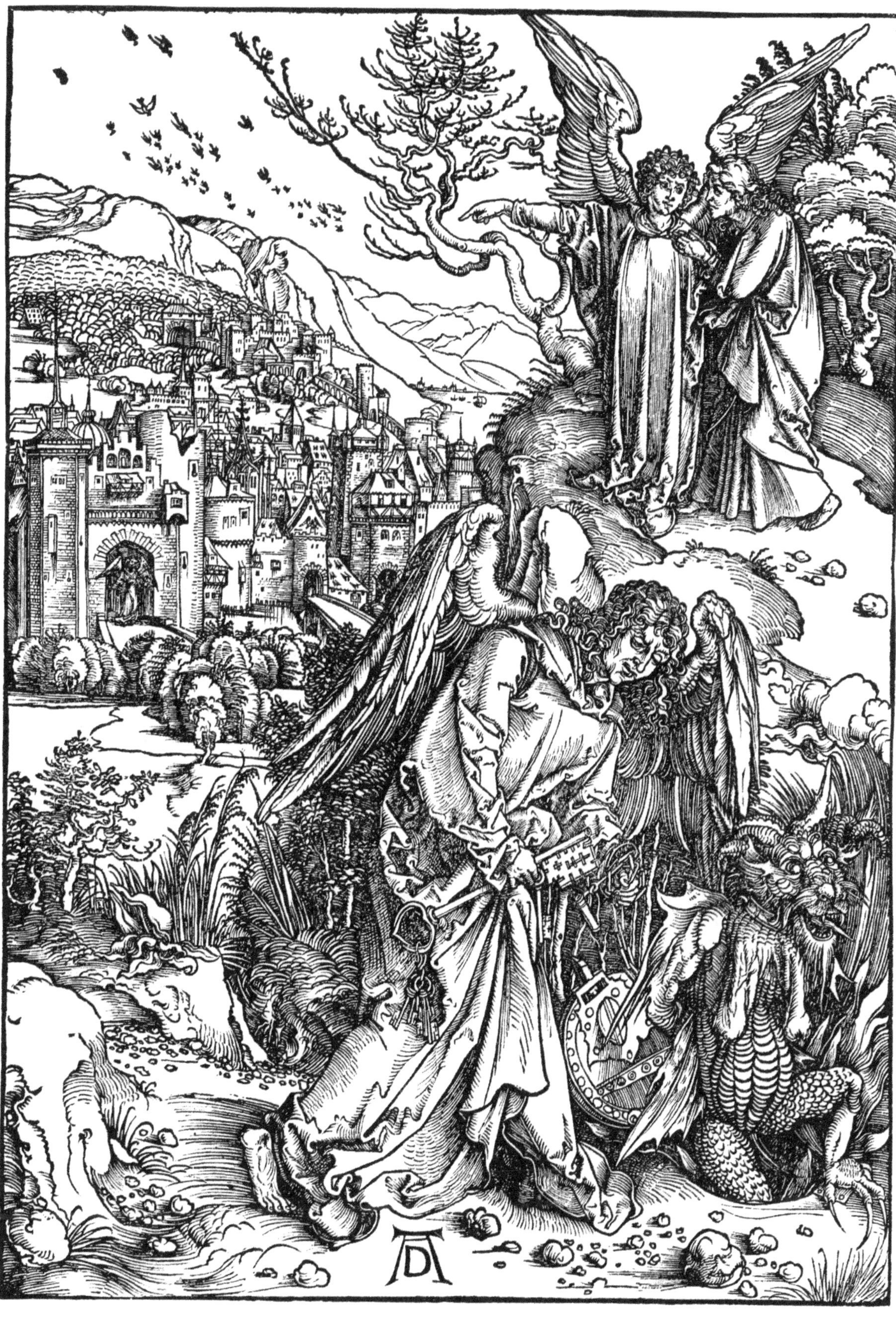

ALBRECHT DÜRER

95. The angel with the key of the bottomless
pit. Albrecht Dürer, 1511.

96

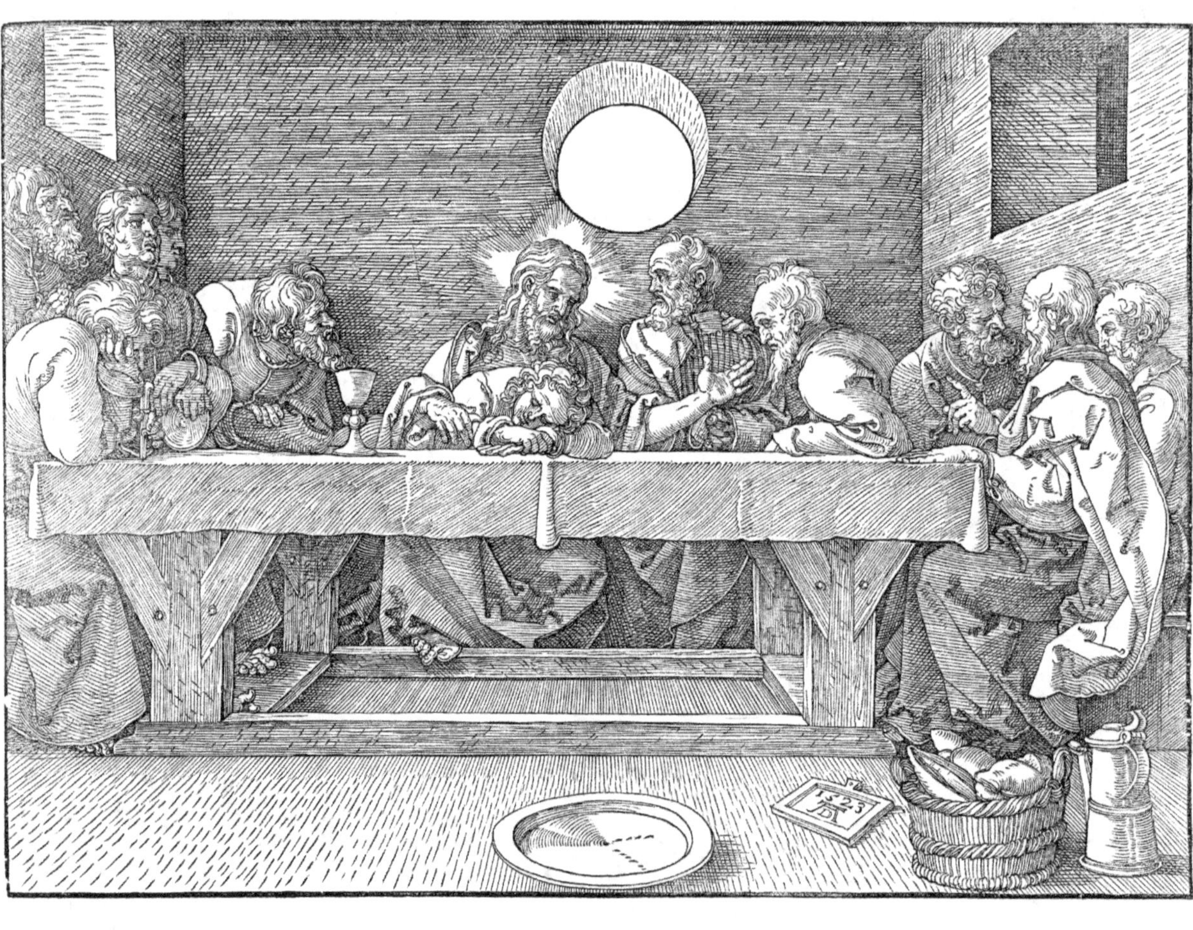

96. Last Supper, Albrecht Dürer, 1523

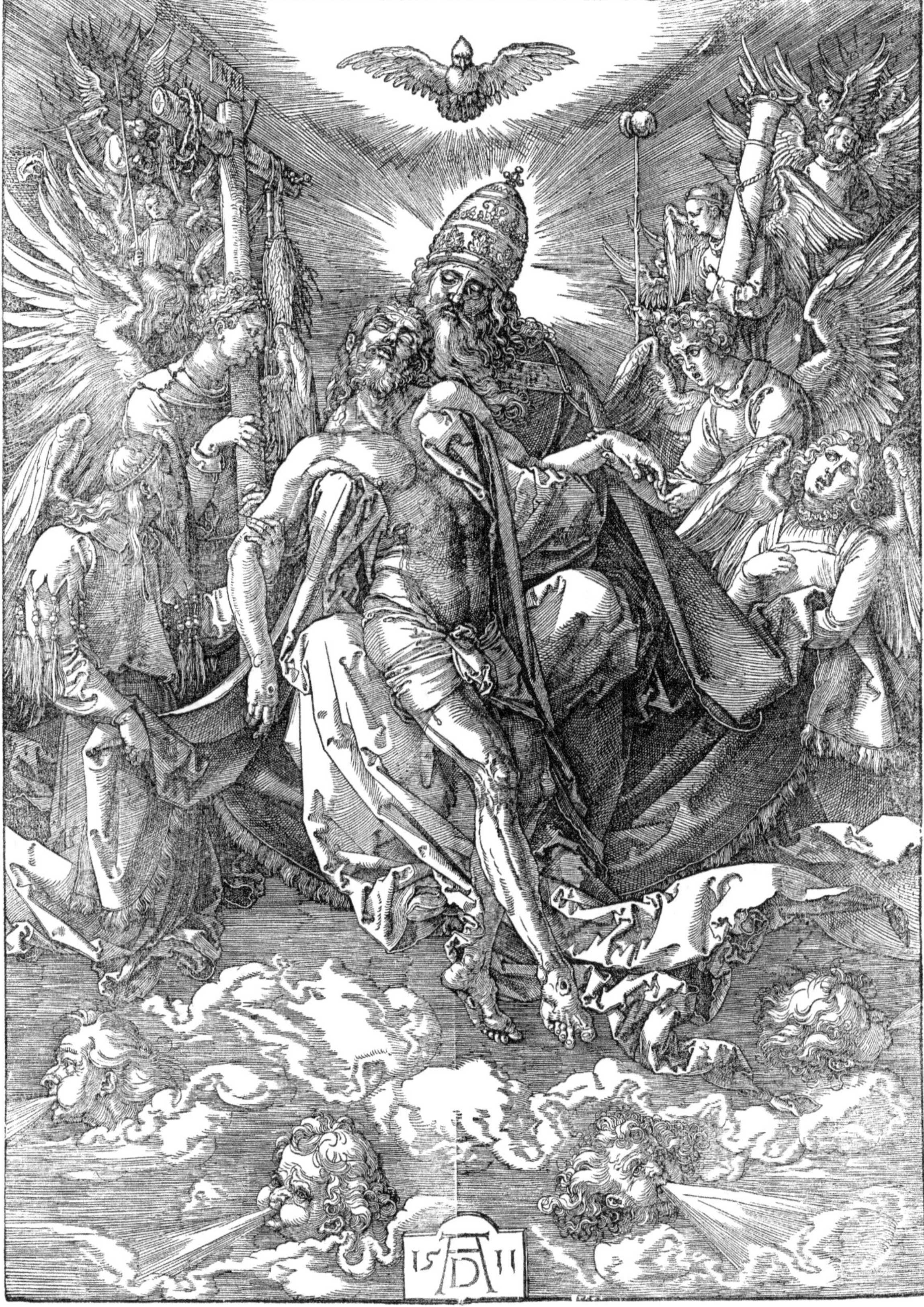

ALBRECHT DÜRER

98

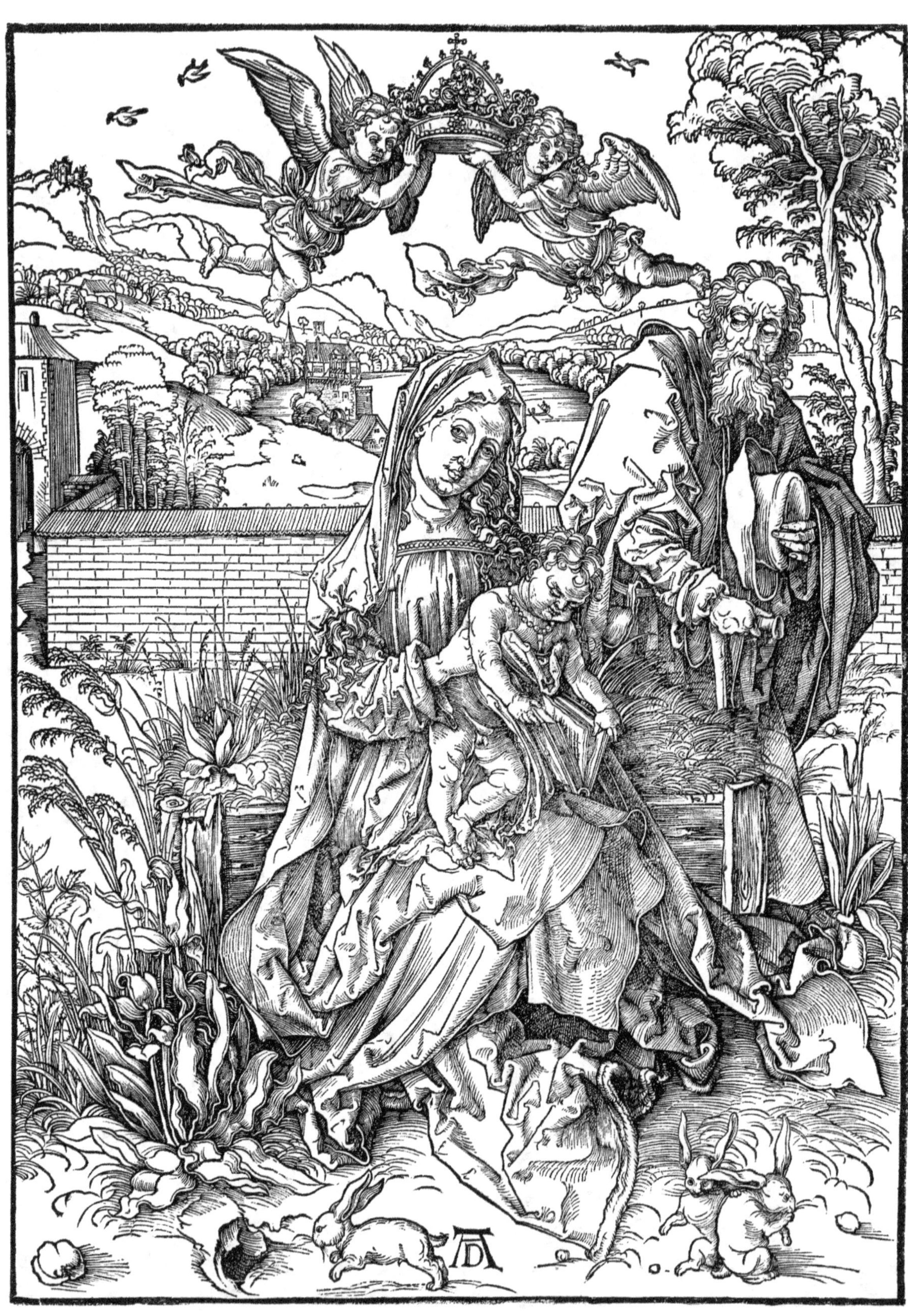

98. *The Holy Family with Three Hares*, Albrecht Dürer, 1495 - 1499

99

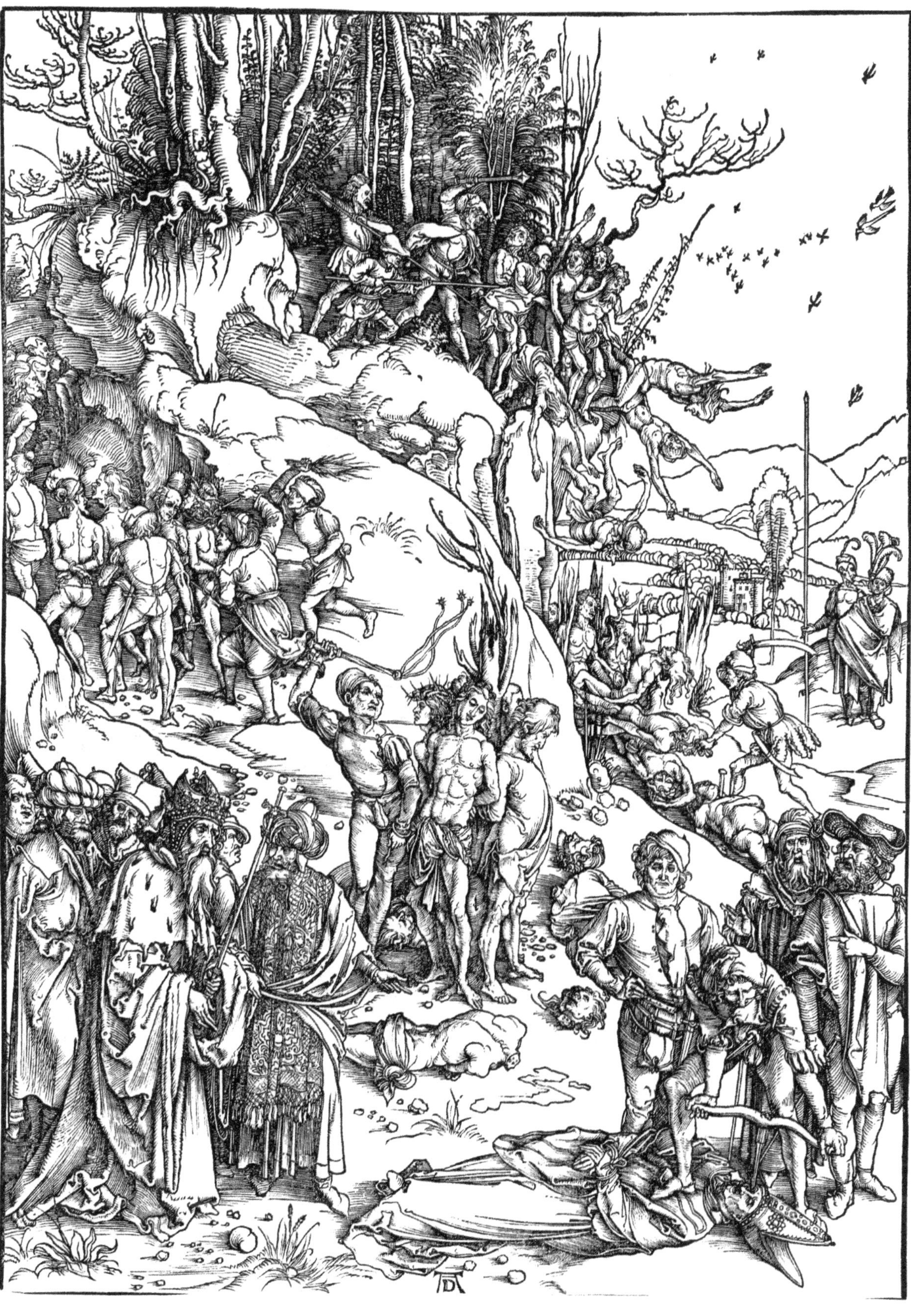

99. The Martyrdom of the Ten Thousand,
Albrecht Dürer, 1494 - 1498

100

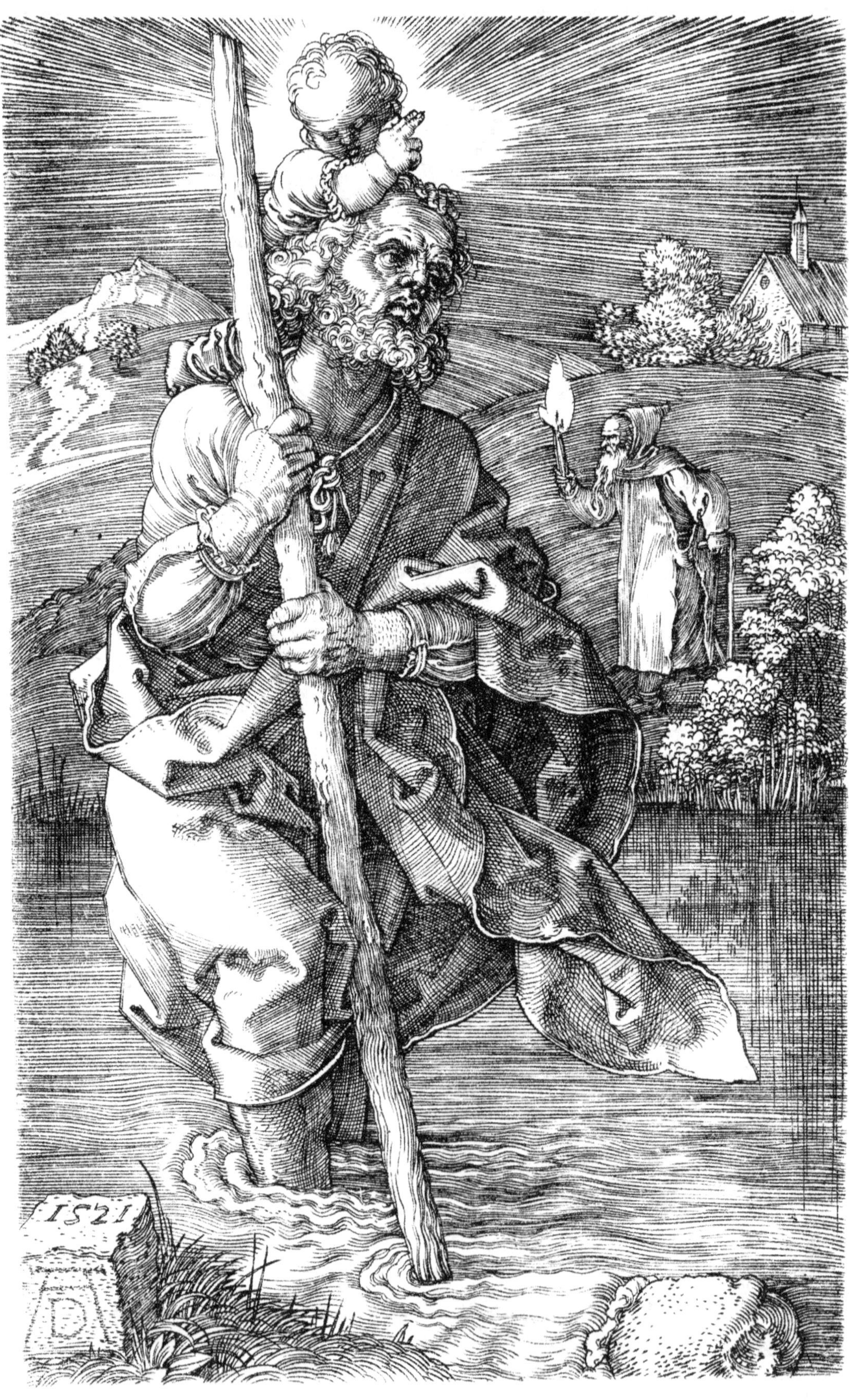

100. *Saint Christopher Facing Right, Albrecht Dürer, 1521*

101

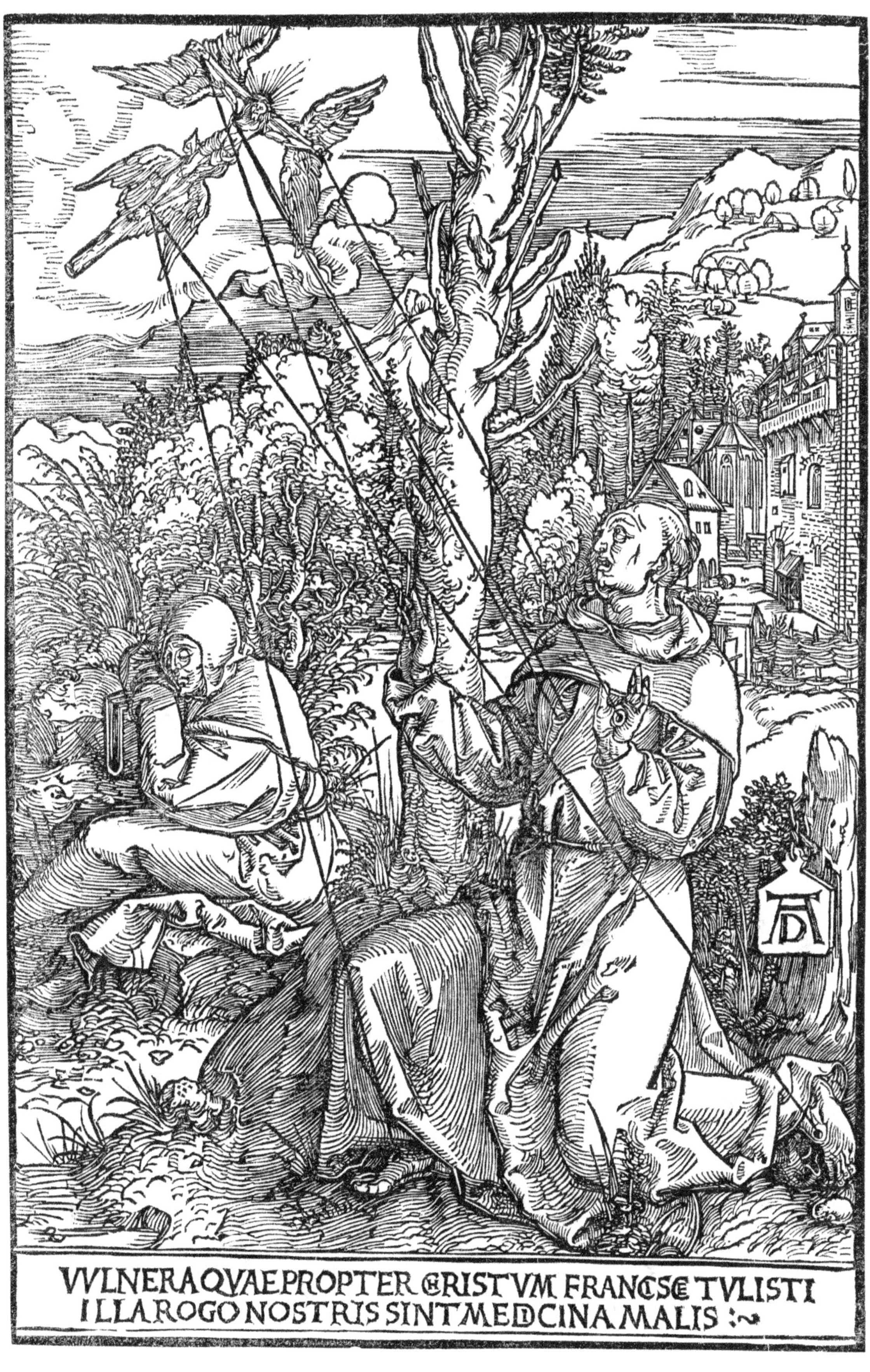

ALBRECHT DÜRER

101 Saint Francis Receiving the Stigmata.
Albrecht Dürer, 1503 - 1504

102

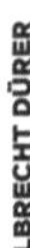

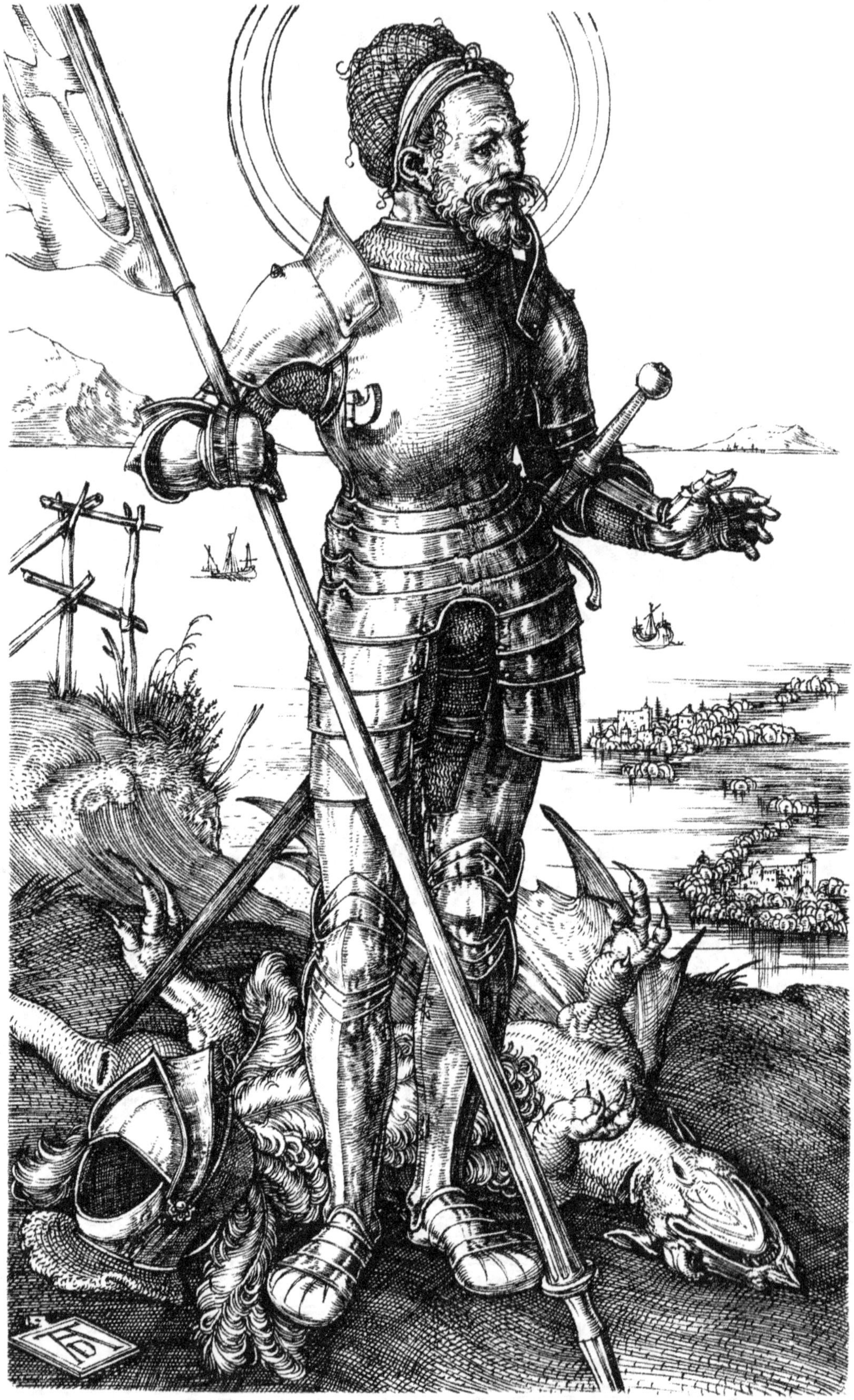

102. Saint George on Foot. Albrecht Dürer.
1500 - 1505

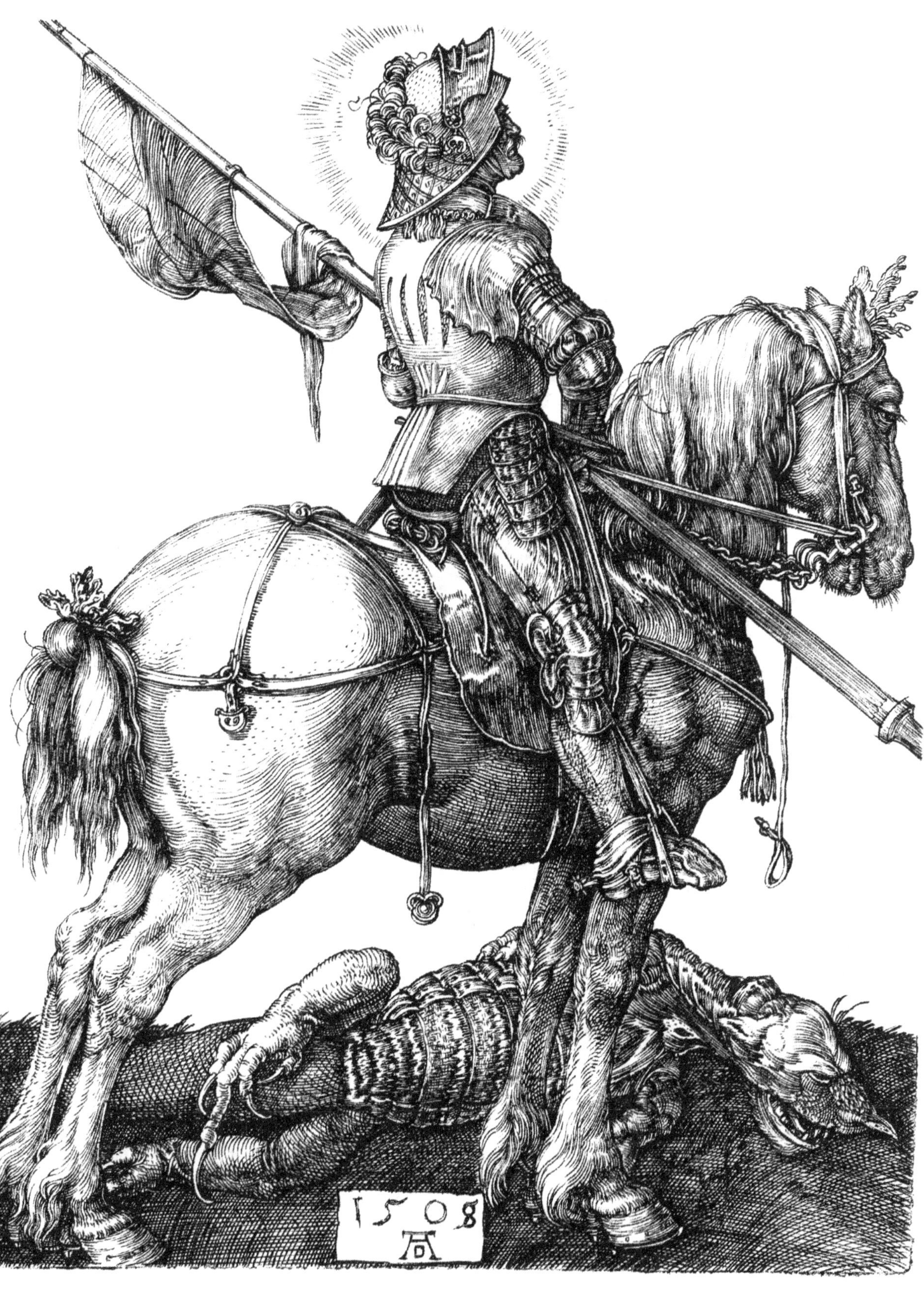

103. Saint George on Horseback, Albrecht Dürer, 1508

104

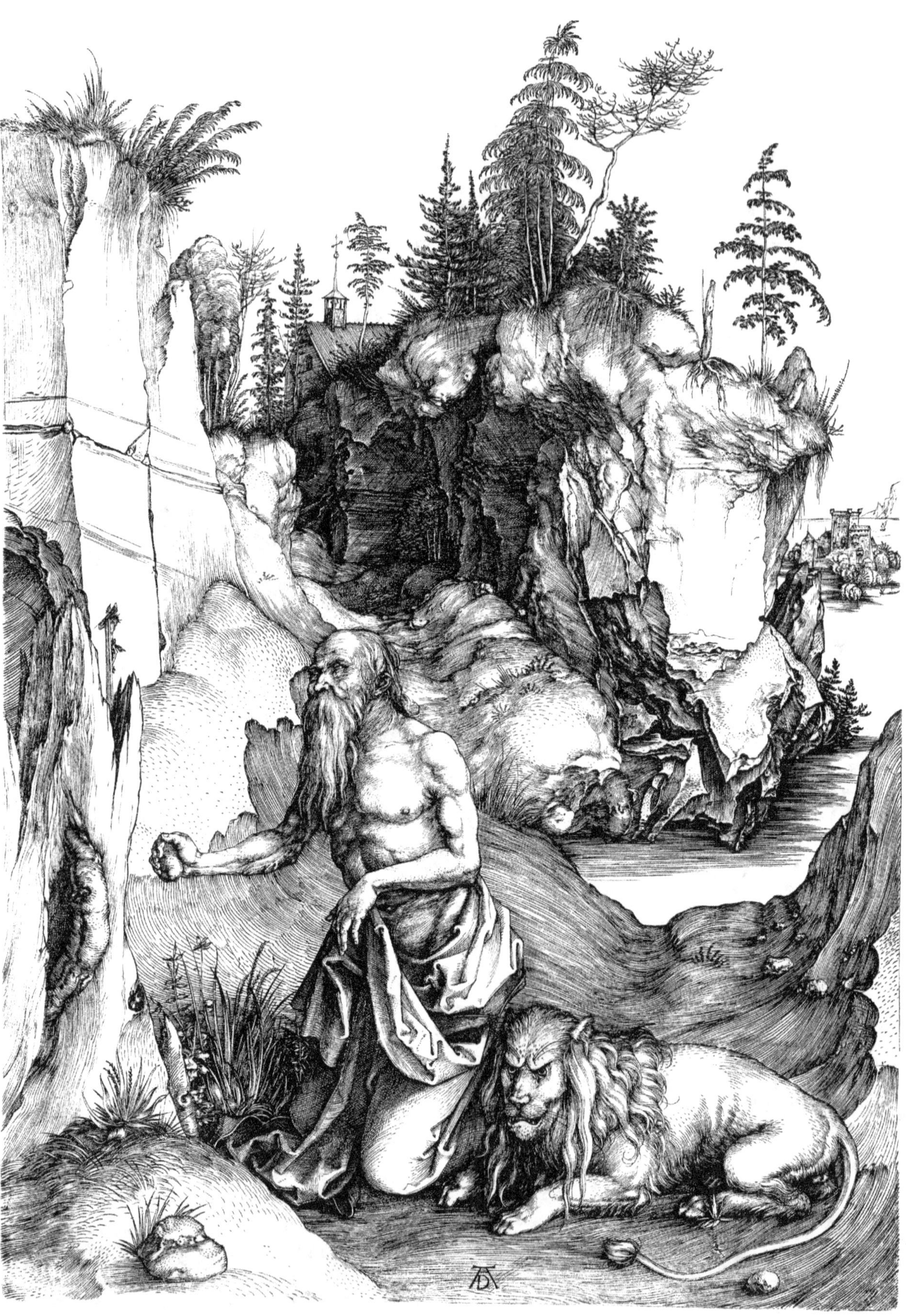

*104. Saint Jerome in the Wilderness, Albrecht
Dürer, 1494 - 1498*

105

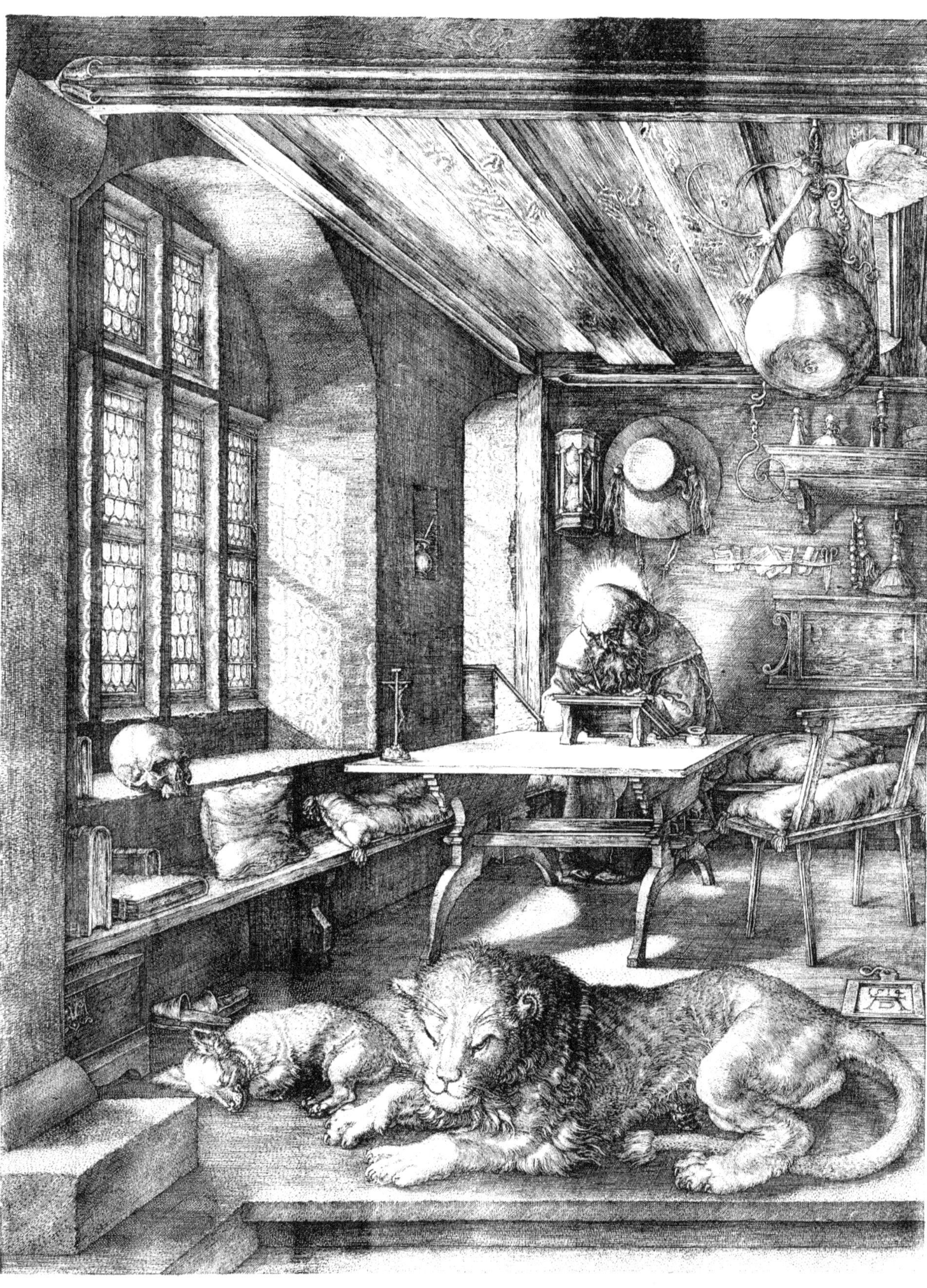

ALBRECHT DÜRER

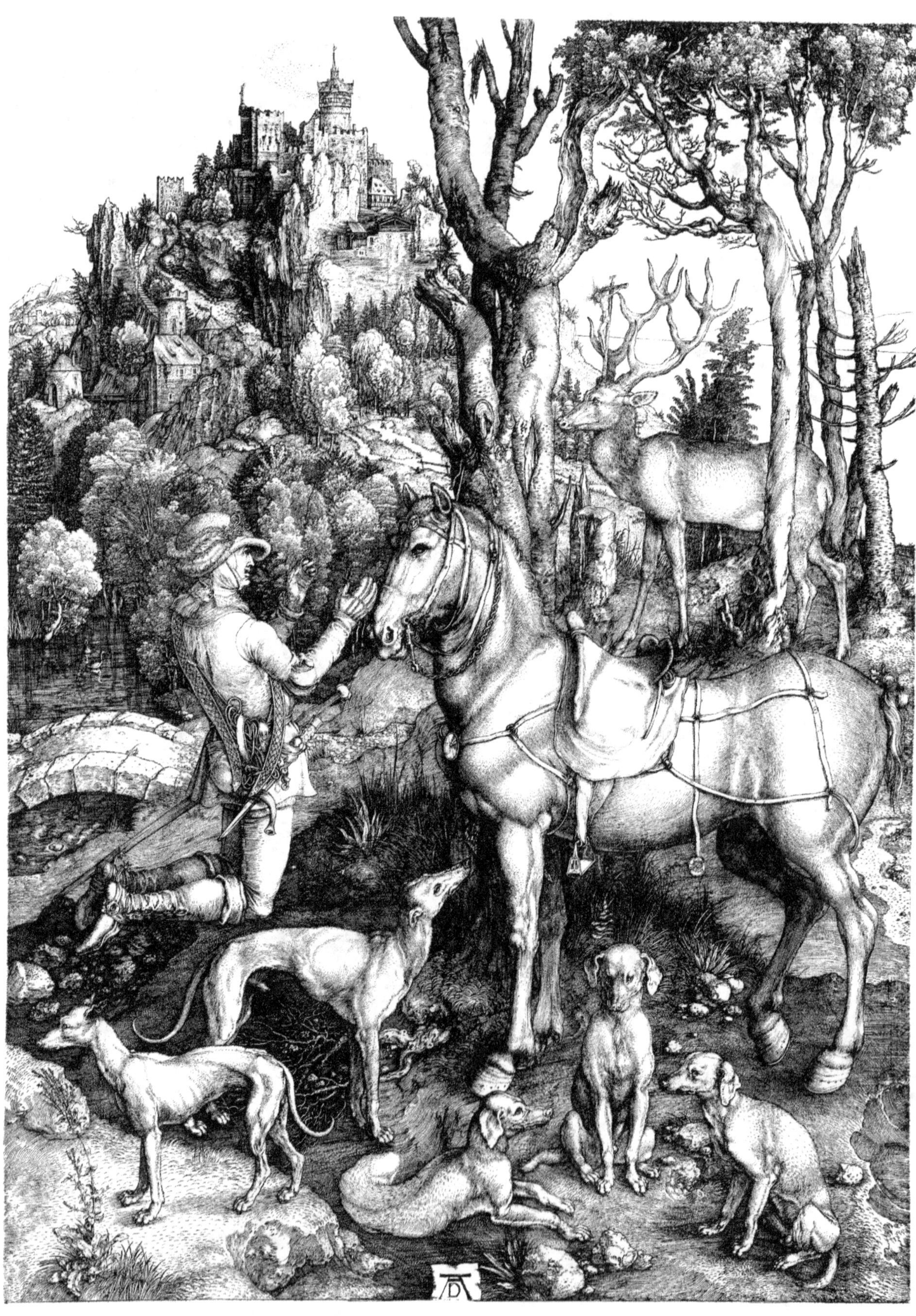

106. St Eustace, Albrecht Dürer, 1499 - 1503

107

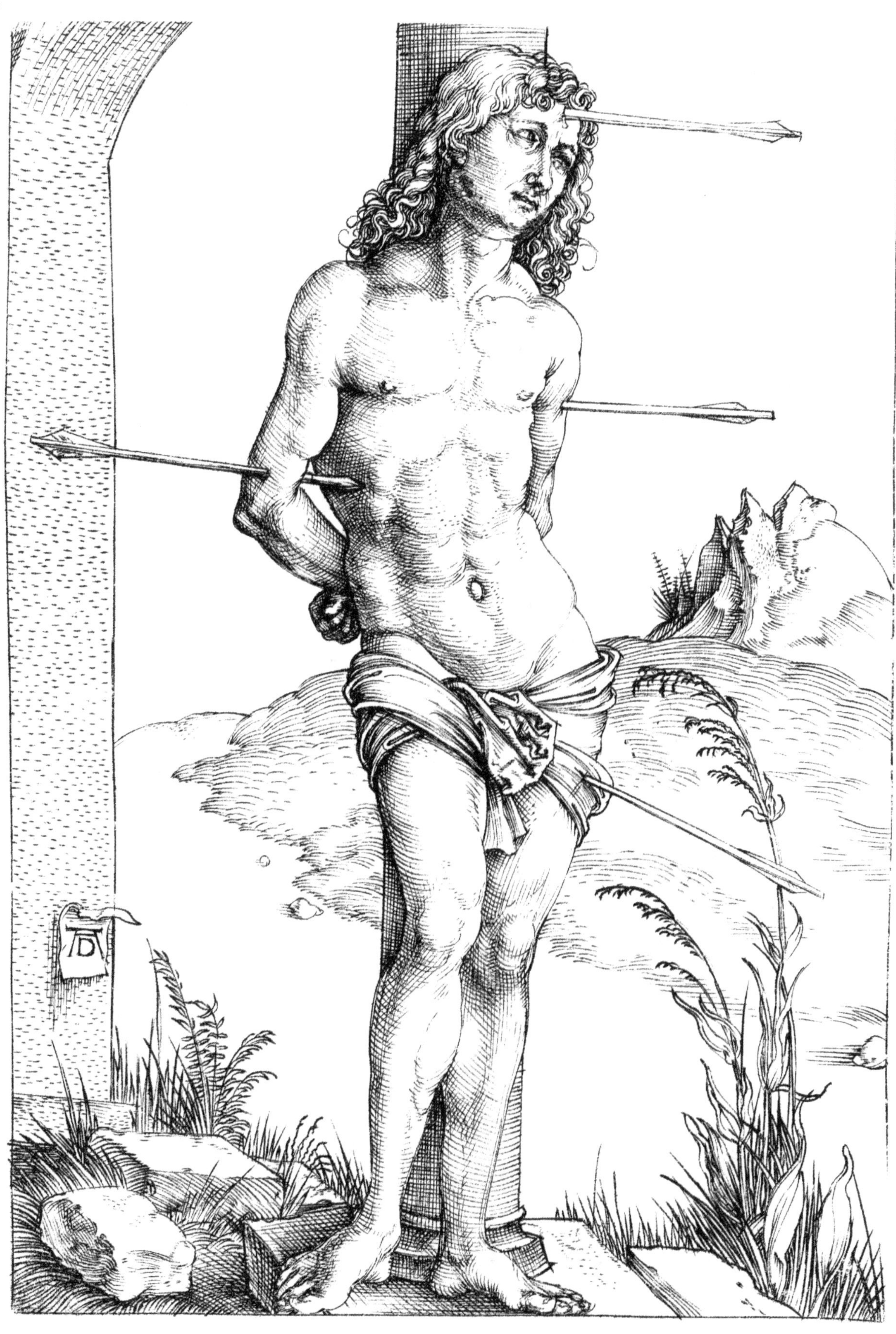

107. The Martyrdom of Saint Sebastian, Albrecht
Dürer, 1497 - 1501

108

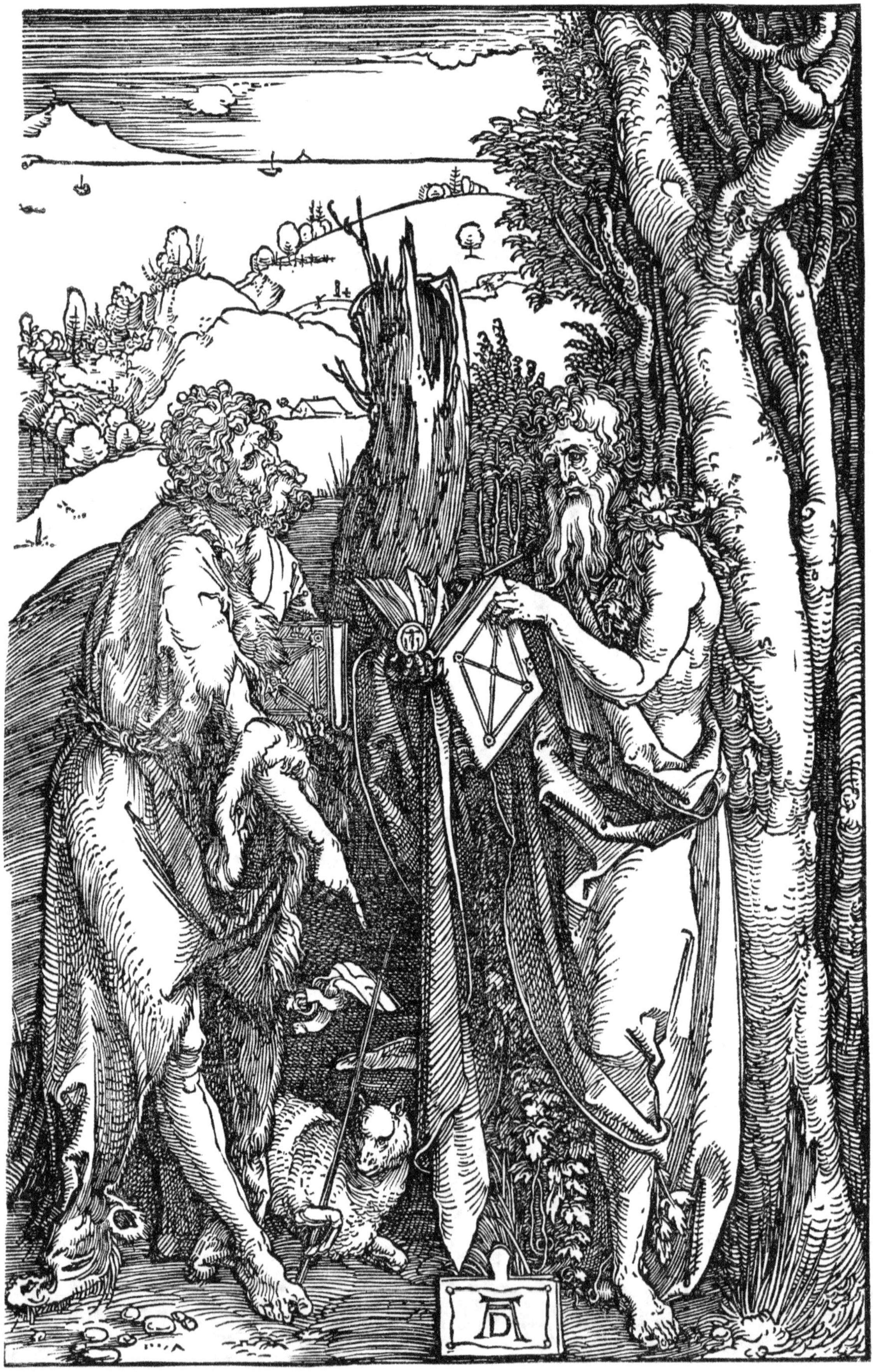

108. John the Baptist with Saint Onuphrius in
the Wilderness, Albrecht Dürer, 1503 - 1504

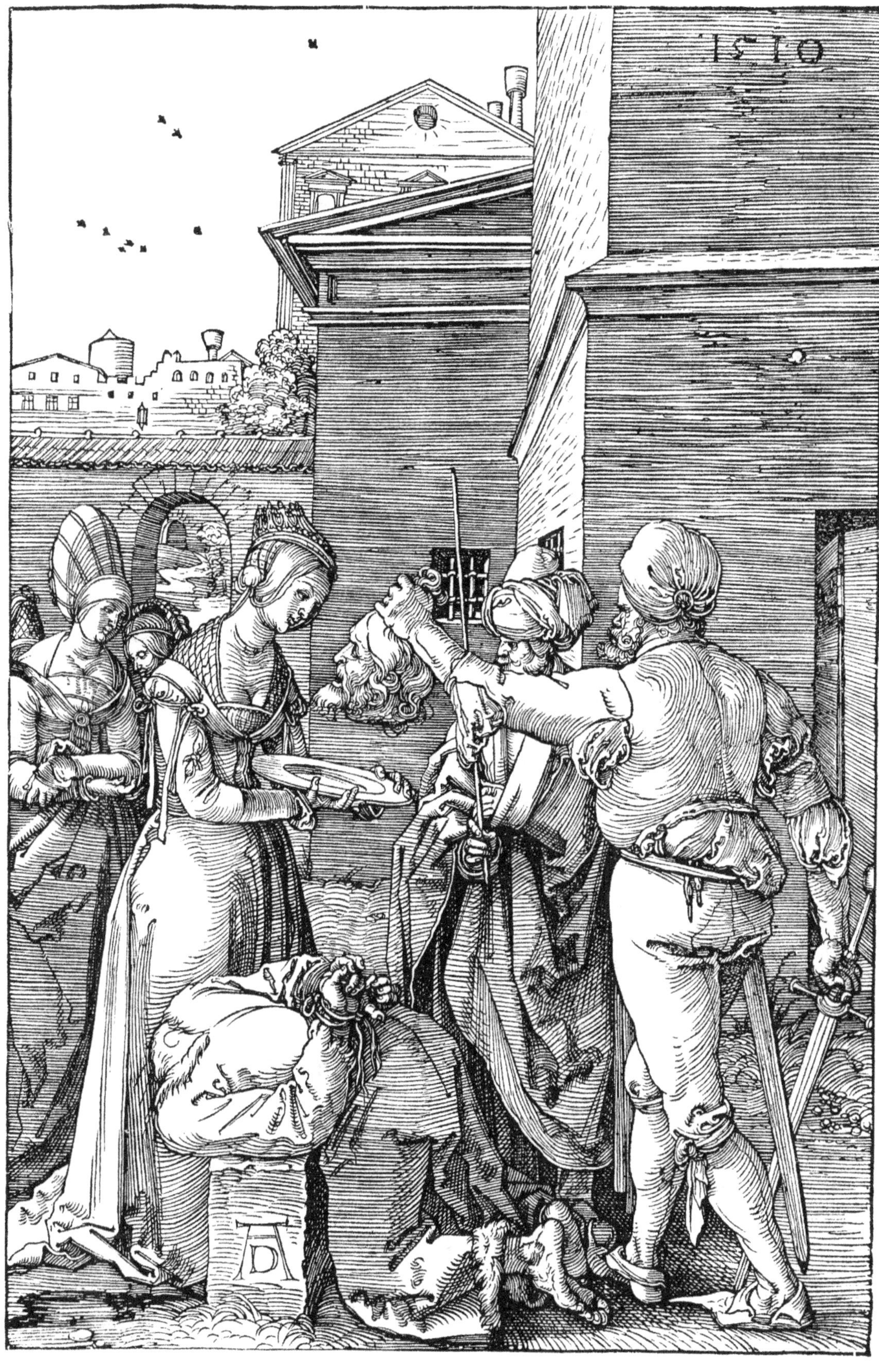

109 The Beheading of Saint John the Baptist.
Albrecht Dürer, 1510.

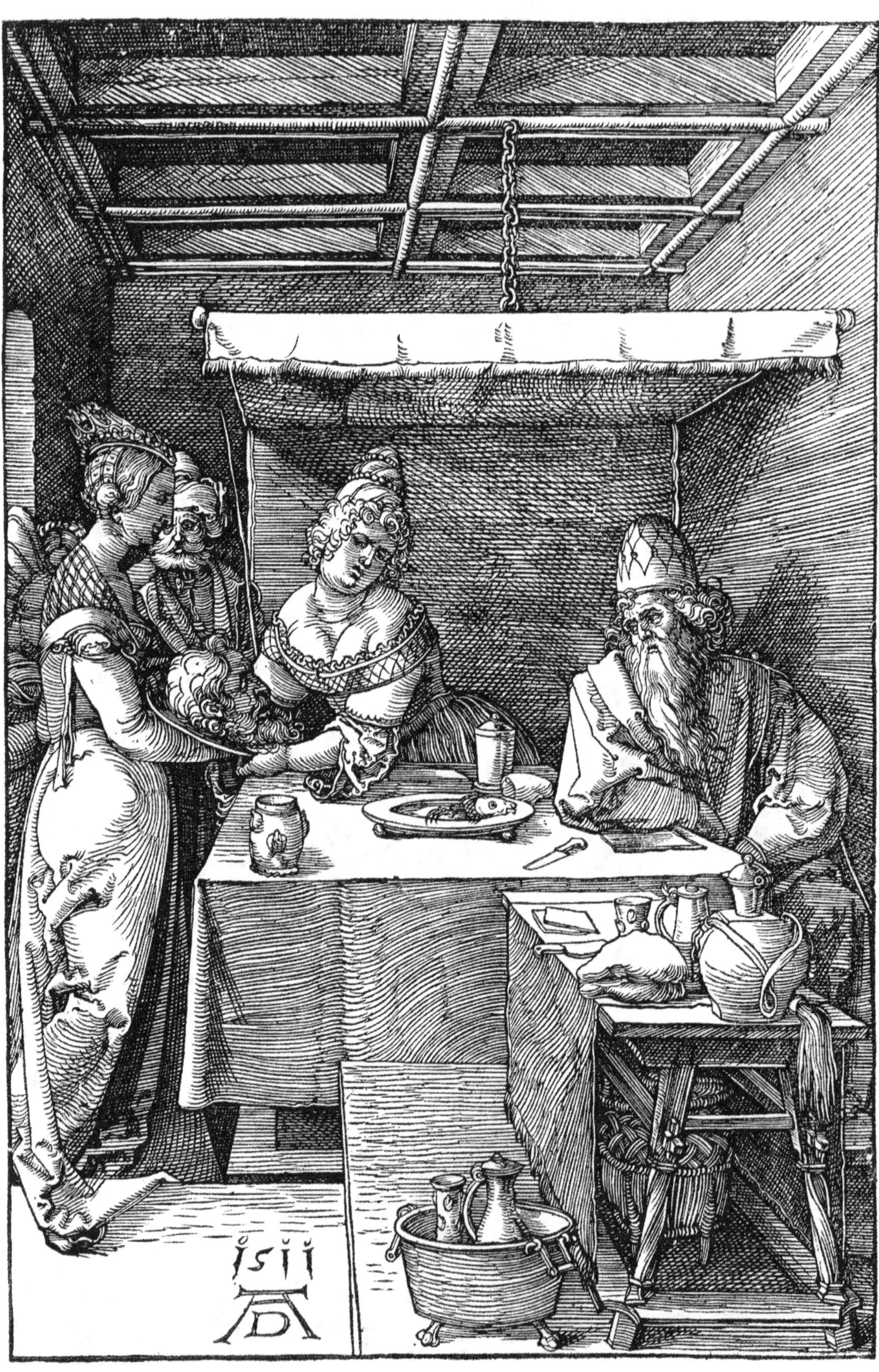

110. *Herodias receives the head of John the Baptist, Albrecht Dürer, 1511*

111

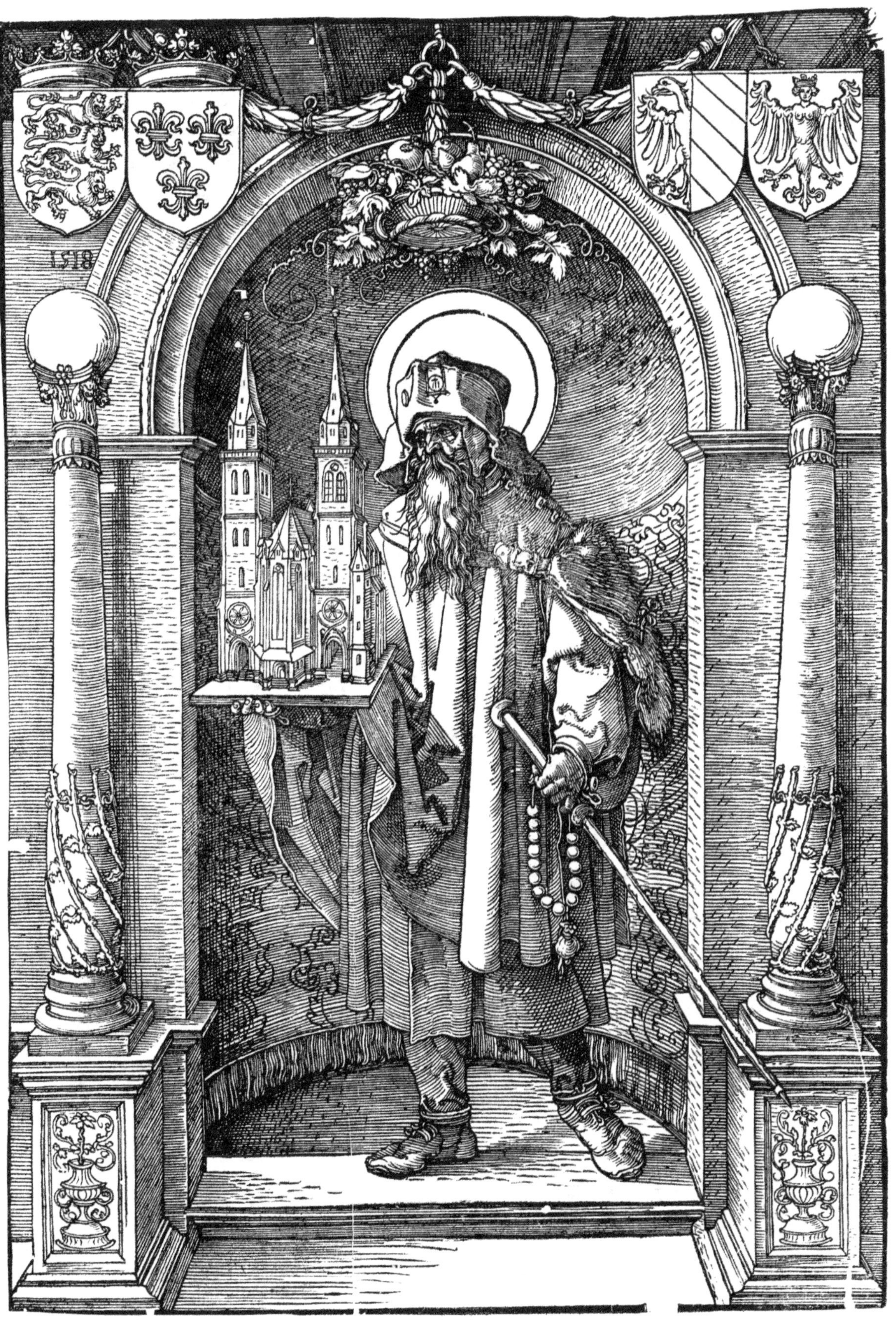

111. Saint Sebald in a Niche, Albrecht Dürer
(attributed to), 1518

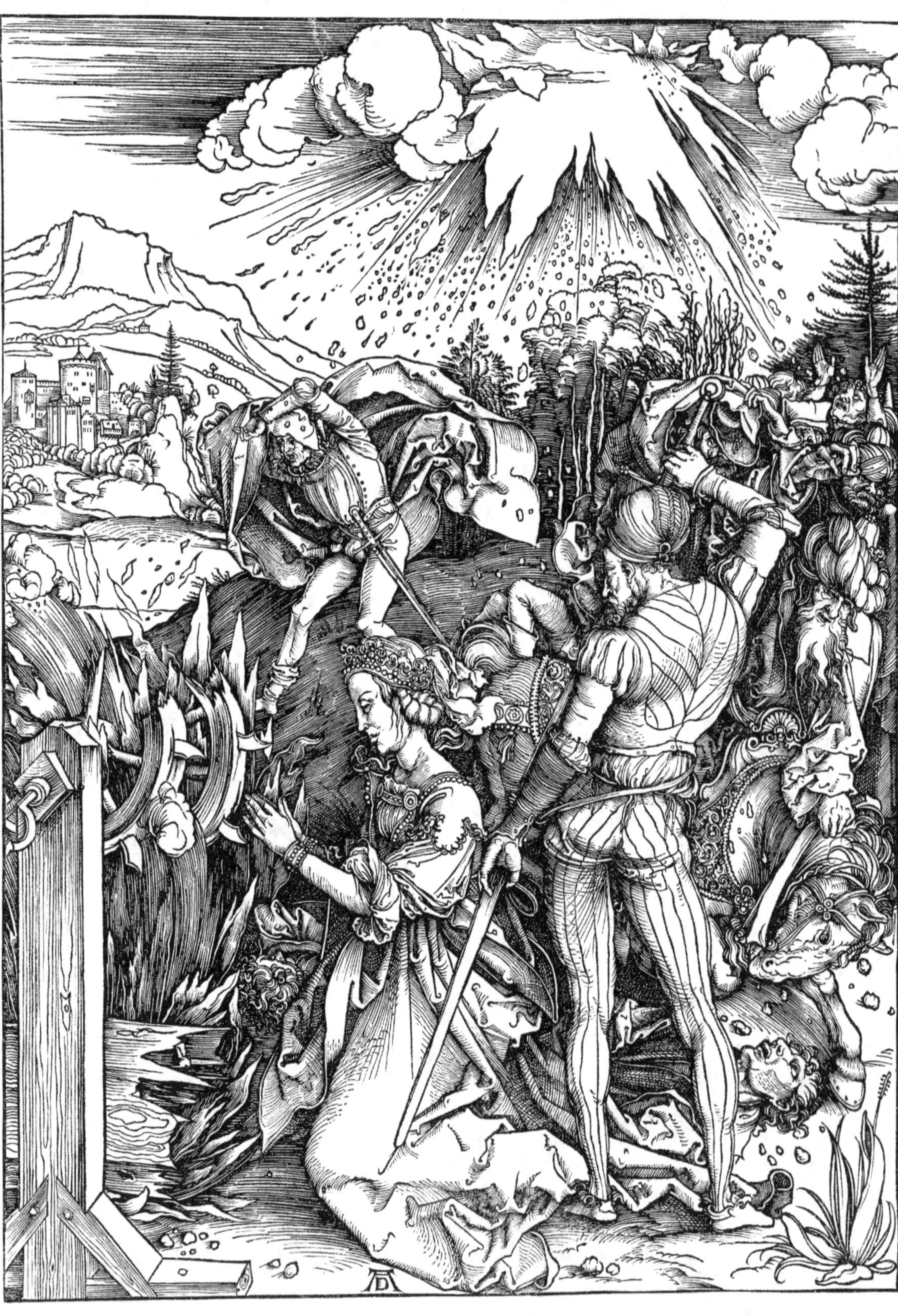

112. *The Martyrdom of Saint Catherine, Albrecht Dürer, 1496 - 1500*

113

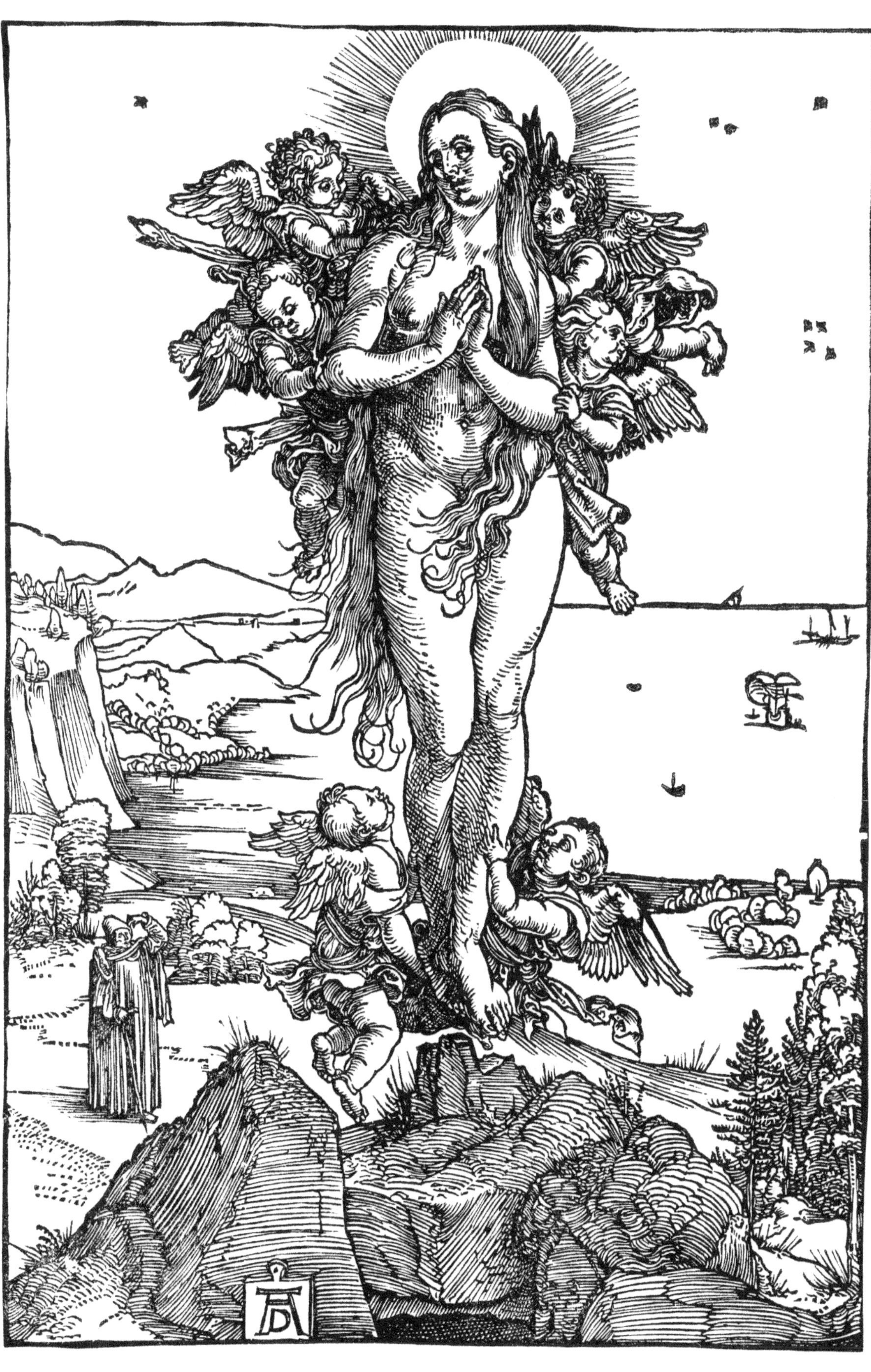

ALBRECHT DÜRER

02

MYTHOLOGY

'Mythology' features familiar faces from Greek and Roman mythology, such as an engraving of Apollo, the god of the Sun, war, and music, and his twin, Diana, the goddess of the Moon, hunting, and childbirth. Albrecht Dürer's incredible ability to capture a sense of grace and movement in the human figure is evident in this captivating image. The great hero, Hercules, also appears in Dürer's woodcut, *Hercules Conquering the Molionide Twins*'. In this tale, Hercules battles Eurytus and Kteatus, twin sons of Poseidon, god of the Sea and the mortal, Molione. They were hatched from a silver egg and became epic warriors. The strength of their conjoined bodies made it almost impossible for them to be defeated. Dürer's highly detailed portrayal of their entangled limbs and armour is a testament to his technical ability.

This chapter also includes various characters who inhabit the mythical world, such as a satyr and a wood nymph, featured in *'The Satyr Family'*. In this artwork, the satyr, a half-man, half-goat, stands beside his woodland nymph partner in a scene of peaceful familial bliss, a far cry from

the drunken debauchery we typically associate with satyrs. Dürer's background of textured and gnarled trees creates the impression we are observing this domestic scene through a clearing in a dark and ancient wood.

Dürer's masterful renderings of these mythological figures and scenes showcase his exceptional technical skill. They breathe life into the timeless legends, allowing us to experience their wonder and complexity anew.

114

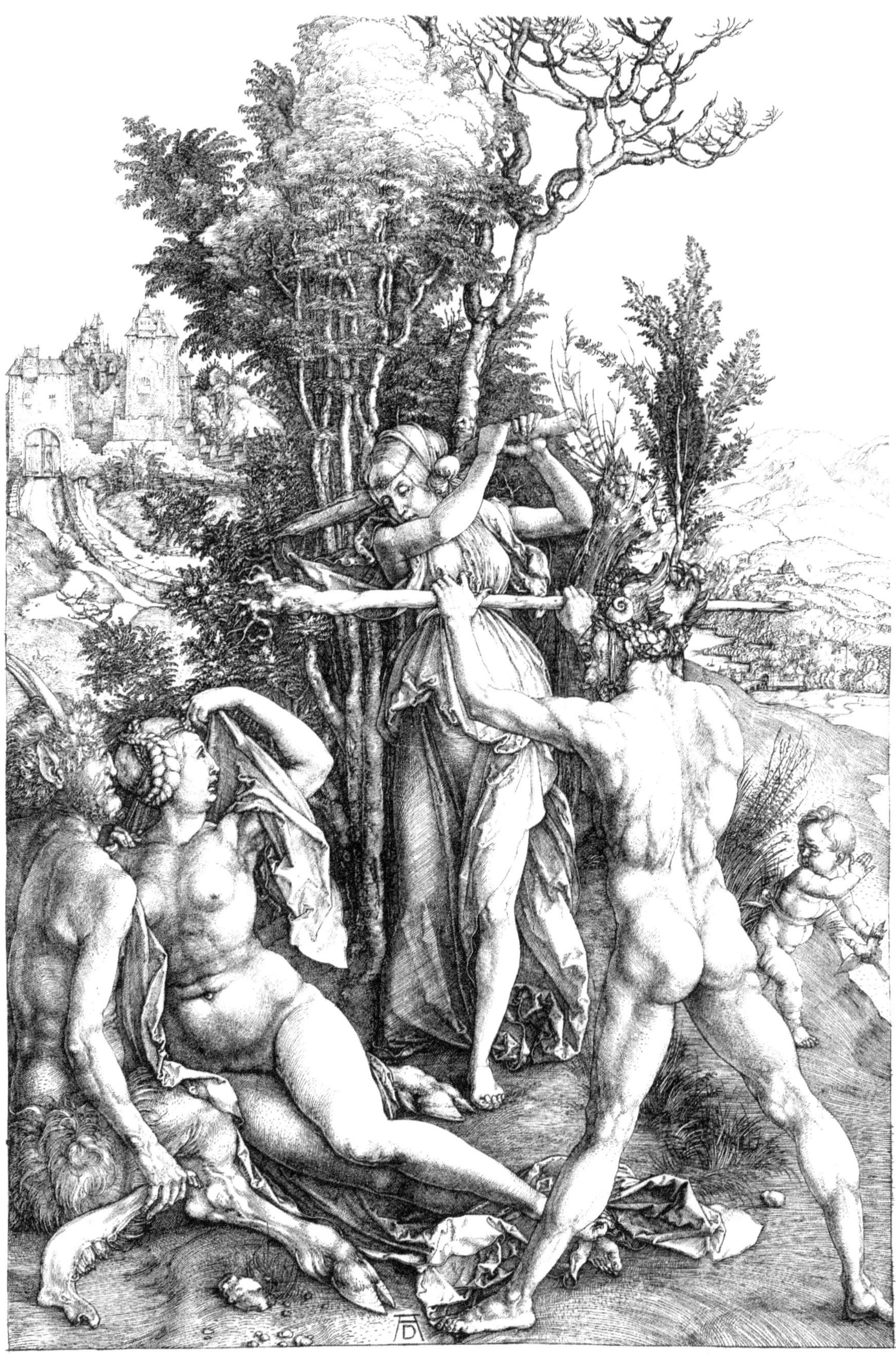

ALBRECHT DÜRER

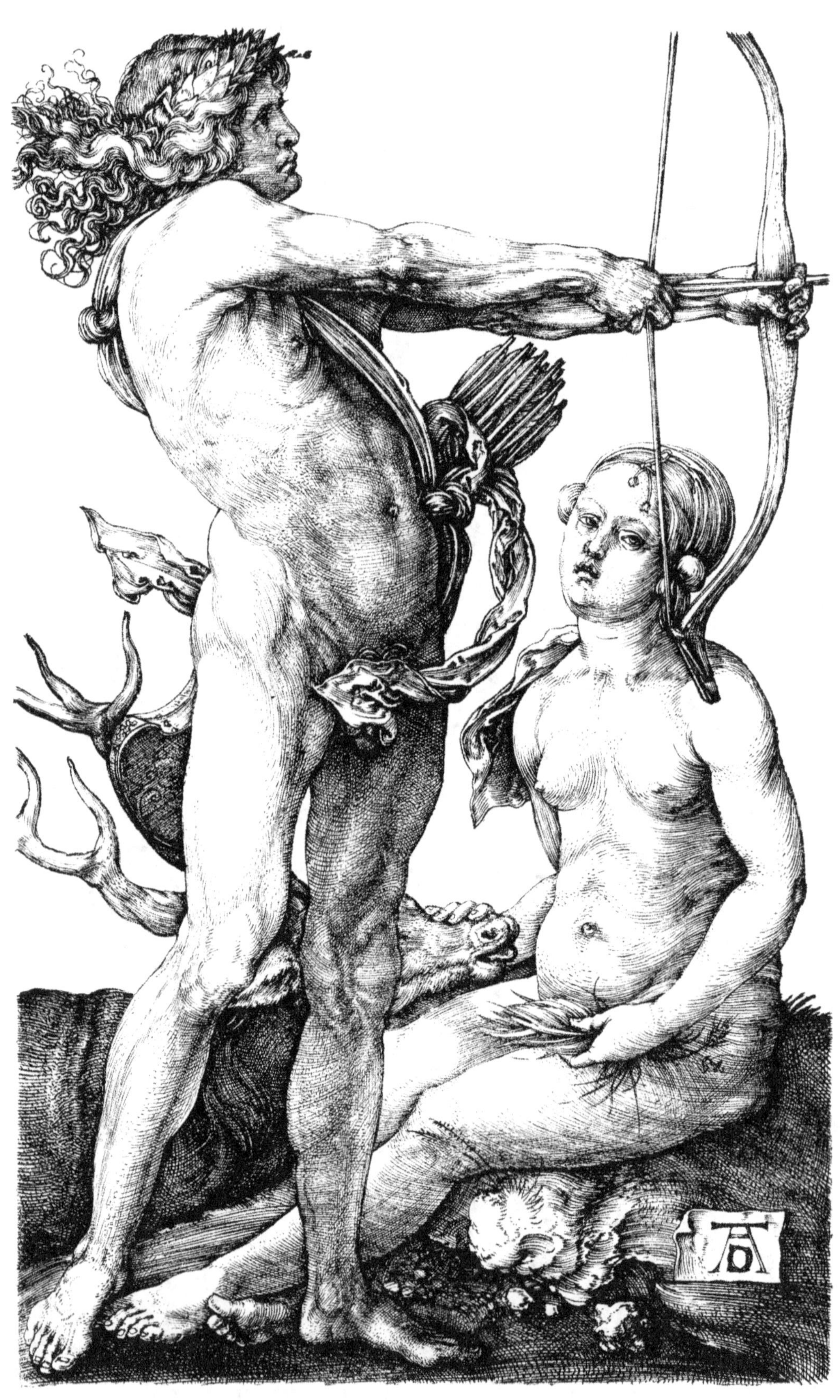

115. *Apollo and Diana, Albrecht Dürer, 1501 - 1506*

116

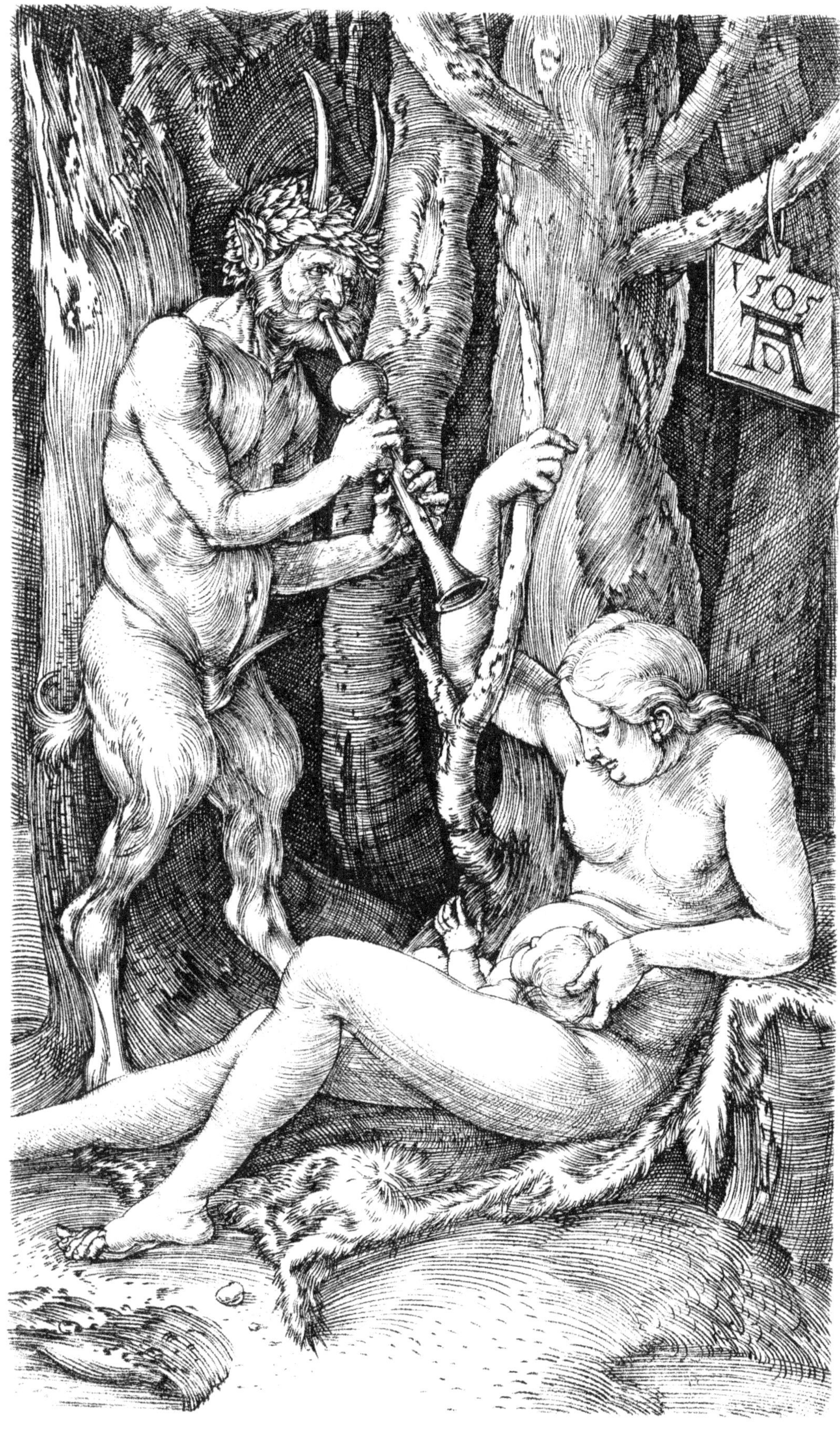

ALBRECHT DÜRER

116. The Satyr Family, Albrecht Dürer, 1505

117

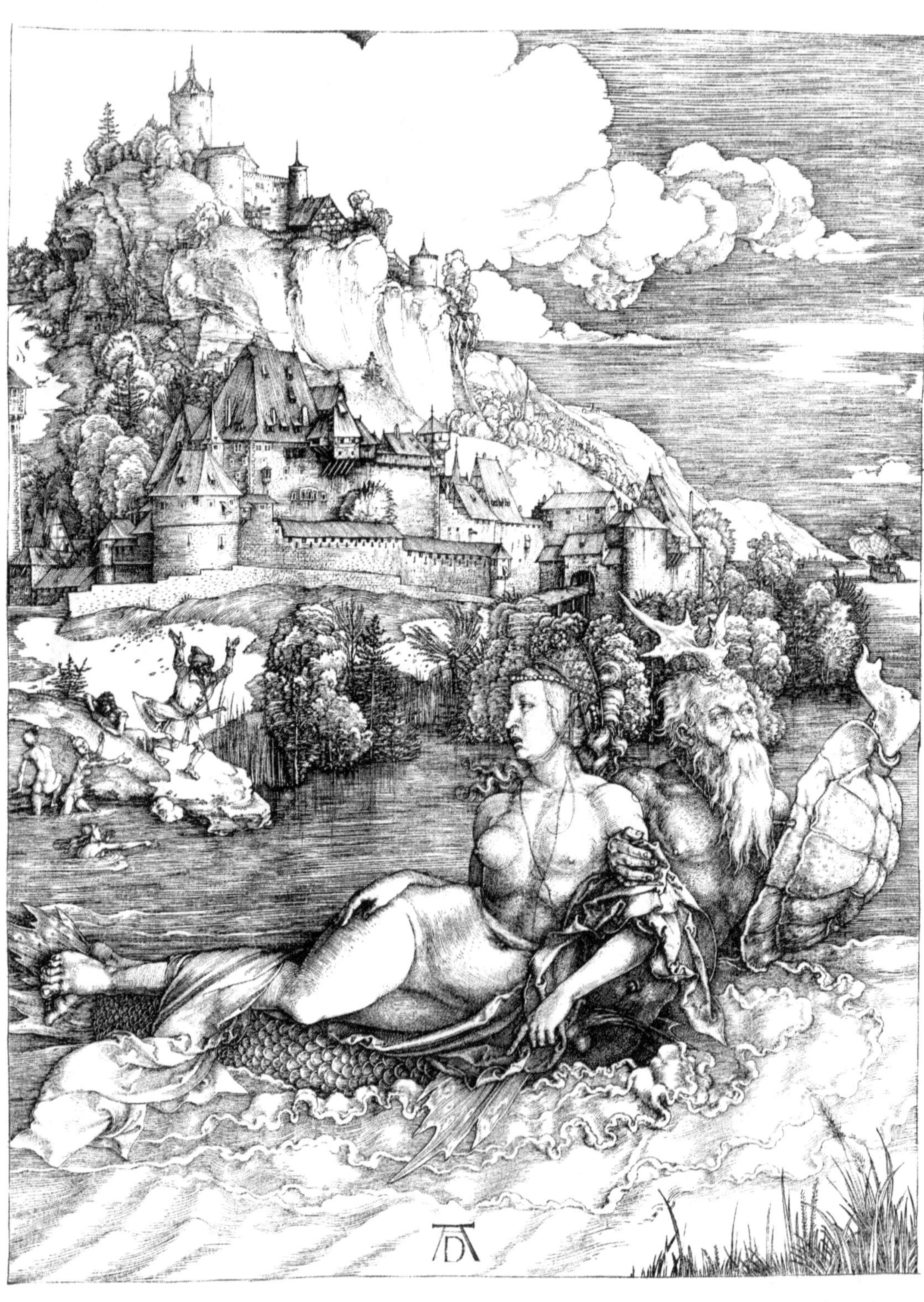

117. Abduction by the Sea Monster, Albrecht
Dürer, 1496 - 1500

118

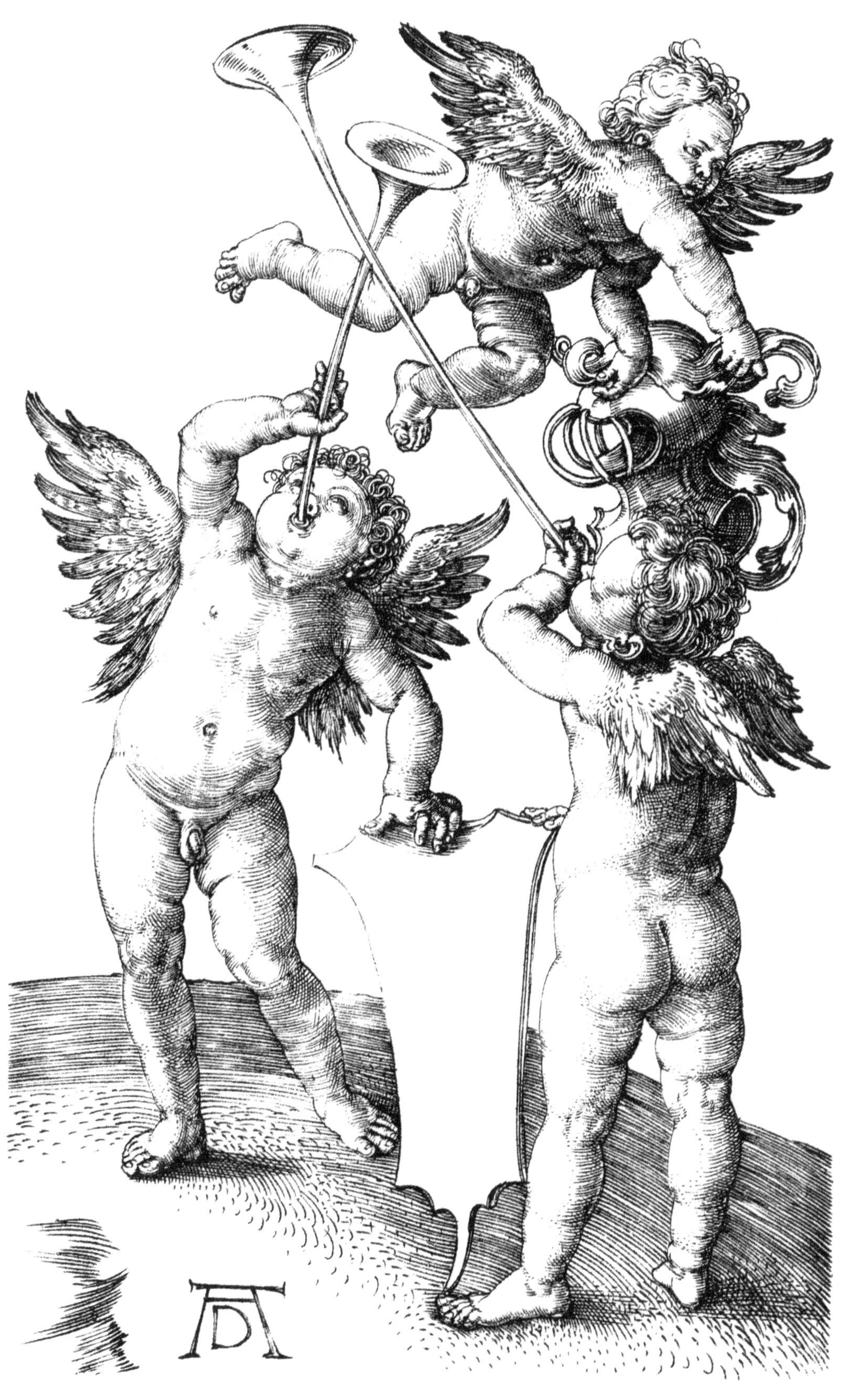

118. Three putti with trumpets, shield and
helmet. Albrecht Dürer, 1498 - 1502

119

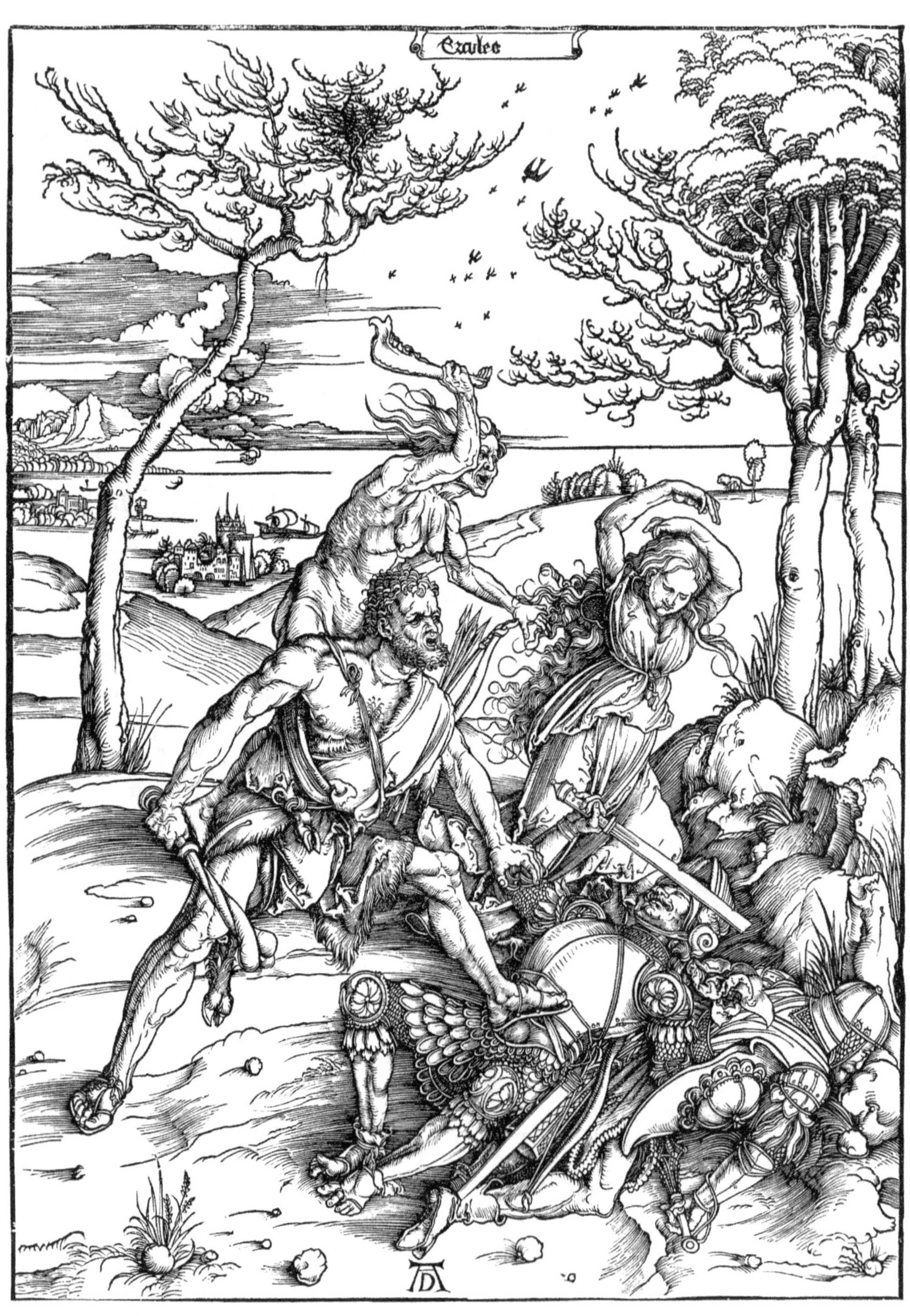

119. Hercules Conquering the Molionide Twins.
Albrecht Dürer, 1494 - 1498

120

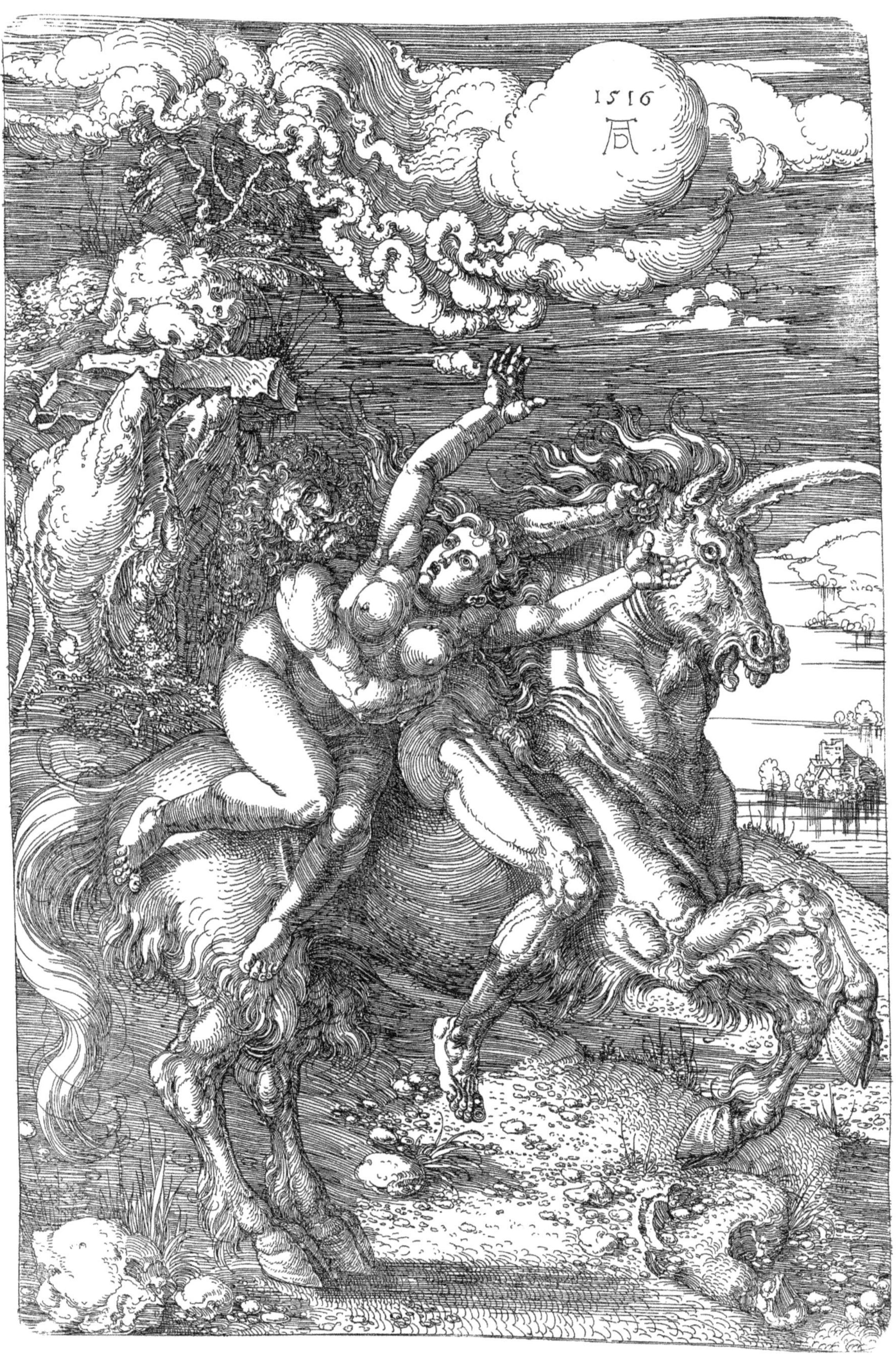

ALBRECHT DÜRER

120. The Abduction of Proserpine on a Unicorn.
Albrecht Dürer, 1516.

03

ALLEGORY

Albrecht Dürer used allegory to enhance his work's depth and meaning and convey complex emotions and concepts. A great example of this is his *Meisterstiche* (Master Engravings). This term refers to three famous pieces, *'Knight, Death and the Devil'* (1513), *'St. Jerome in His Study'* (1514) and *'Melencolia I'* (1514). The use of shadow, light and texture makes these images excellent examples of Dürer's incredible technical ability. These works are not a series or companion pieces, but renowned art historian Friedrich Lippmann theorised they are linked by the virtues they represent: the moral, the spiritual and the intellectual.

The *'Knight, Death and Devil'* describes a Christian's life navigating the hostile secular world. In this engraving, death rides a pale horse and brandishes an hourglass, a symbol of the shortness of life—the goat-headed devil leers at the knight, who rides on, unconcerned and secure in his faith.

In *'St. Jerome in His Study,'* (featured in the chapter, Biblical Scenes and Saints), the Saint is depicted in a moment of theological reflection, surrounded by religious and academic paraphernalia.

Saint Jerome is often depicted with a lion he befriended after removing a thorn from its paw. Dürer's perspective and lighting create a sense of depth and a calm, studious atmosphere.

The rich detail and symbolism of *'Melencolia I'* is a topic of significant debate. Erwin Panofsky, an art historian known for his studies in iconography, says it describes *"the life of the secular genius in the rational and imaginative worlds of science and art"*. The female character, possibly a personification of melancholia, sits despondently beside a putto and a dog. Tools and objects relating to the creative arts and academic study surround them; their meaning has fascinated and intrigued audiences for centuries.

Through these masterful engravings, Dürer showcases his technical prowess and invites viewers to engage with profound moral, spiritual, and intellectual questions, reflecting the enduring power of allegory in art.

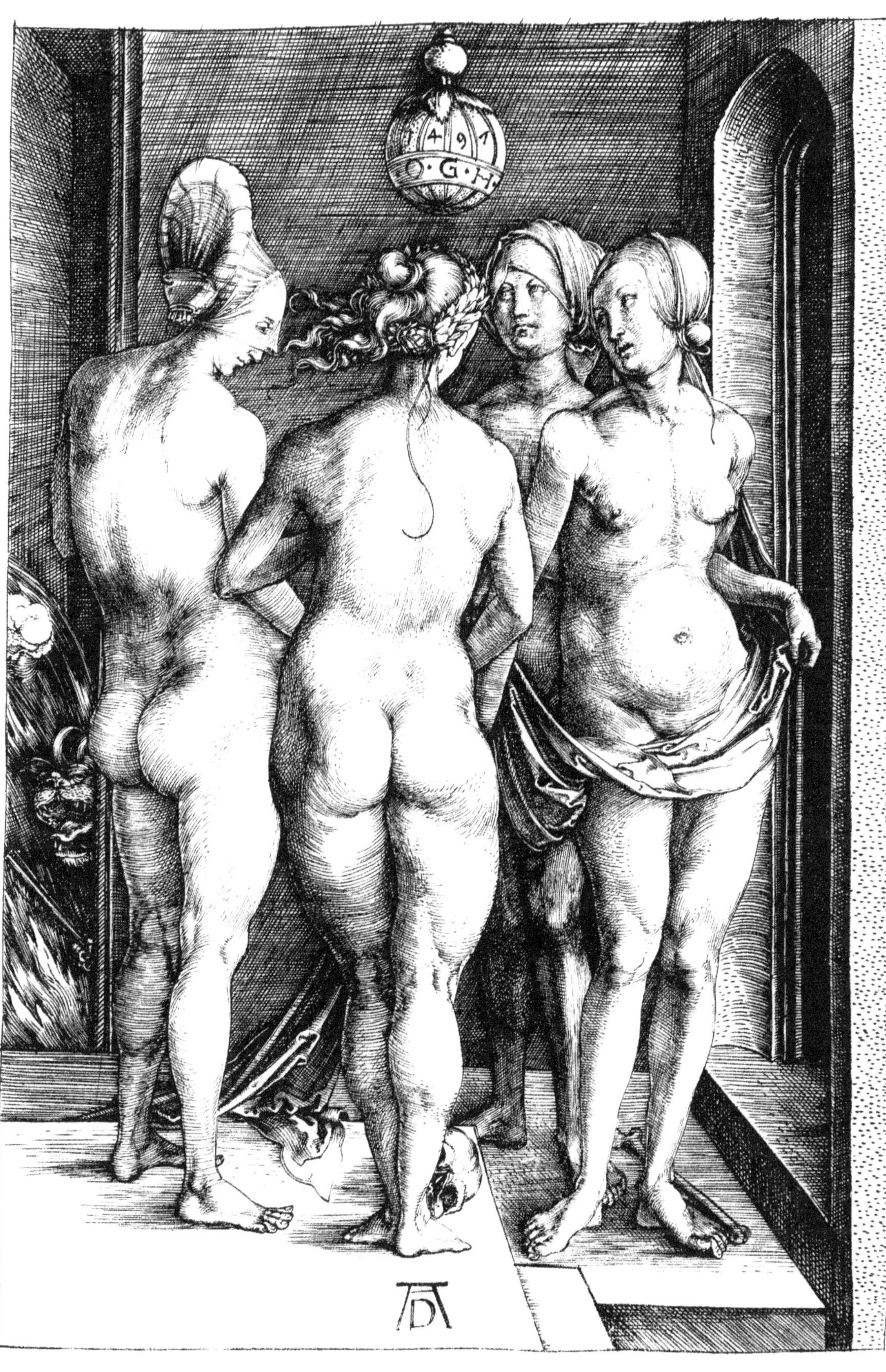

121. *The Four Witches (The Four Naked Women), Albrecht Dürer, 1497*

122

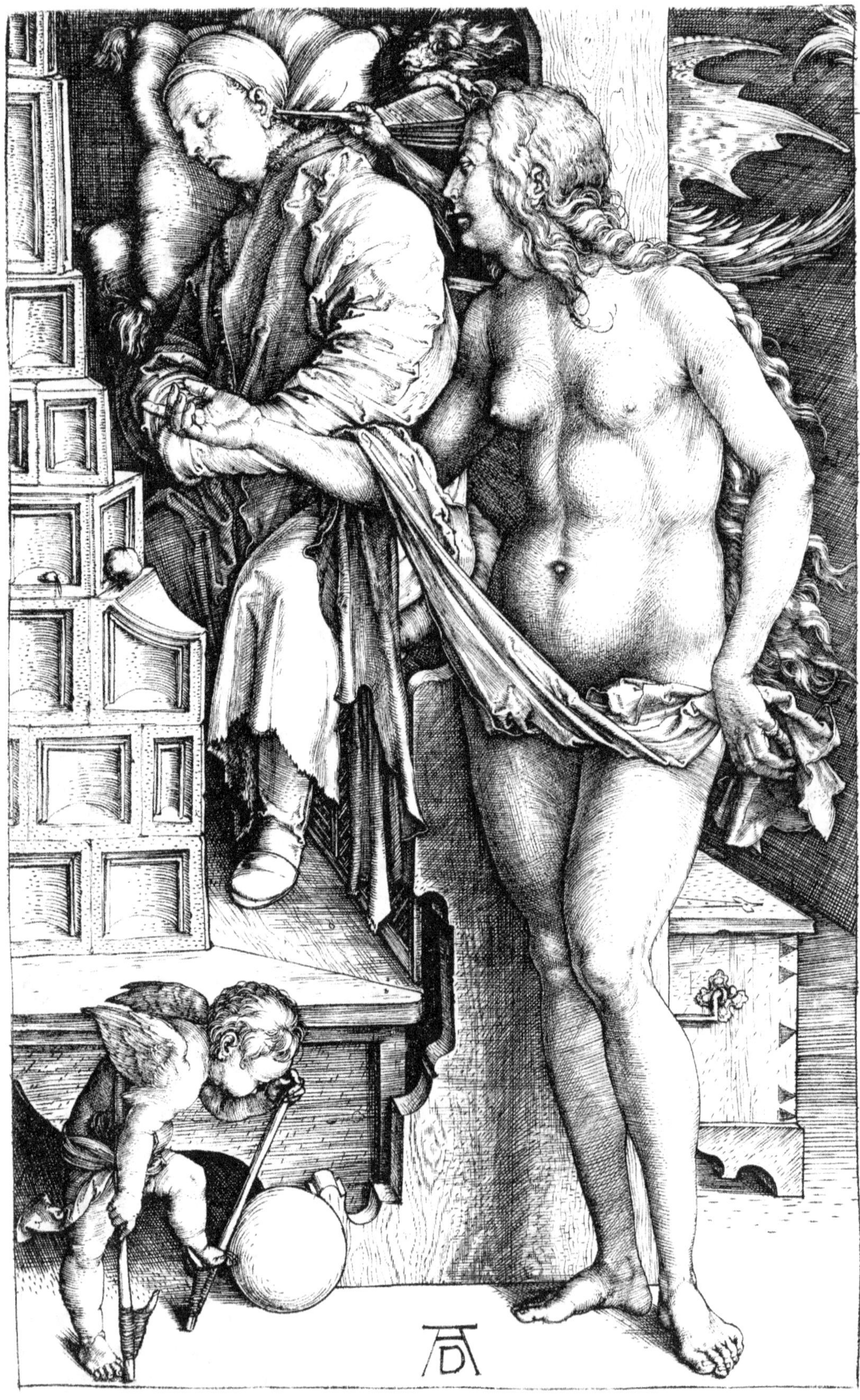

122. *The Dream of the Doctor, Albrecht Dürer.*
1496 - 1500

123

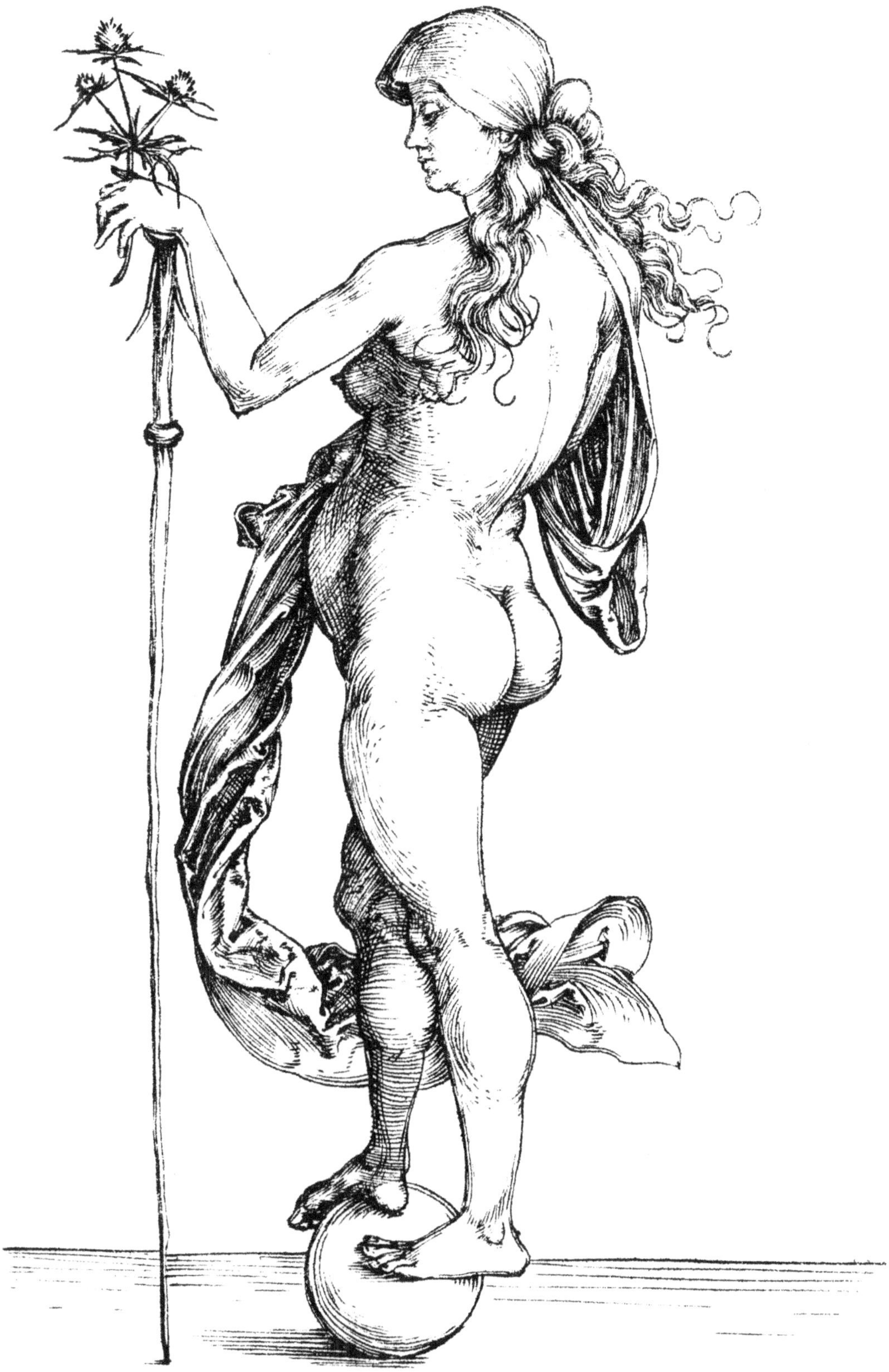

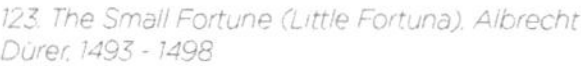

ALBRECHT DÜRER

123. The Small Fortune (Little Fortuna), Albrecht Dürer, 1493 - 1498

124

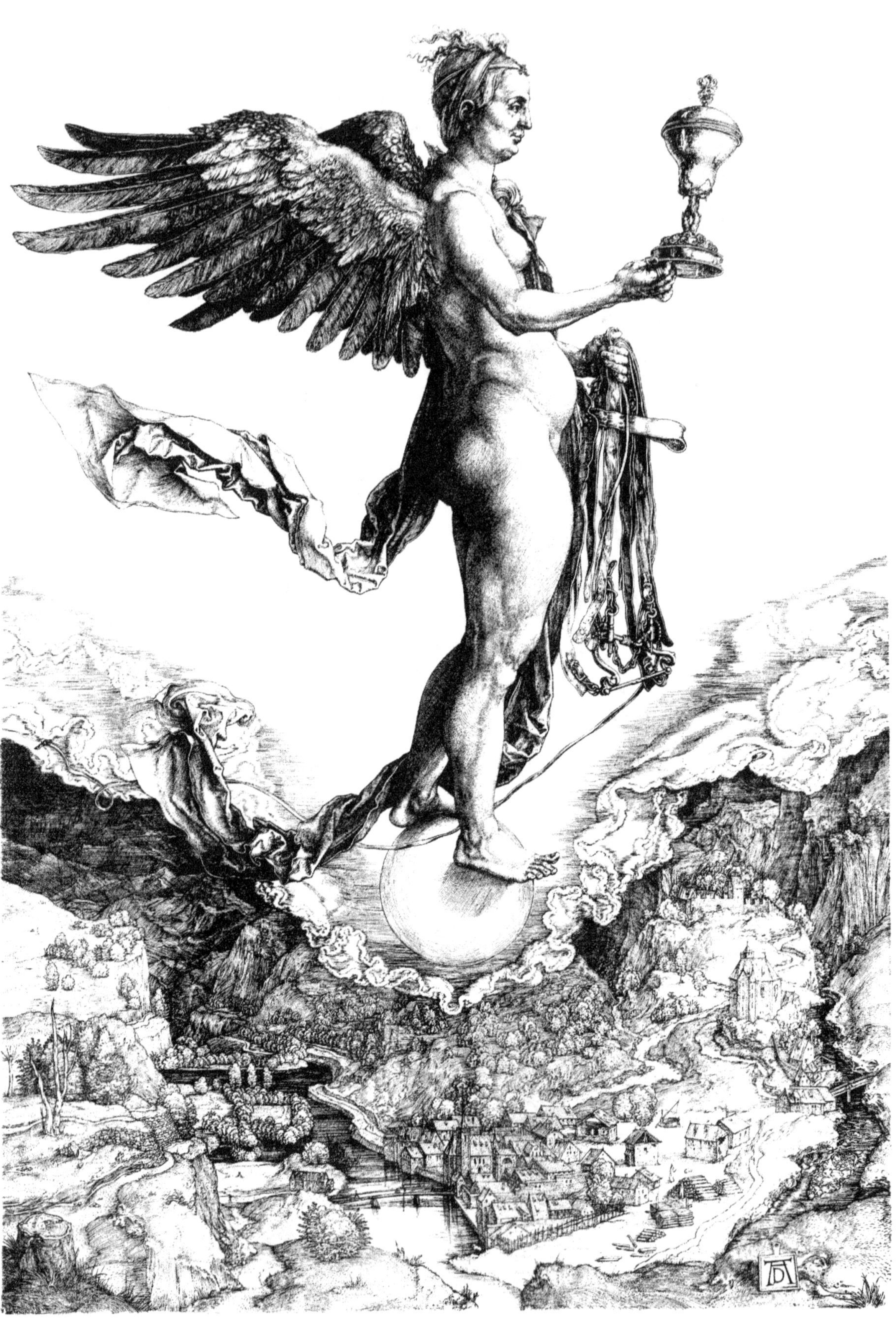

*124 Nemesis (The Great Fortune), Albrecht
Dürer, 1499 - 1503*

125

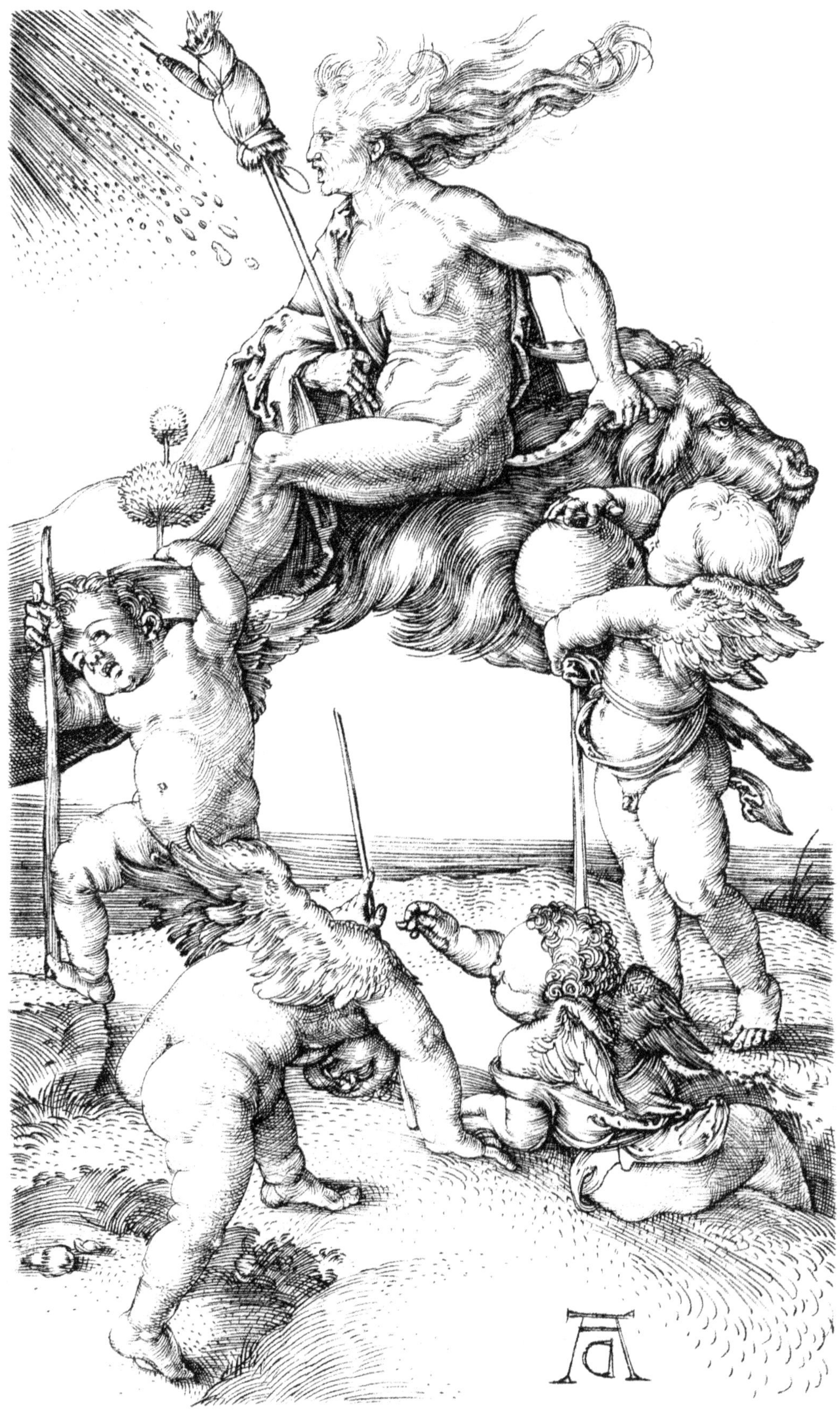

ALBRECHT DÜRER

126

ALBRECHT DÜRER

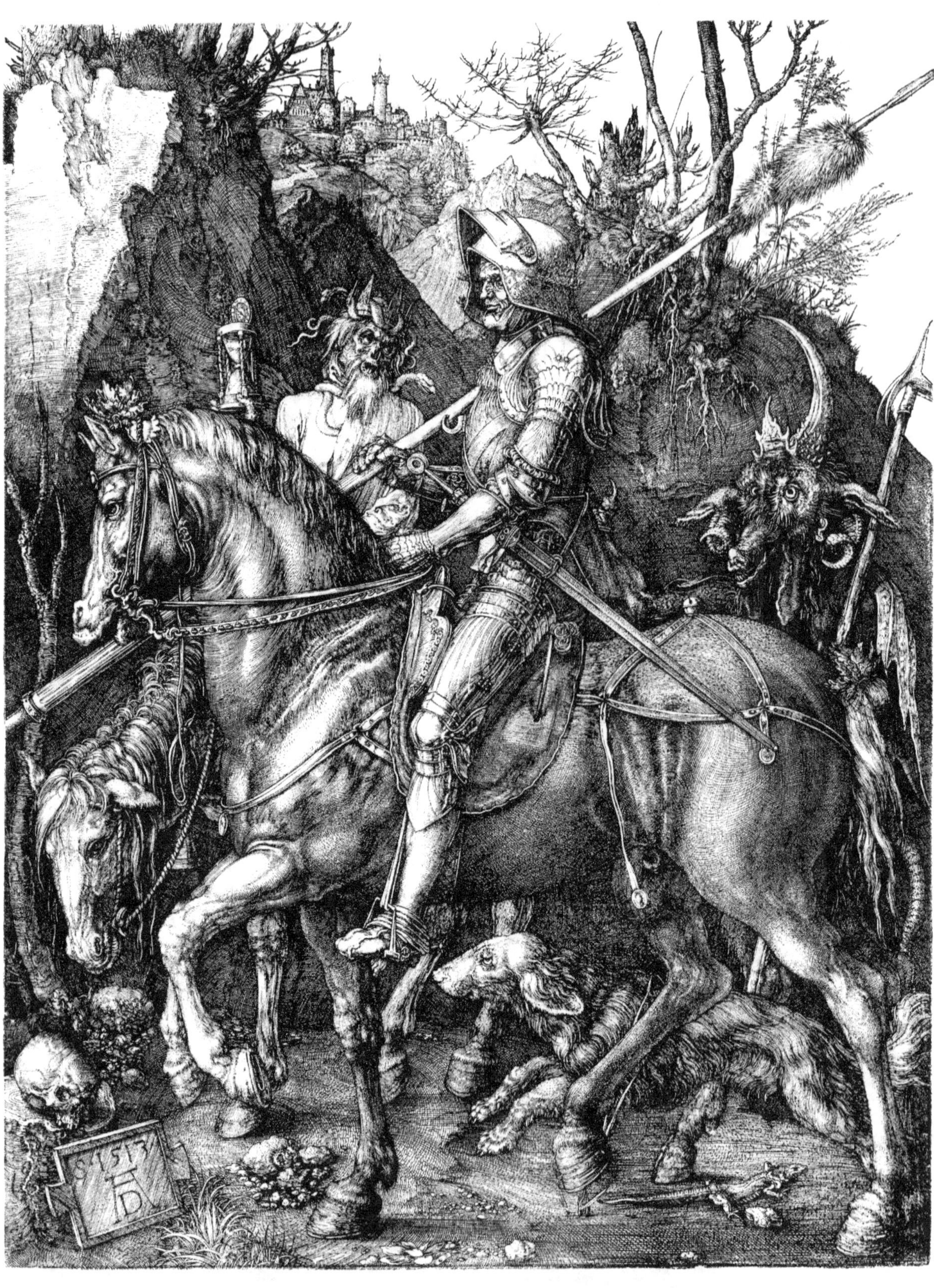

126. *Knight, Death, and the Devil*, Albrecht
Dürer, 1513

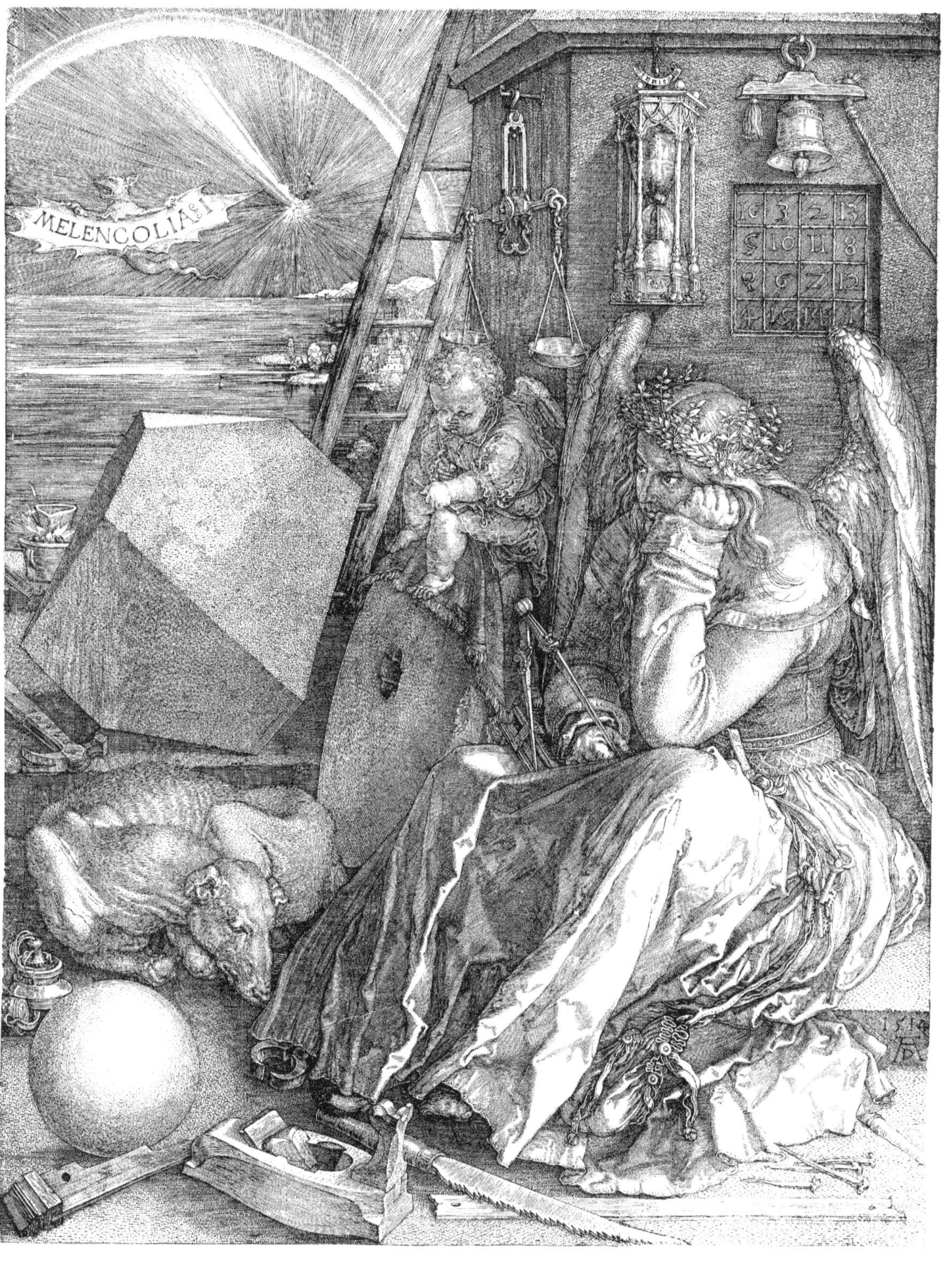

ALBRECHT DÜRER

04

MAN AND BEAST

'Man and Beast' presents a rich tapestry of individuals from various walks of life in diverse situations. This chapter also features mesmerising depictions of animals, highlighting Dürer's incredible ability to capture the essence of both human and animal subjects.

'The Men's Bath' is a woodcut describing a social scene at the communal bathhouse. Some of the bathers are recognisable: Albrecht Dürer is on the left leaning against the tap, and his friend Willibald Pirckheimer is drinking on the far right. The figures in the centre are thought to be Lukas and Stephan Paumgartner, friends of Dürer. A man stands outside the bathhouse watching the group. This piece is an example of Dürer's great skill in depicting the male figure in various poses, but it also represents the five senses; Dürer watching the two musicians represents hearing, Prickheimer's drinking signifies taste, and the figures in the foreground, holding a back scraper

for touch, and flower for smell. The man looking into the bathhouse from outside signifies sight. *'The Small Horse'* and *'The Large Horse'* are a pair of companion prints depicting idealised images of horses. *'The Small Horse'* is standing in profile, in a heraldic pose reminiscent of classic equestrian statues. The horse's open mouth and raised forelimb hint at the animal's power and movement, currently constrained by the groom and its close surroundings. *'The Large Horse'* is a naturalised image of a horse; its stance is calm and still, with incredible detail of the animal's mane, tail, muscles and textured coat.

Dürer's mastery of depicting human and animal forms offers a captivating glimpse into the diverse and intricate world he envisioned.

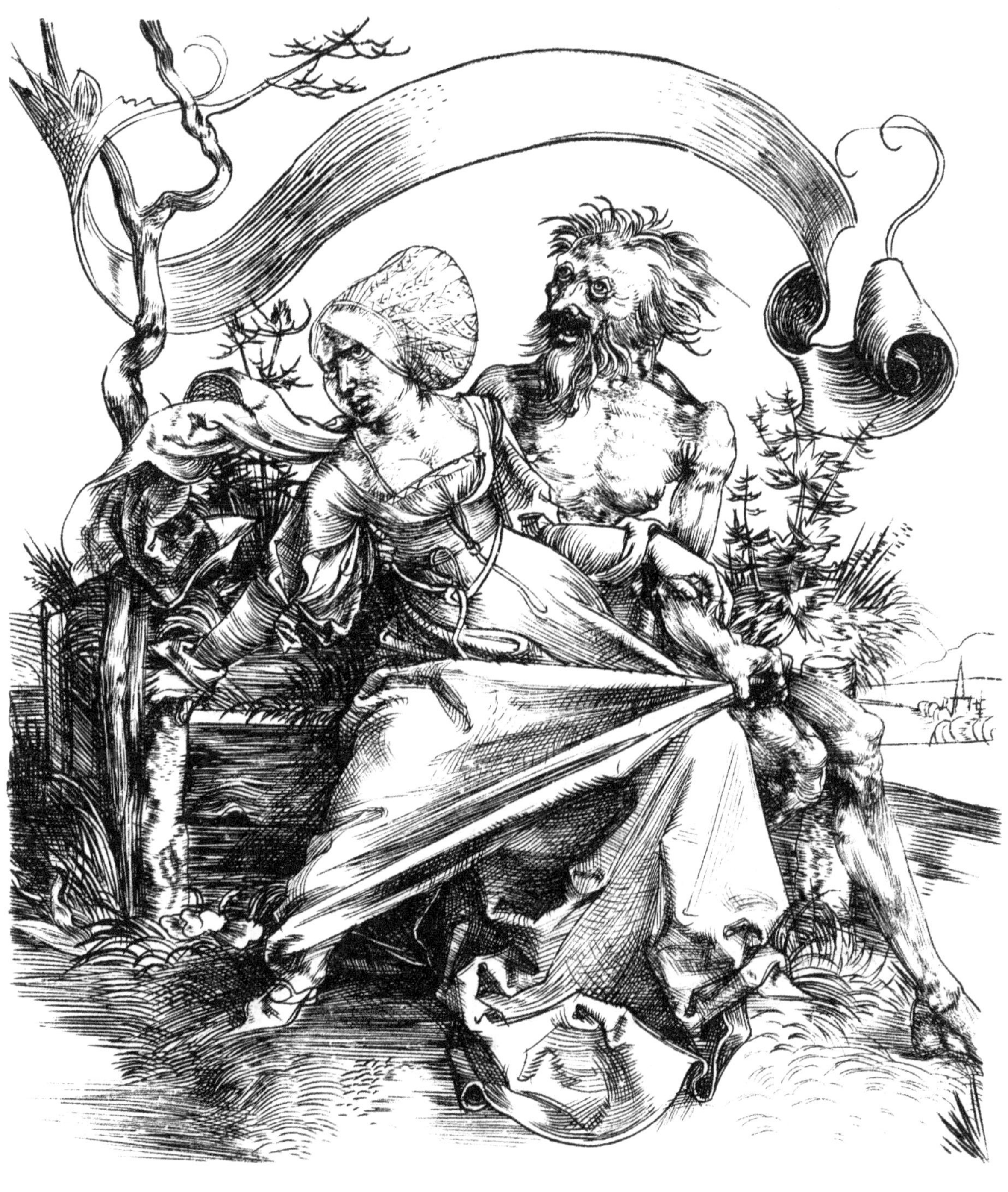

128. The Ravisher, Albrecht Dürer, 1493 - 1497

ALBRECHT DÜRER

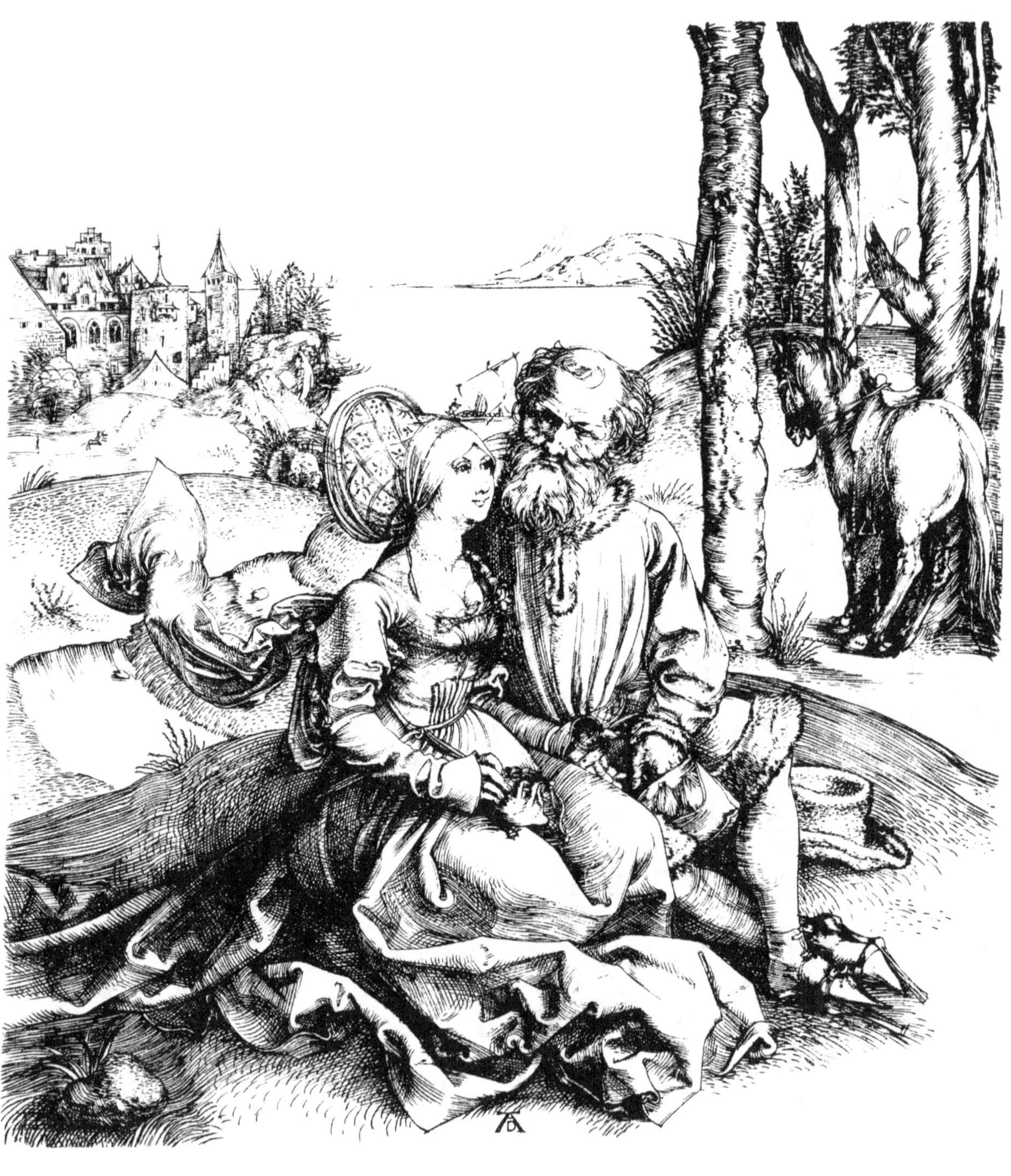

*129. The Offer of Love (or The Ill-Assorted
Couple), Albrecht Dürer. 1493 - 1497*

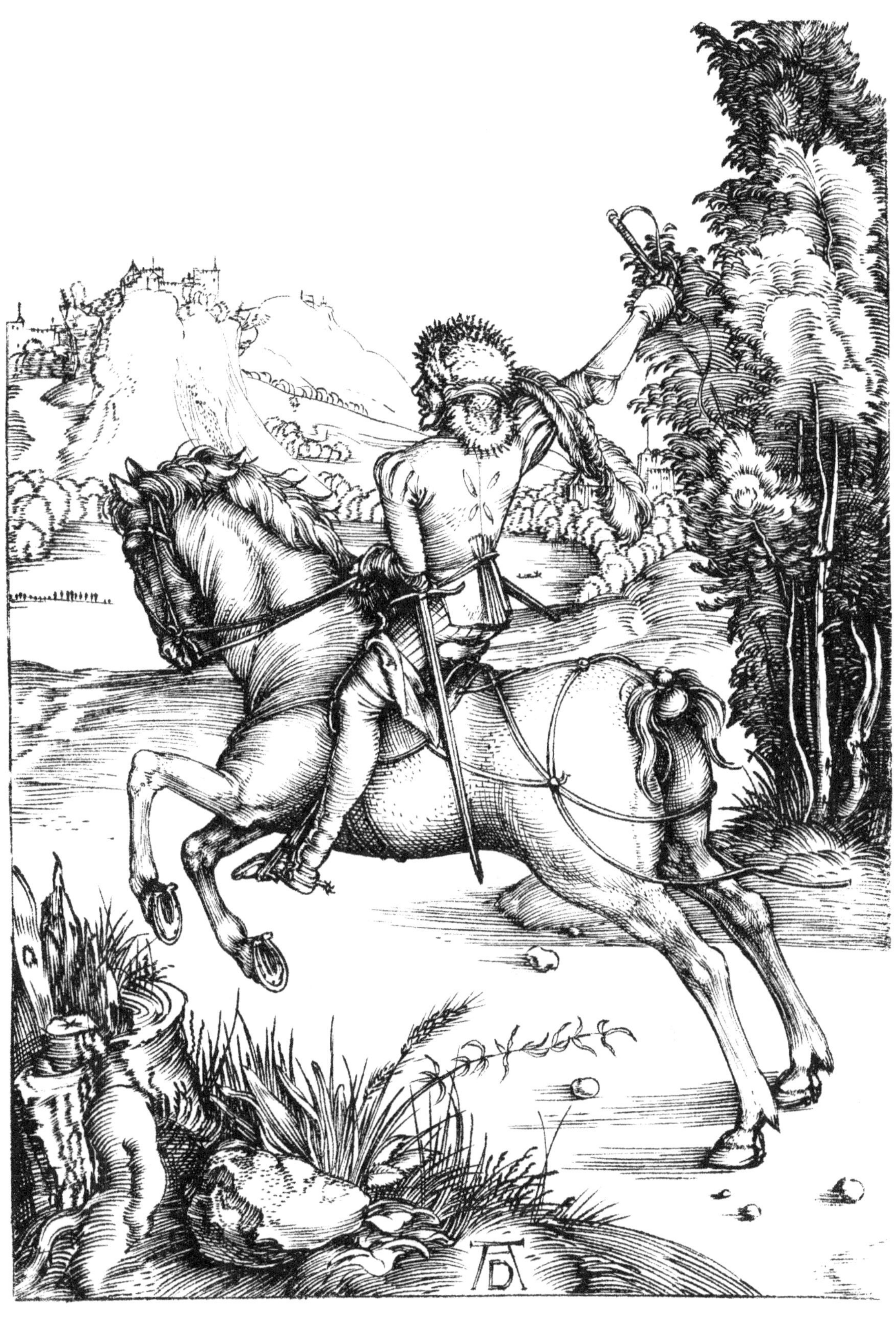

130. The Little Courier, Albrecht Dürer, 1494
- 1498

131

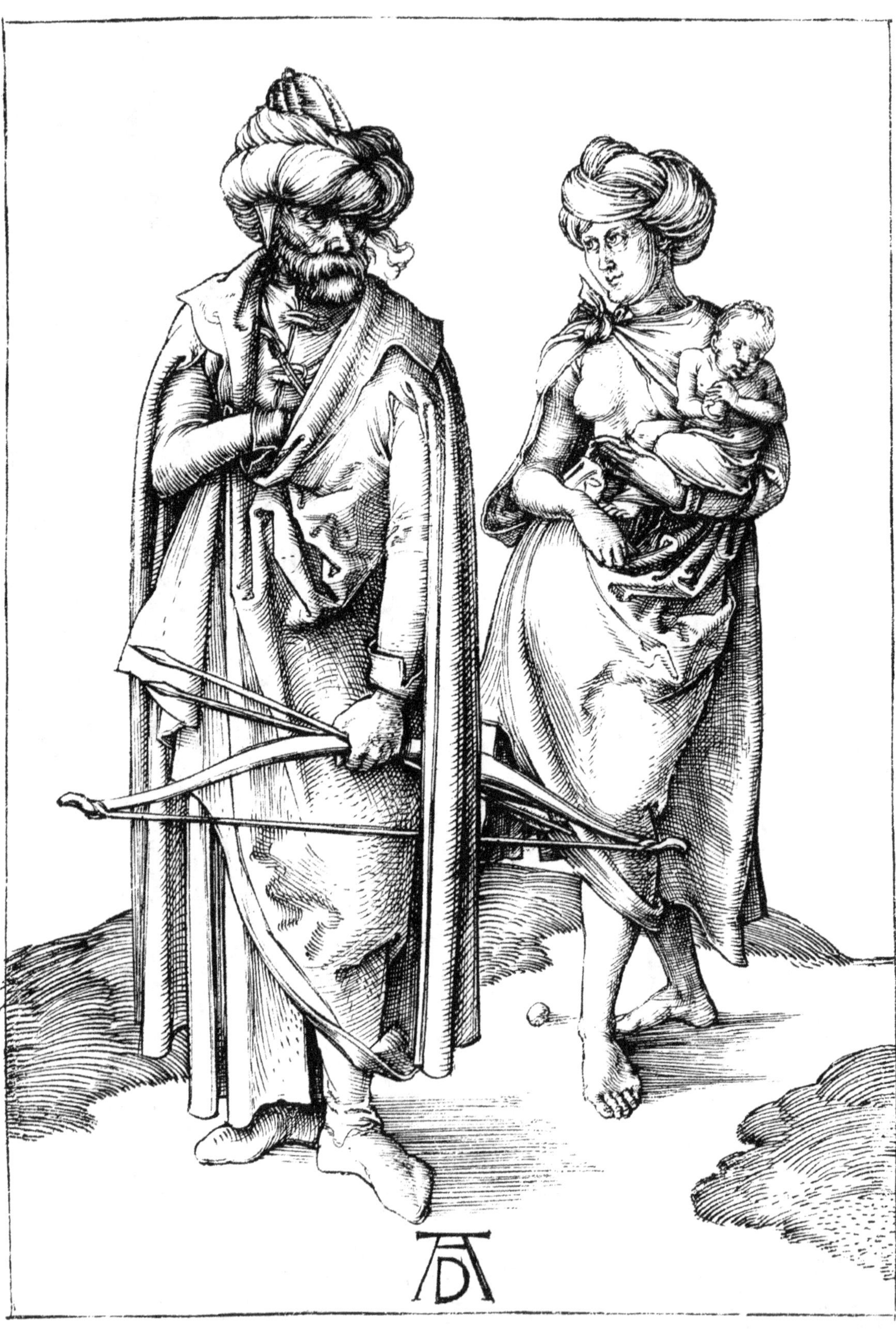

131. The Turkish Family, Albrecht Dürer, 1495

132

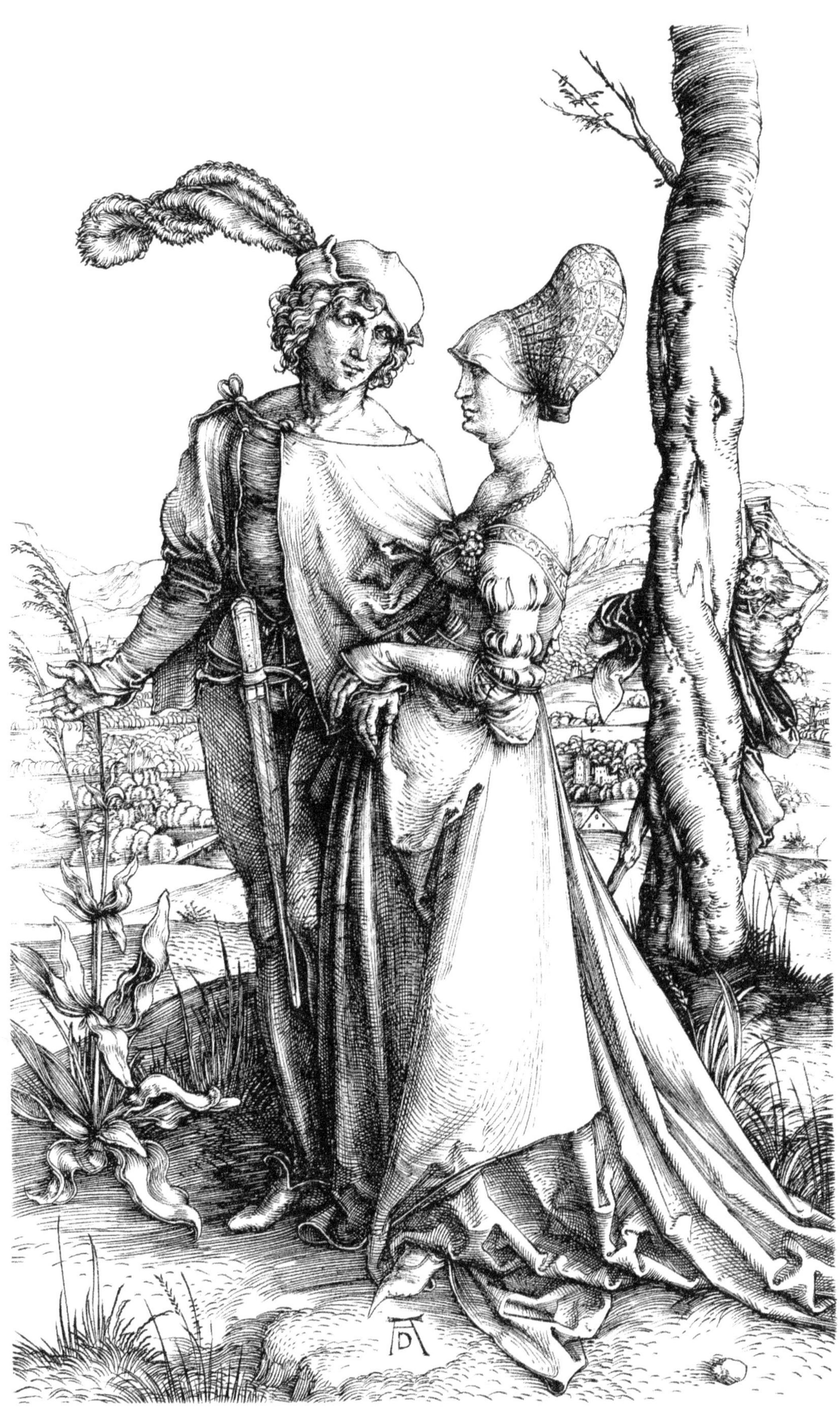

ALBRECHT DÜRER

133

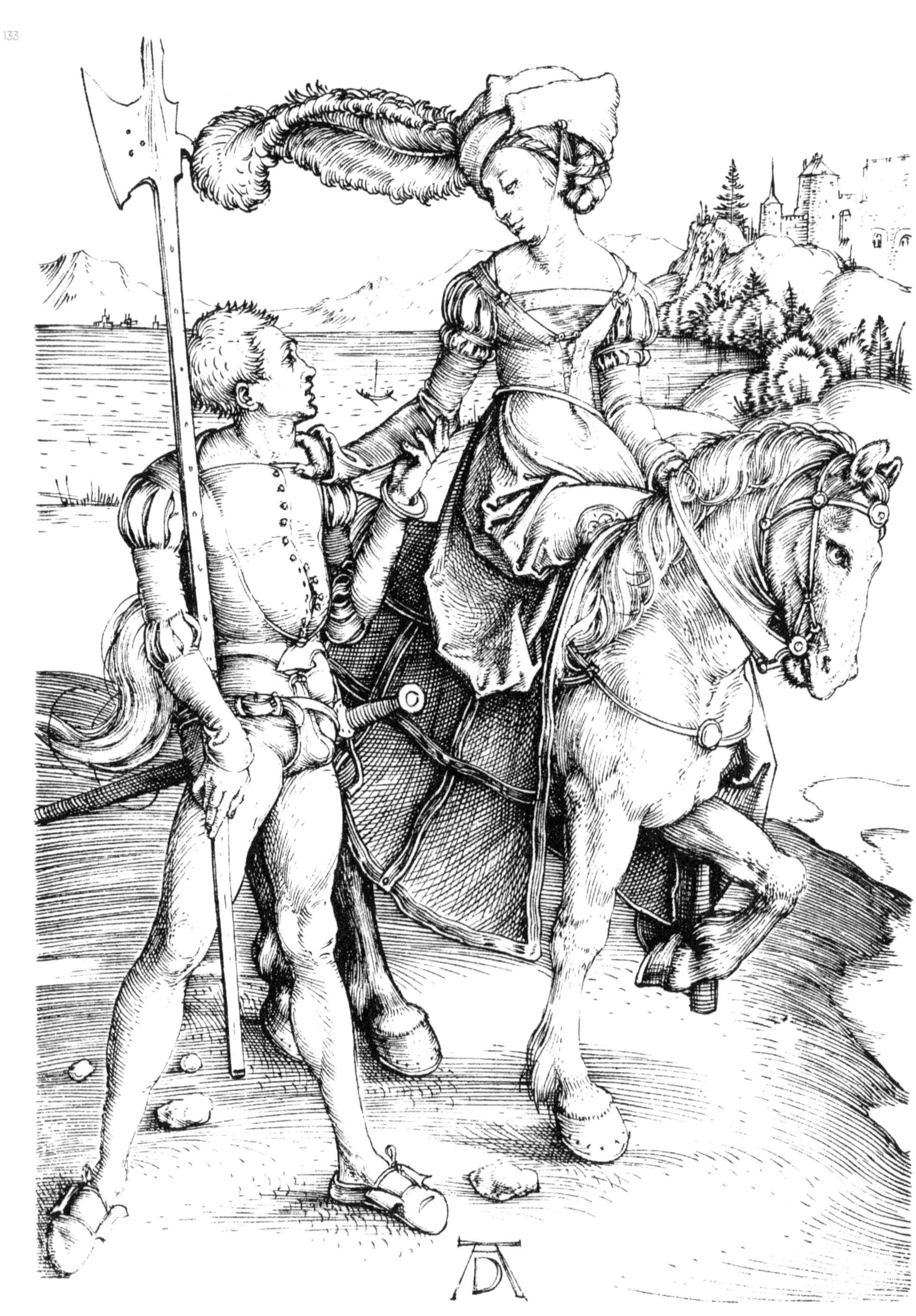

133. Woman on Horseback and Soldier,
Albrecht Dürer, 1495 - 1499

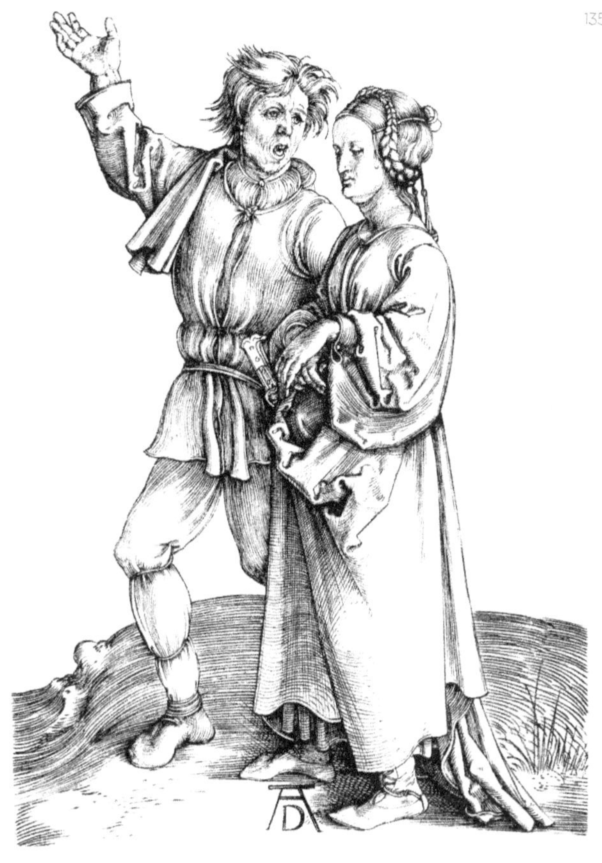

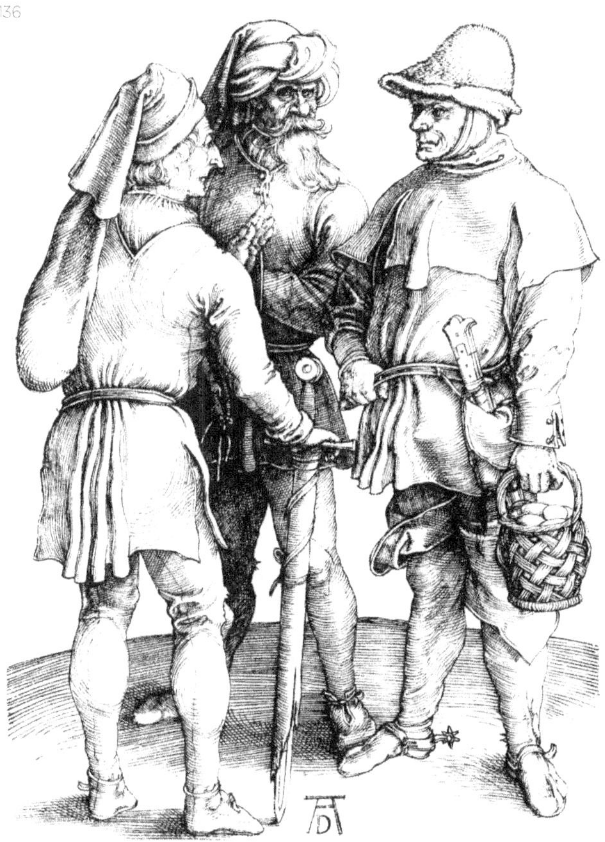

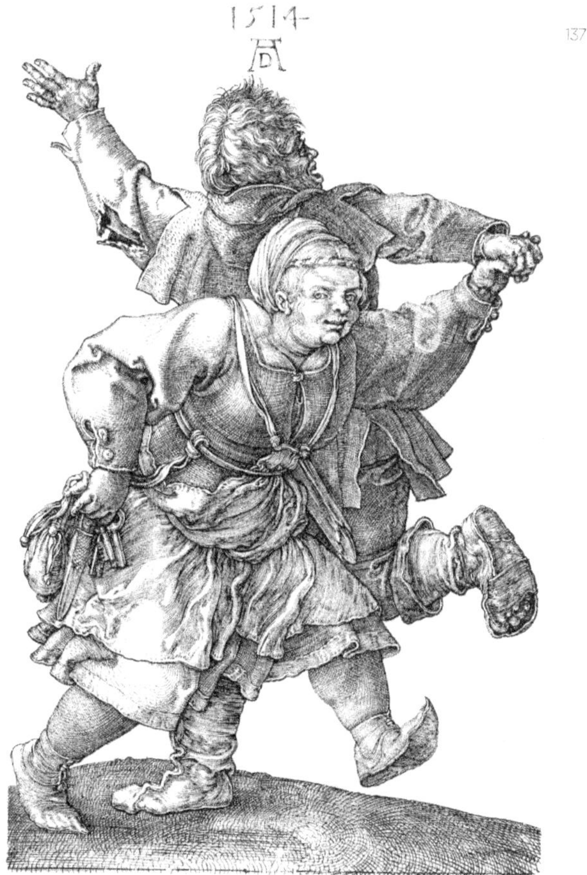

134. *The Cook and his Wife. Albrecht Dürer, 1494 - 1498*

135. *The Peasant and his Wife. Albrecht Dürer, 1495 - 1499*

136. *Three Peasants in Conversation. Albrecht Dürer, 1495 - 1499*

137. *Dancing Peasant Couple. Albrecht Dürer, 1514*

138

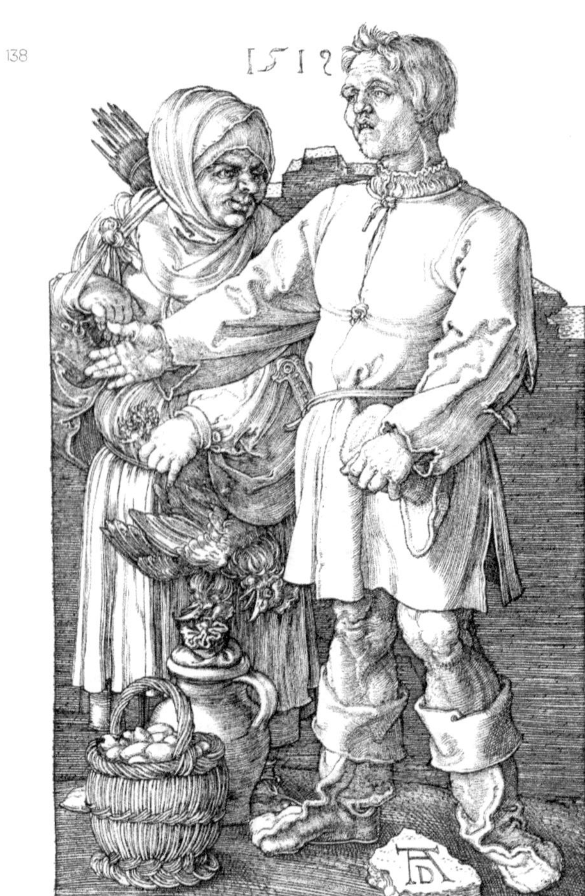

139

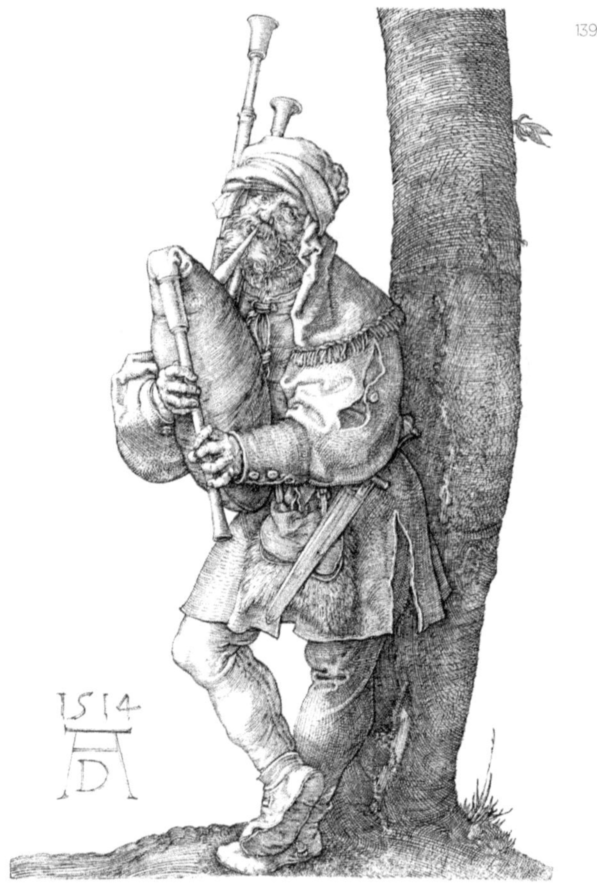

140

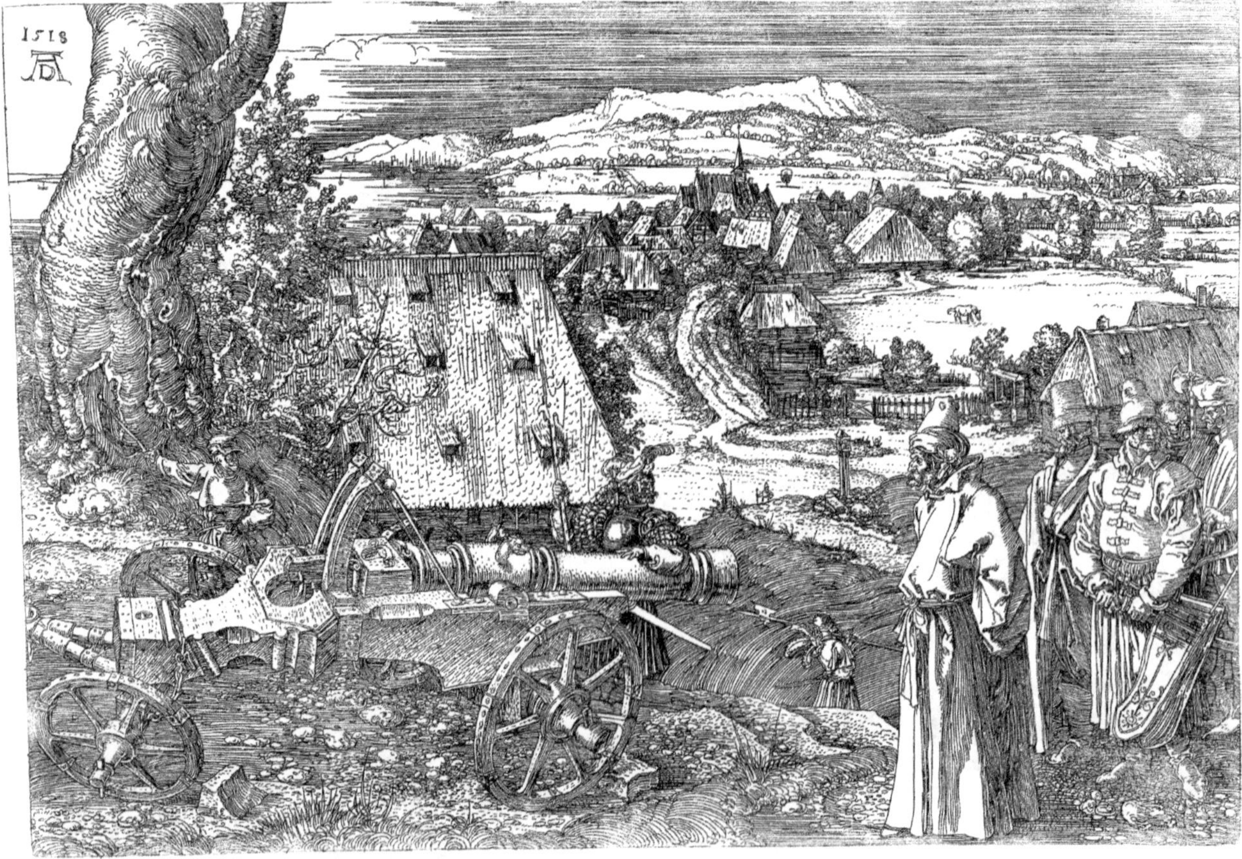

138. *Peasant couple at the market*, Albrecht Dürer, 1519

139. *The Bagpiper*, Albrecht Dürer, 1514

140. *Landscape with cannon*, Albrecht Dürer, 1518

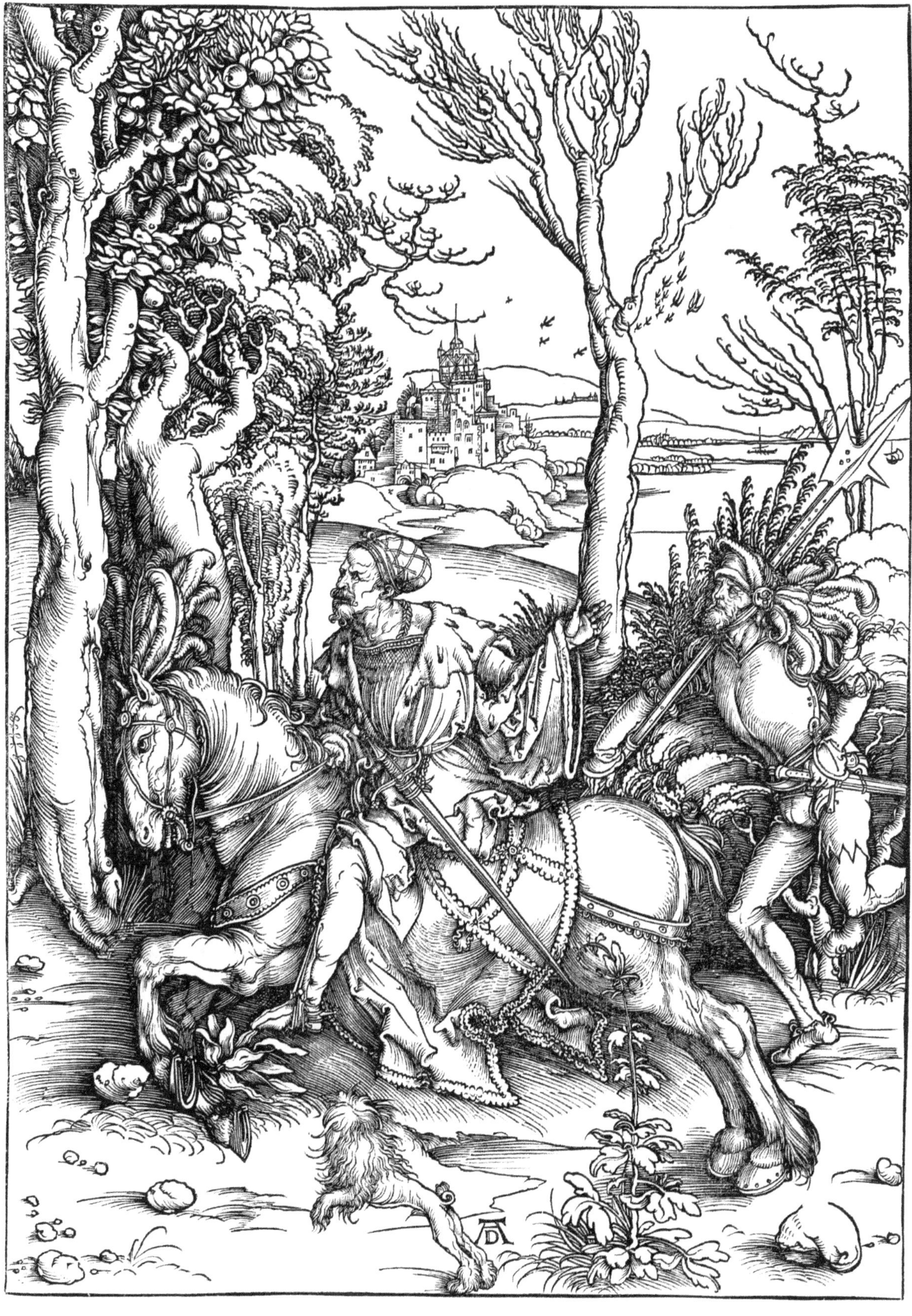

ALBRECHT DÜRER

142

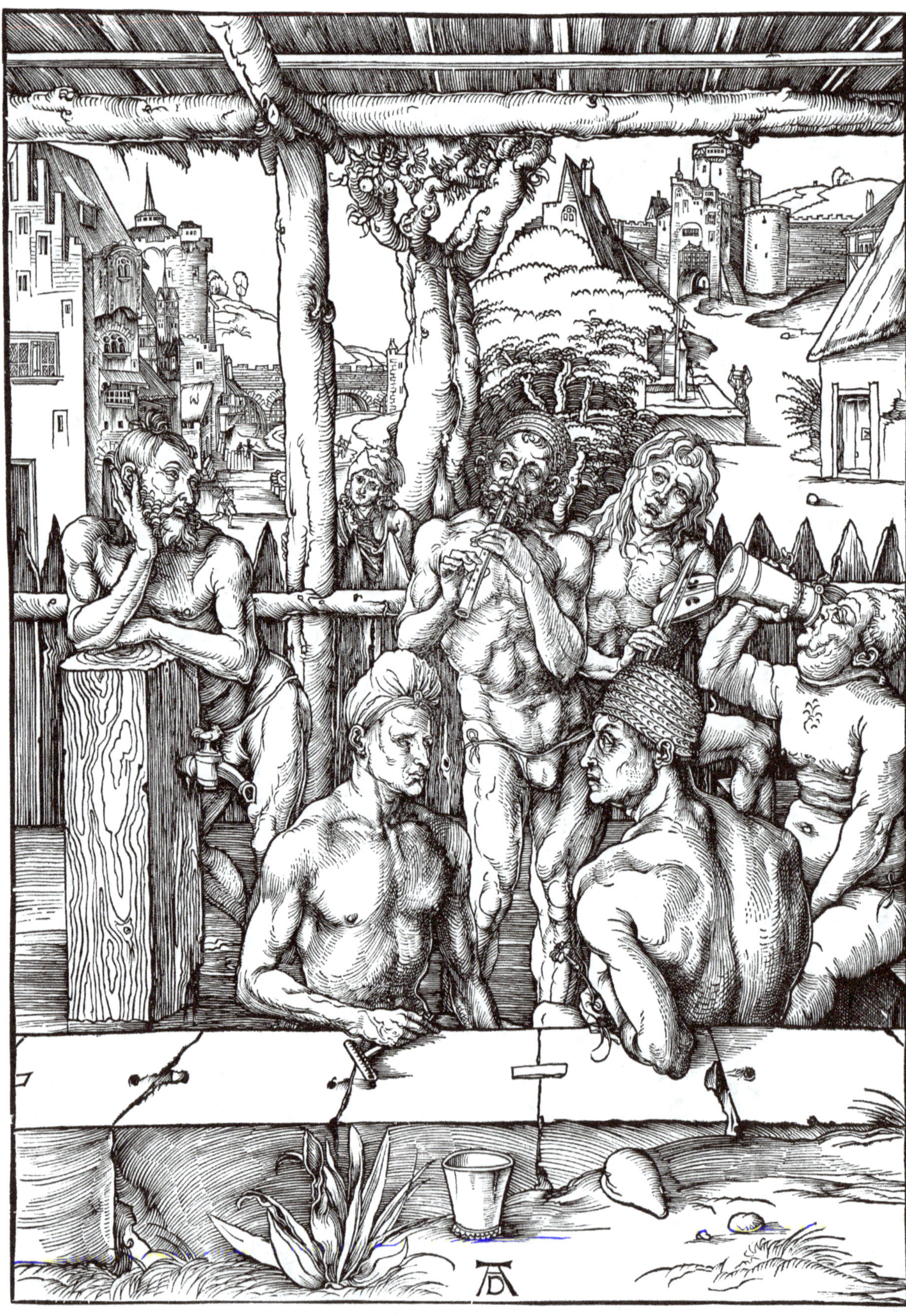

142 *The Men's Bath, Albrecht Dürer, 1496 - 1497*

143

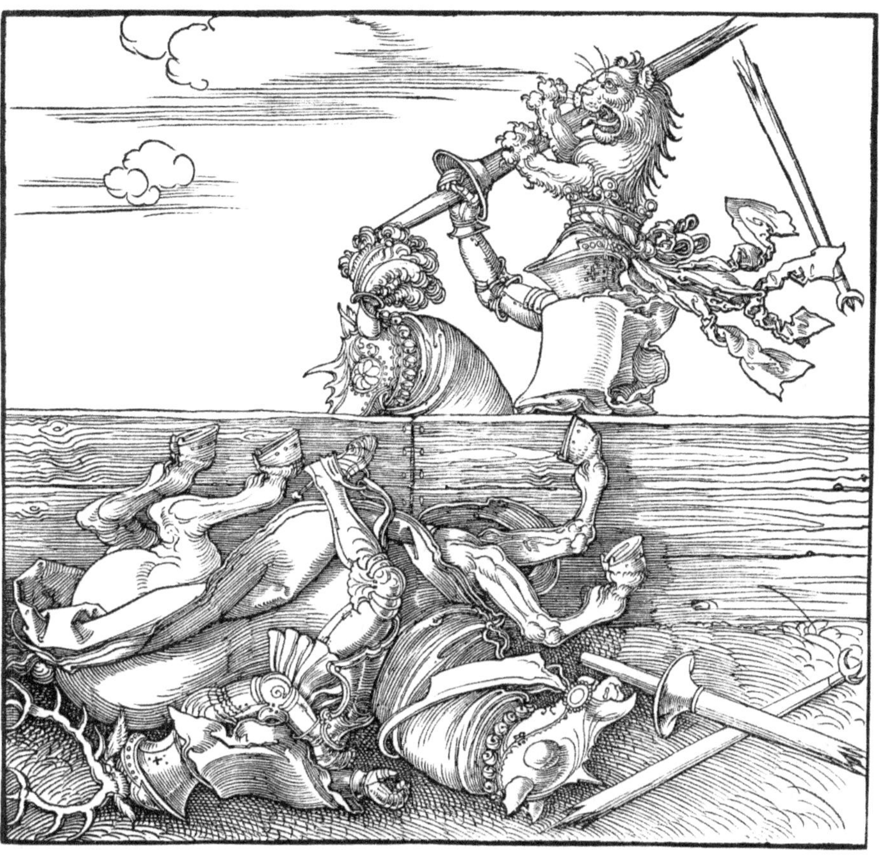

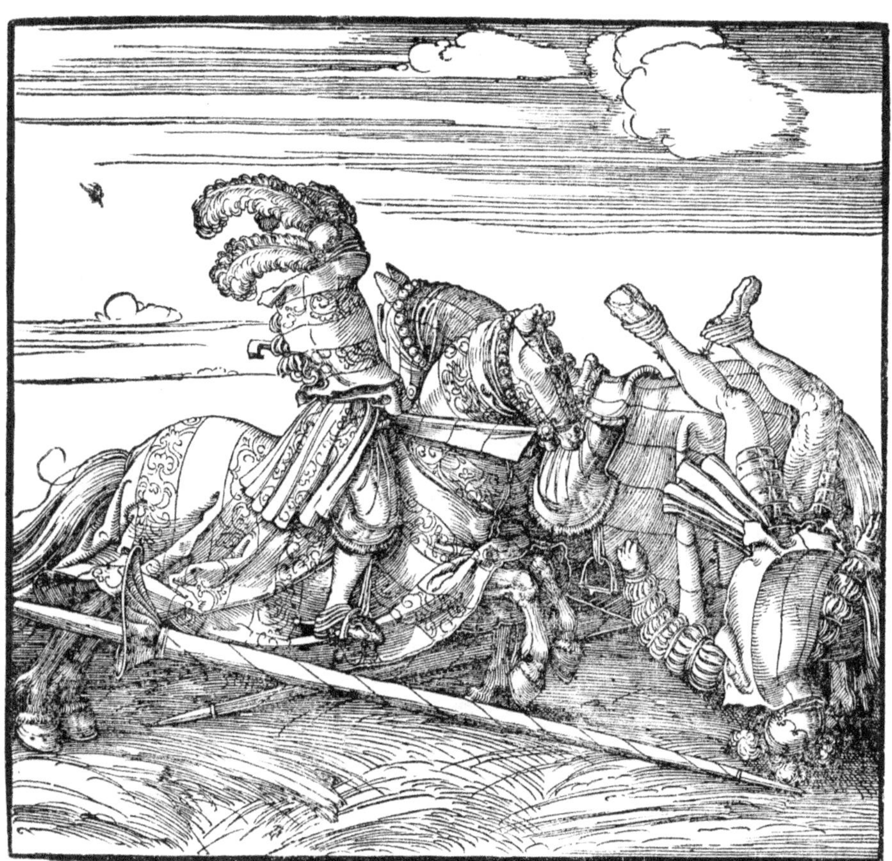

144

143. *Italian Joust of Peace Between Jacob de Heere and Freydal, Albrecht Dürer, 1517-1518*

144. *Freydal Jousting with Lord Niclas von Firmain, Albrecht Dürer, 1517 - 1518*

ALBRECHT DÜRER

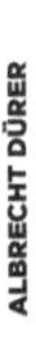

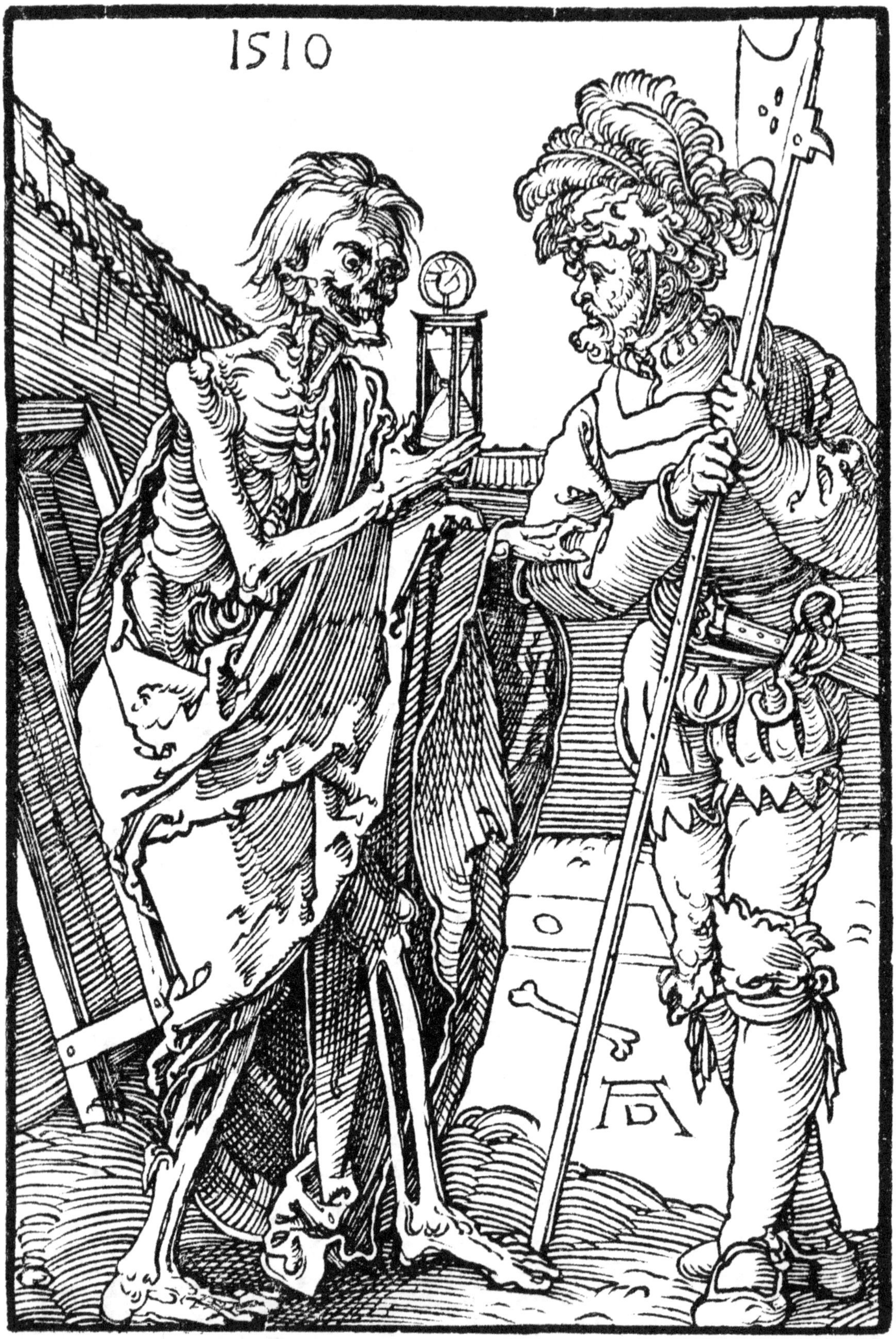

145. *The Soldier and Death, Albrecht Dürer, 1510*

146

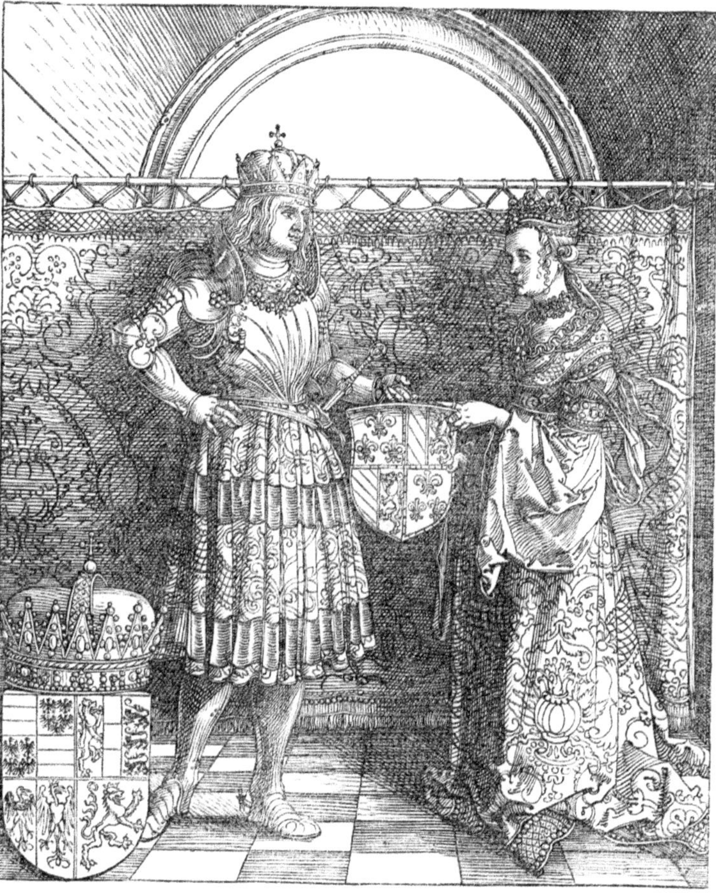

147

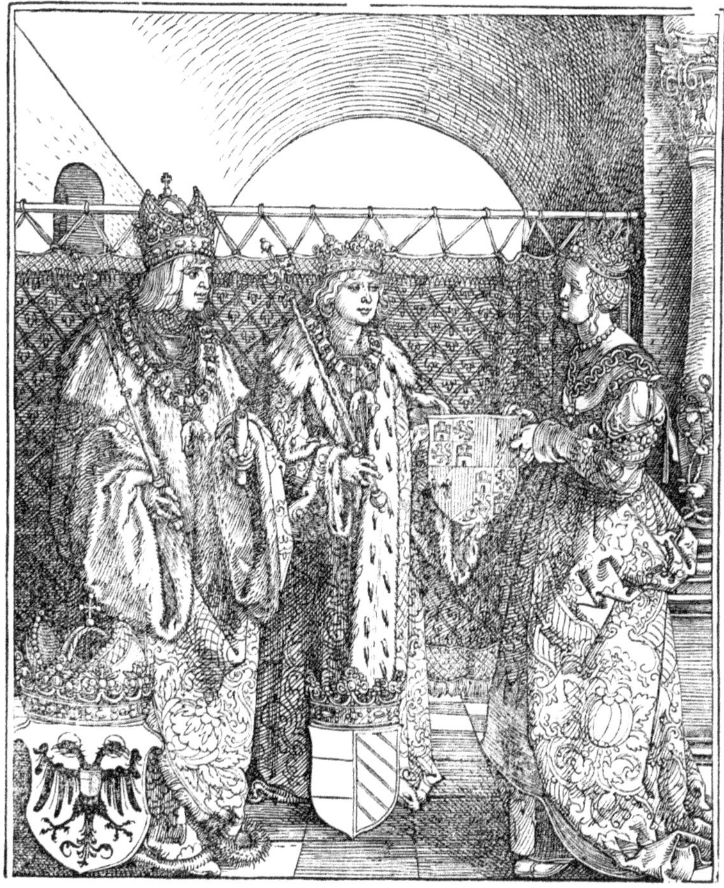

146. The Burgundian Marriage Maximilian
marries Mary of Burgundy, Albrecht Dürer, 1515

147. The Spanish Marriage, Philip the Fair
marries Joanna of Castile, Albrecht Dürer, 1515

148

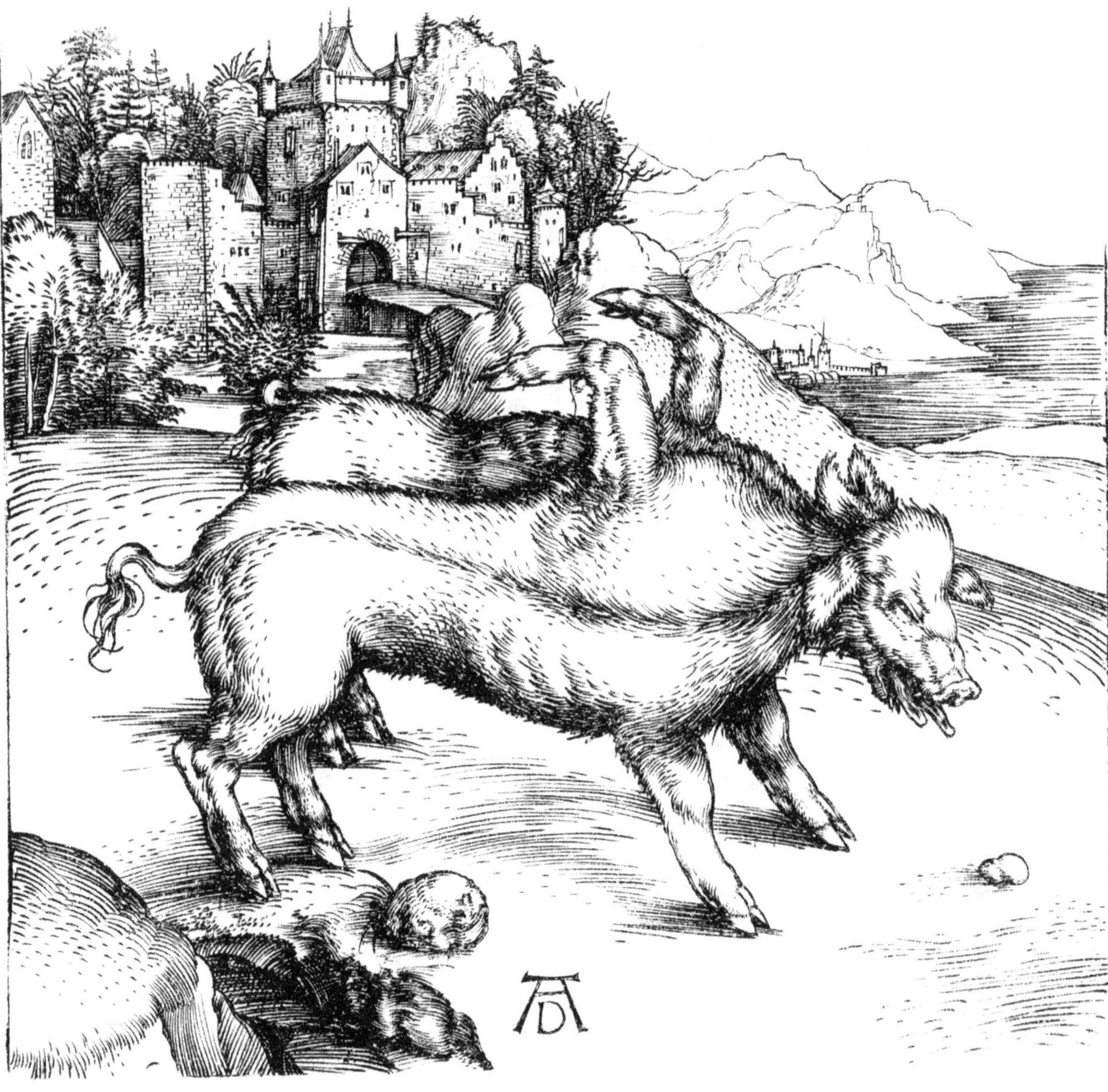

148. The Monstrous Pig of Landser, Albrecht
Dürer, 1496

Nach Christus gepurt.1513. Jar.Adi.j.May. Hat man dem grofmechtigen Kunig von Portugall Emanuell gen Lysabona pracht auß India/ein sollich lebendig Thier. Das nennen sie Rhinocerus.Das ist hye mit aller seiner gestalt Abcondertset.Es hat ein farb wie ein gespreckelte Schildtkrot. Vnd ist võ dicken Schalen vberlegt fast fest.Vnd ist in der größ als der Helfandt Aber nydertrechtiger von paynen/vnd fast werhafftig.Es hat ein scharff starck Horn vorn auff der nasen/Das begyndt es alweg zu wetzen wo es bey staynen ist.Das dosig Thier ist des Helffantz todt feyndt.Der Helffandt furcht es fast vbel/dann wo es In ankumbt/so laufft Im das Thier mit dem kopff zwischen dye fordern payn/vnd reyst den Helffandt vnden am pauch auff vñ erwürgt In/des mag er sich nit erwern.Dann das Thier ist also gewapent/das Im der Helffandt nichts kan thün.Sie sagen auch das der Rhynocerus Schnell/ fraydig vnd Listig sey.

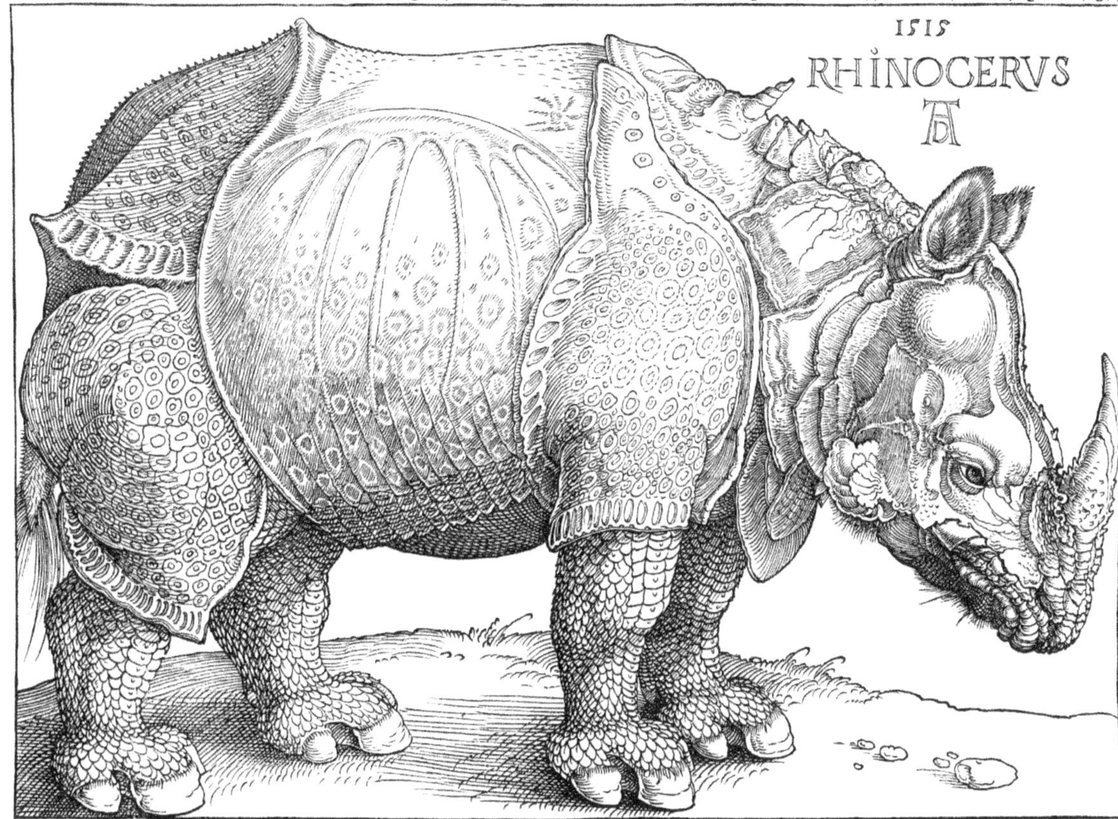

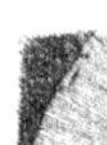

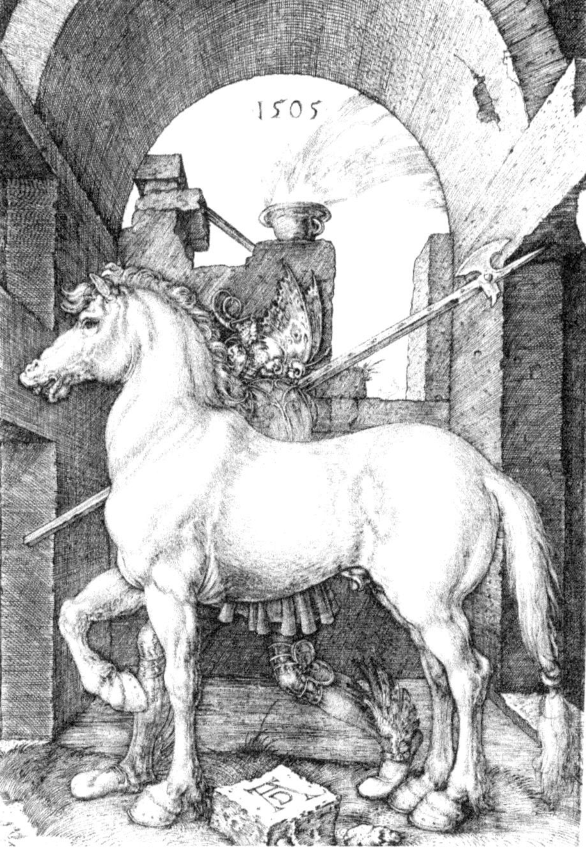

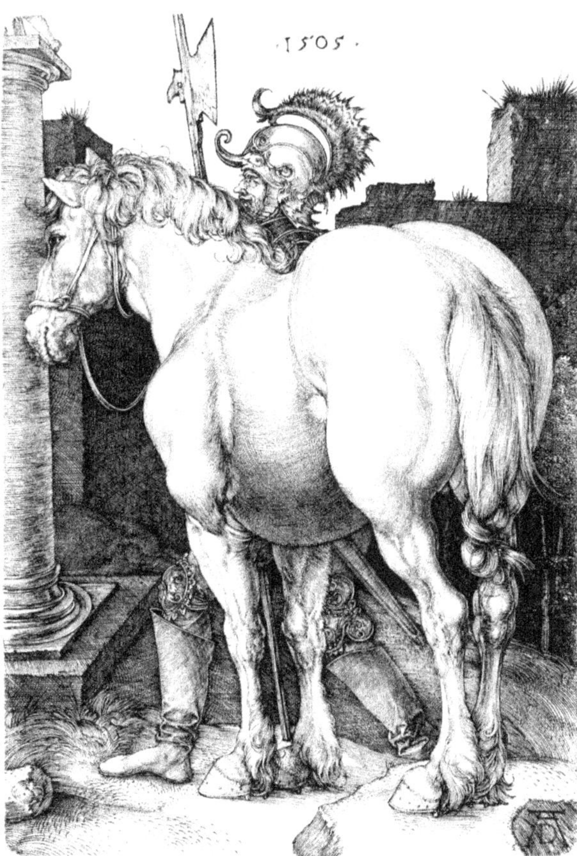

ALBRECHT DÜRER

05

HERALDRY

Heraldry, with its rich history and intricate designs, played a pivotal role in medieval society as a symbol of status and identity. For Albrecht Dürer, these emblems were not just symbols of power but a canvas for his artistic mastery. Dürer's fascination with heraldic devices is evident in his meticulous engravings and drawings, where he infused traditional elements with his unique artistic vision.

The concept of a coat of arms originated in medieval Europe. It was designed to identify individuals in combat whose identities were concealed by their armour. The term "coat of arms" itself stems from the surcoat, a garment worn over armour adorned with the bearer's heraldry. Each design was a unique combination of colour, pattern, and design that reflected the individual's heritage and potentially their land ownership and alliances.

A typical coat of arms contains several key elements. At the centre is a shield featuring an emblem representing the owner's family. The shield design can also be divided into sections with different emblems. Flanking the shield are two figures serving as 'supporters'. People or animals in dynamic poses are most common, but supporters can be anything from botanicals to columns. They stand on a 'compartment' that complements the overall design, whether brickwork, a river, or grass. Above the shield sits a helmet and a crest. The crest could contain feathers or intricate designs in the shape of animals, people, or objects like horns. All crests are designed to amplify the wearer's presence and status. The design and placement of the helmet on the arms traditionally denote the bearer's status. Below the shield, a Latin phrase or motto is displayed on a scroll, summarising an individual's belief or purpose.

Through Dürer's attention to detail and creative talents, he ensures that the coat of arms is not only a declaration of lineage and allegiance but also a testament to his artistry.

152

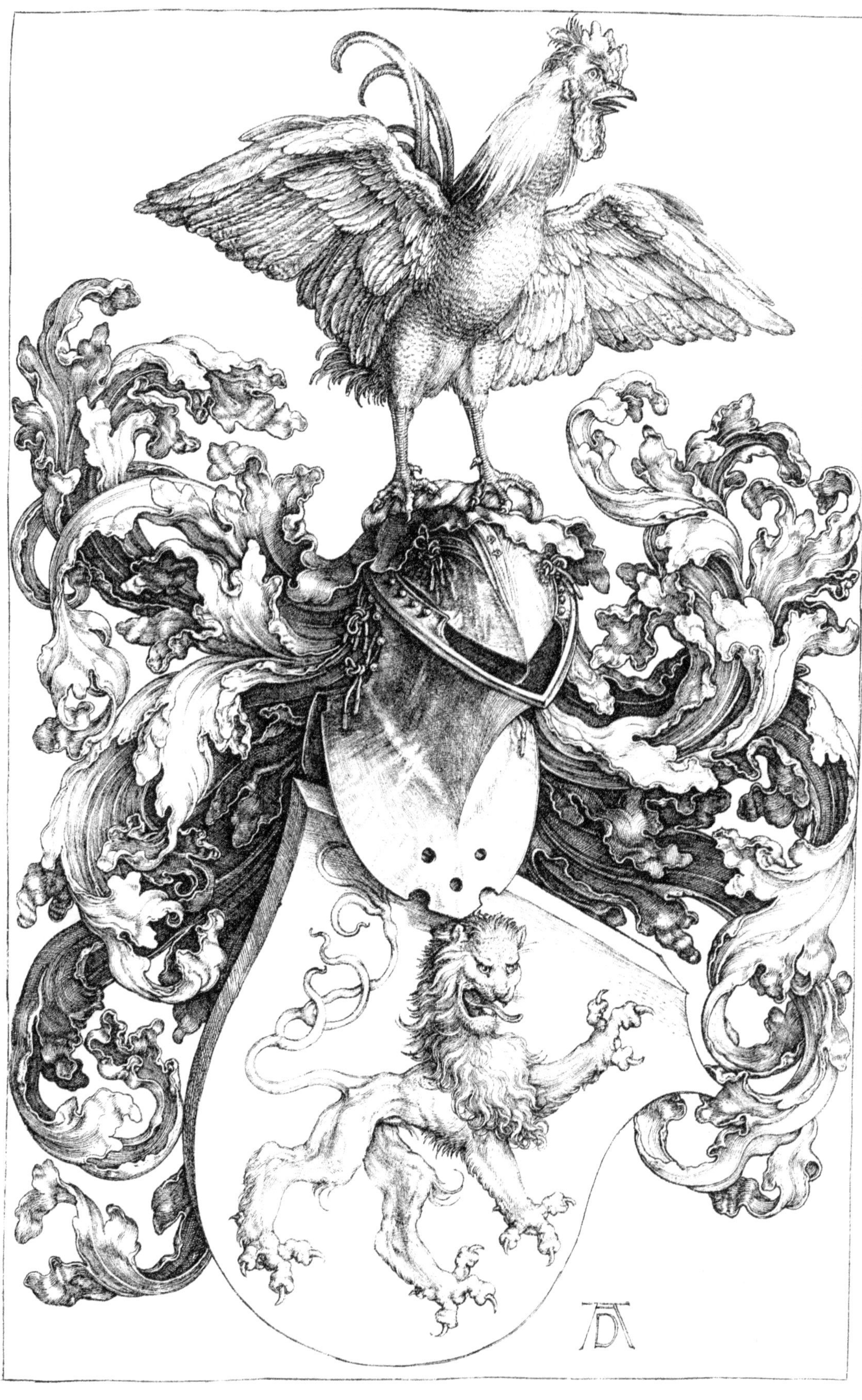

152. Coat of arms with rooster. Albrecht Dürer.
1500 - 1505

153

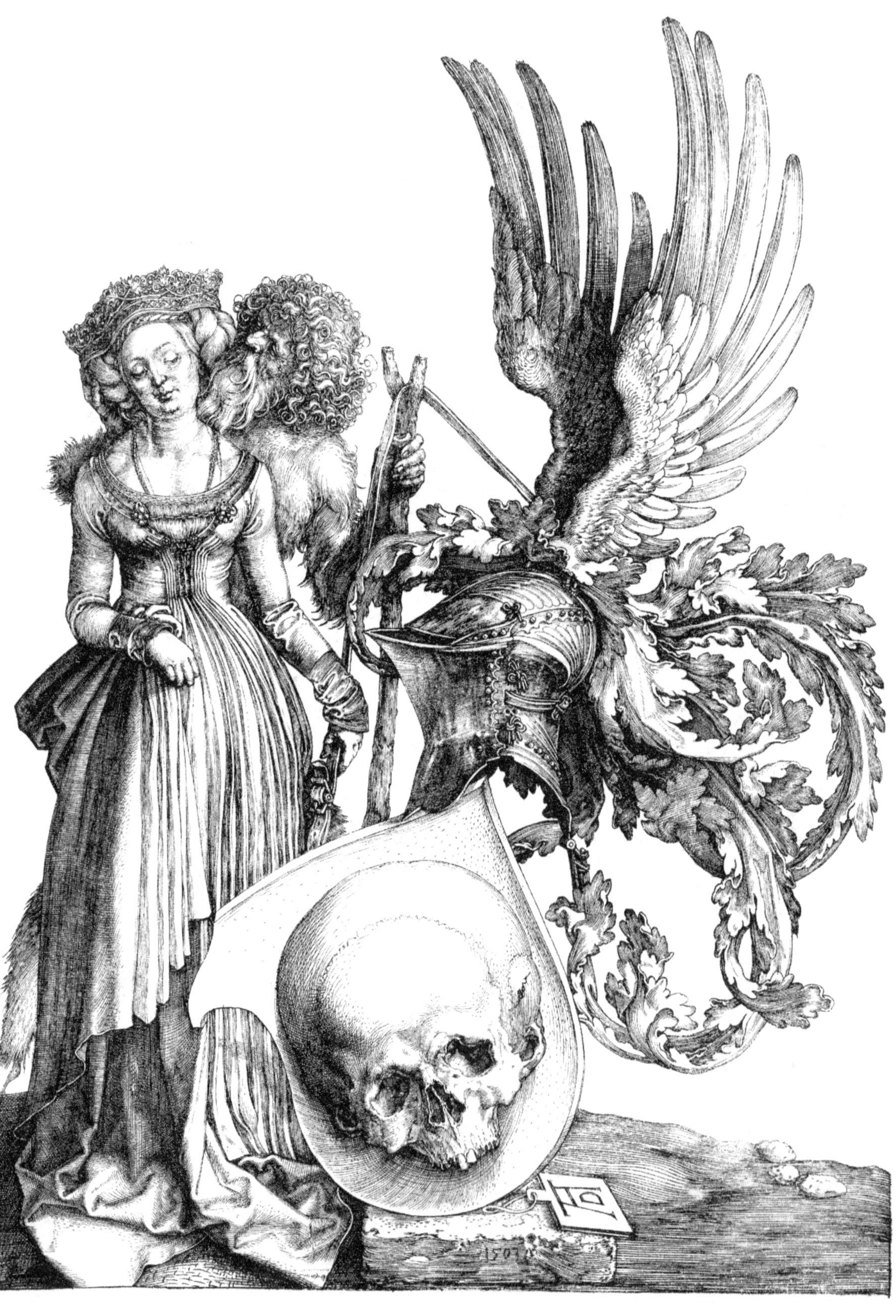

153. Coat of arms with woman and wild man,
Albrecht Dürer, 1503

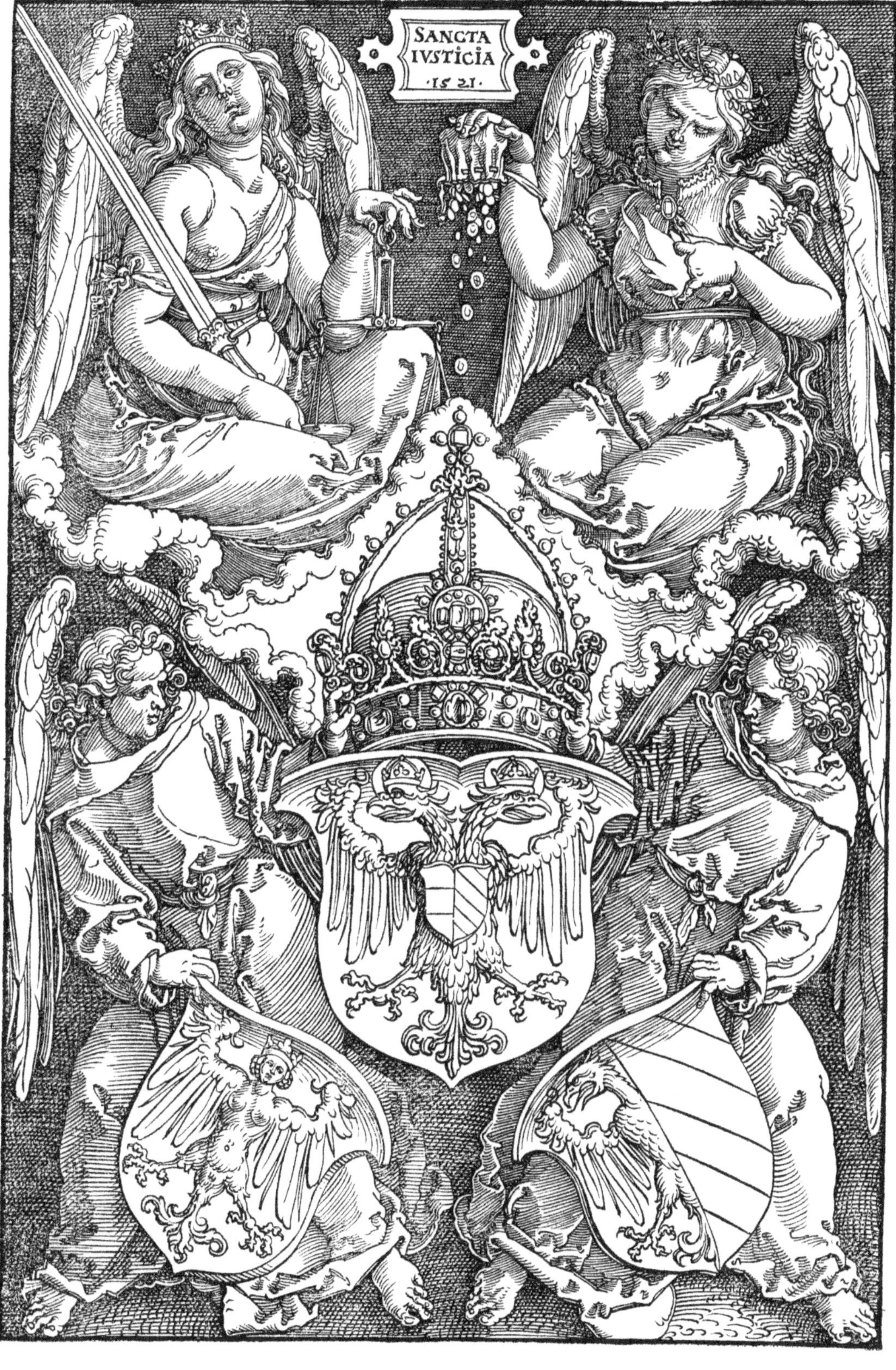

154. Allegory with the coat of arms of the
Empire and two coats of arms of the city of
Nuremberg, Dürer, 1521

155

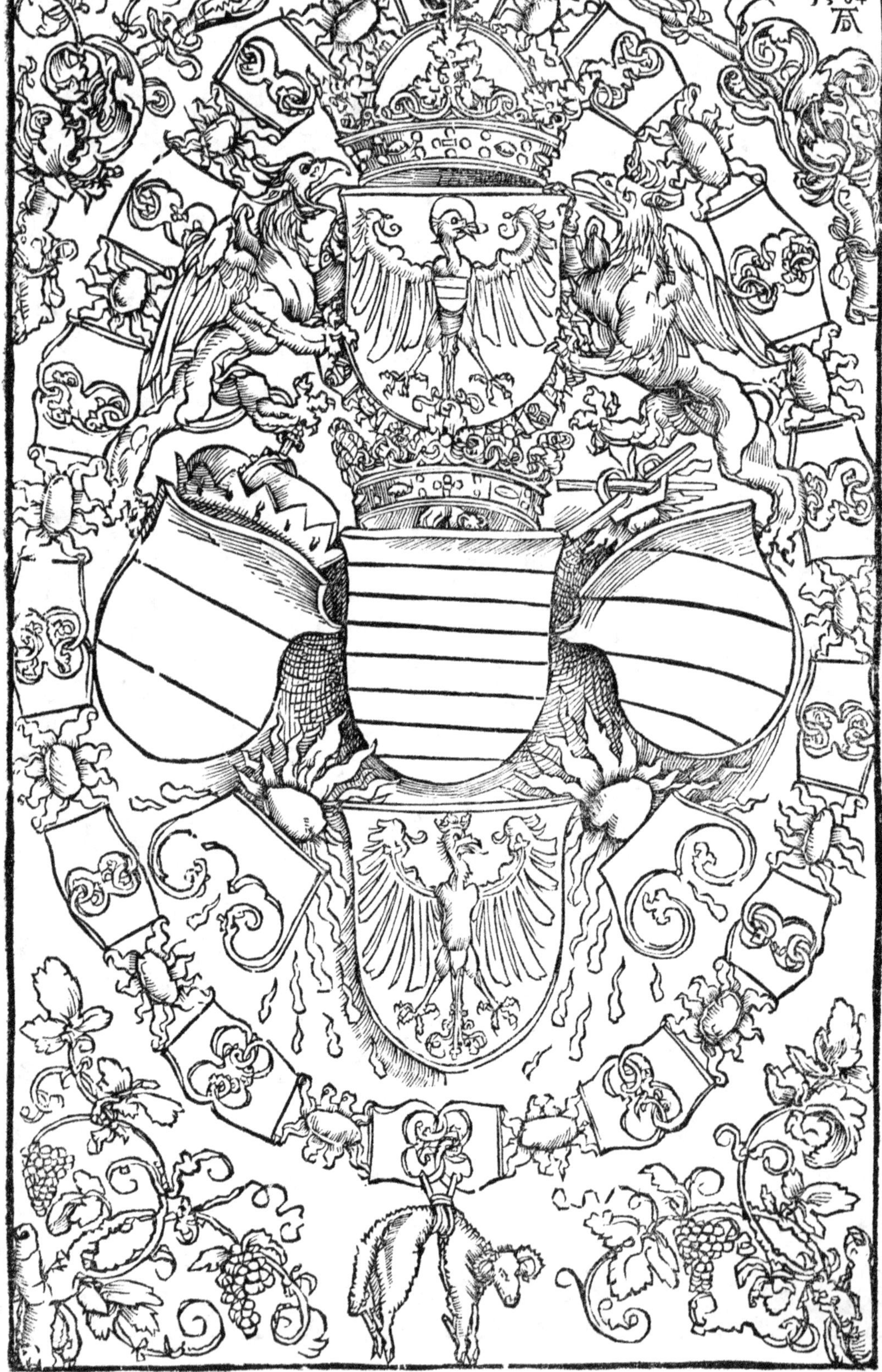

155. Coat of arms of Roman king Maximilian,
Albrecht Dürer, 1550 - 1600

156

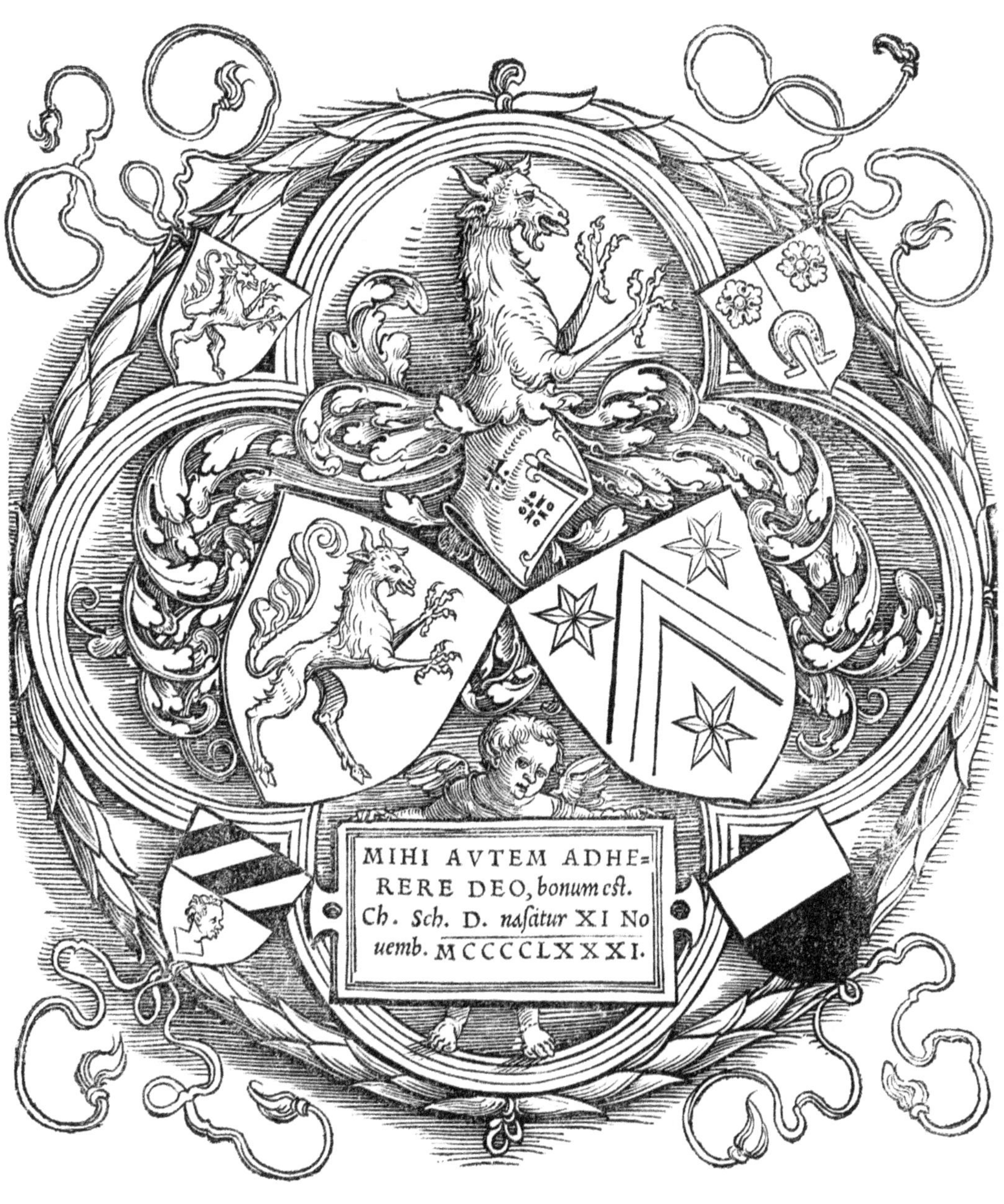

ALBRECHT DÜRER

*156 Coats of arms of the Scheurl and Zinger
families, Albrecht Dürer (school of), 1481 - 1523*

06

PORTRAITS BY DÜRER

Dürer's skill at capturing facial characteristics gives each of his portraits a powerful sense of vitality. 'Portraits by Albrecht Dürer' features his friends, patrons, and prominent people of the day. Below are brief introductions to some of the individuals depicted.

Willibald Pirckheimer (*Fig. 159*) was a lawyer, author, humanist and counsellor from a wealthy and prominent family. He was a significant patron of the arts and a close friend of Albrecht Dürer. Pirckheimer was a scholar who curated a famous personal library and used this portrait as a bookplate for the books in his collection.

Phillip Melanchthon (*Fig. 160*) was a humanist, reformer, theologian, and educator. He was also a friend and collaborator of religious reformist Martin Luther. In 1525, he visited Nuremberg and stayed with Dürer's friend, Willibald Pirckheimer, which could be where he met Dürer. Melanchthon was an admirer of Dürer's work and owned several of his prints. This image of Melanchthon was one of the last portrait prints Dürer made.

Erasmus of Rotterdam (*Fig. 161*) was a Roman Catholic reformer and leading Dutch humanist. He admired Albrecht Dürer and praised his skills in graphic arts, highlighting Dürer's ability to achieve impressive effects without colour. In Dürer's portrait, Erasmus is writing in his study, surrounded by books symbolising his intellect. On the table sits a vase of lilies, suggesting the purity of his mind. A framed Latin and Greek inscription emphasises his humanistic interests because humanists believe Greek and Latin classics teach people all the lessons needed to lead a moral life.

Ulrich Varnbüler (*Fig. 162*) was a German civil servant and scholar. The inscription indicates he was a close friend of Dürer, and the artist intended to preserve the likeness of his friend for posterity. Dürer's attention to detail and bold composition create an impression of a lively, vivid individual.

Through these portraits, Dürer not only captures the likenesses of his contemporaries but also offers a window into his time's vibrant intellectual and cultural milieu.

157

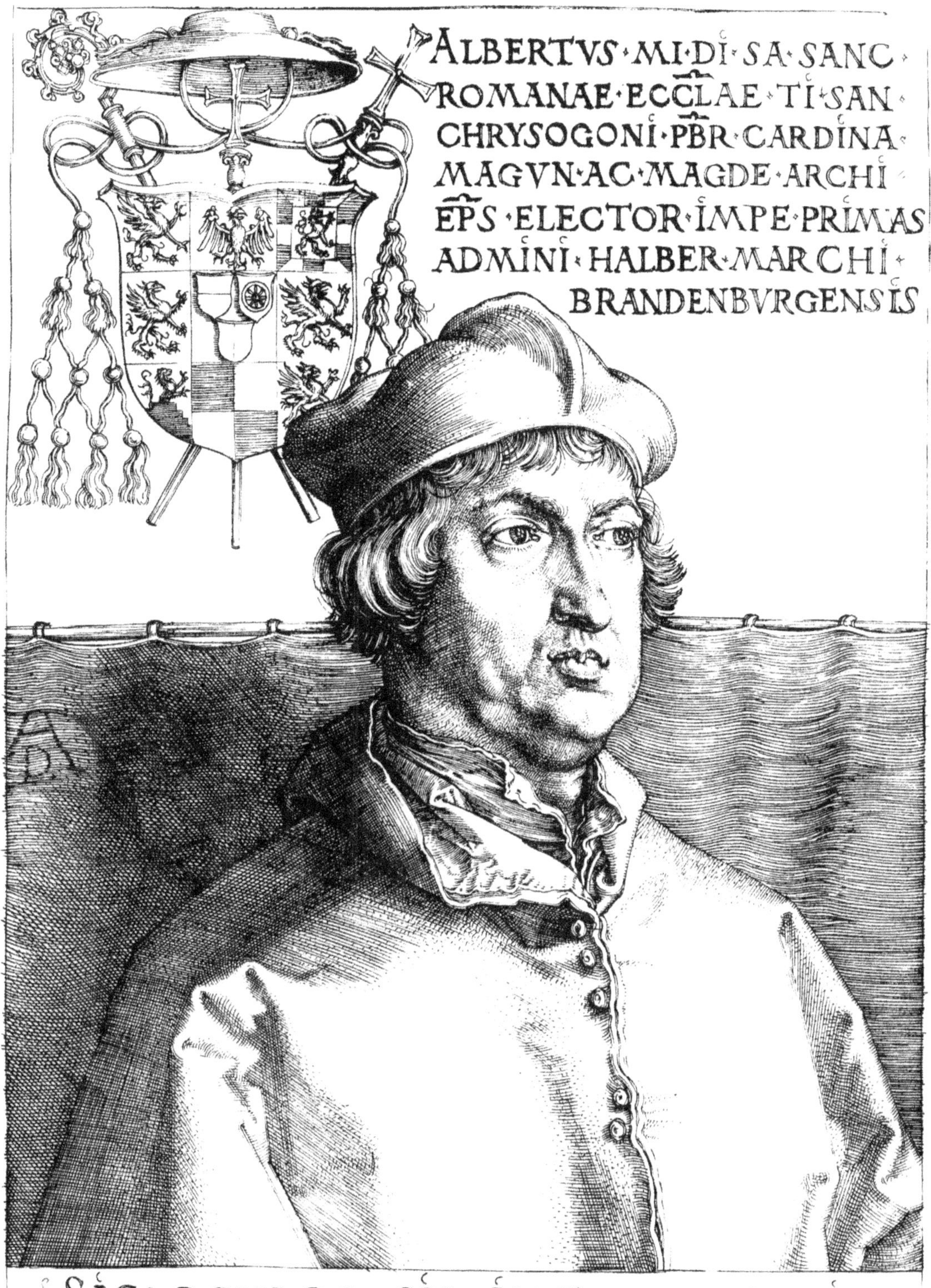

157. Portrait of Cardinal Albert of Brandenburg
at the age of 29. Albrecht Dürer, 1519

ALBRECHT DÜRER

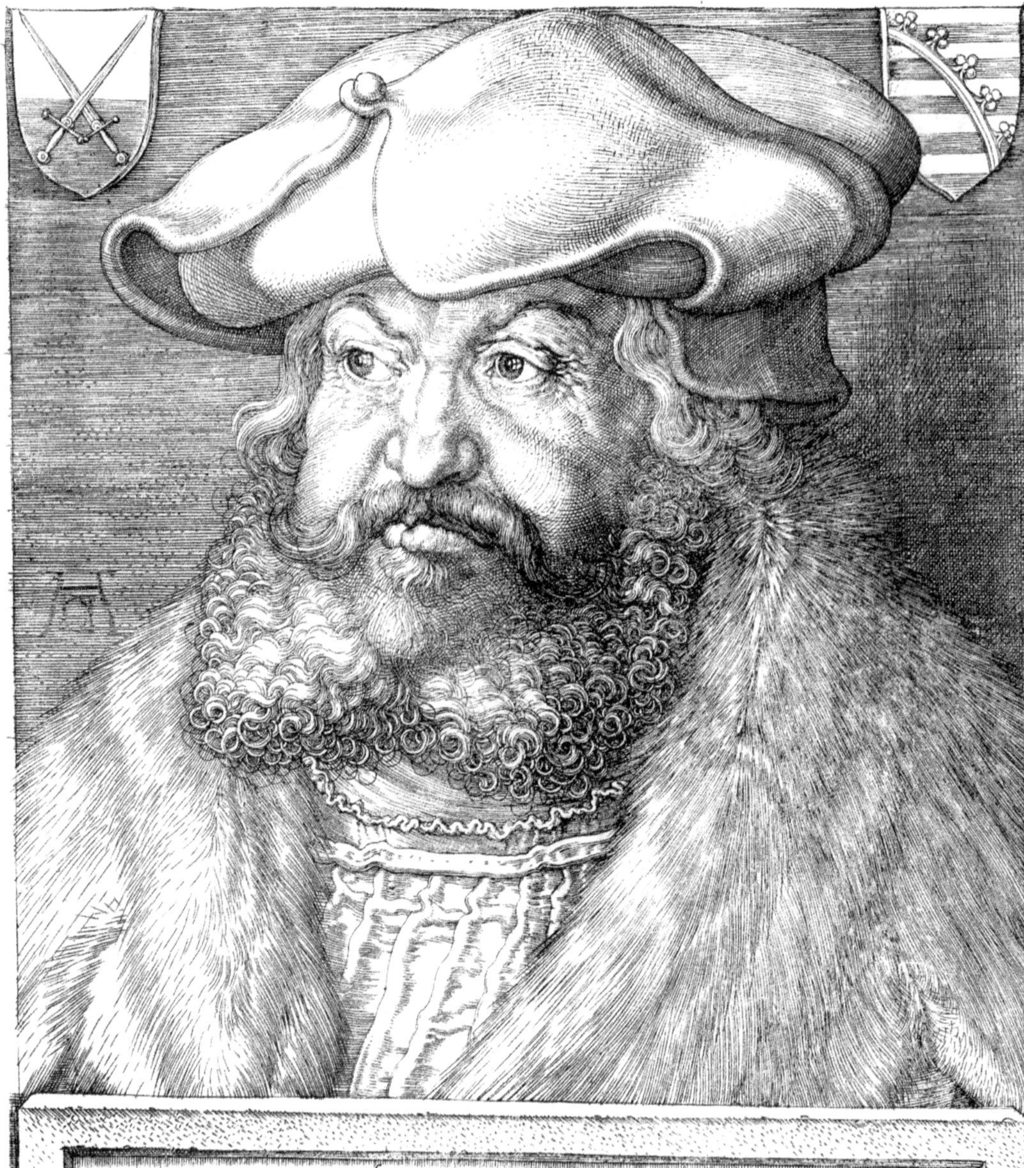

*158. Portrait of Frederick III the Wise, Elector of
Saxony. Albrecht Dürer, 1524*

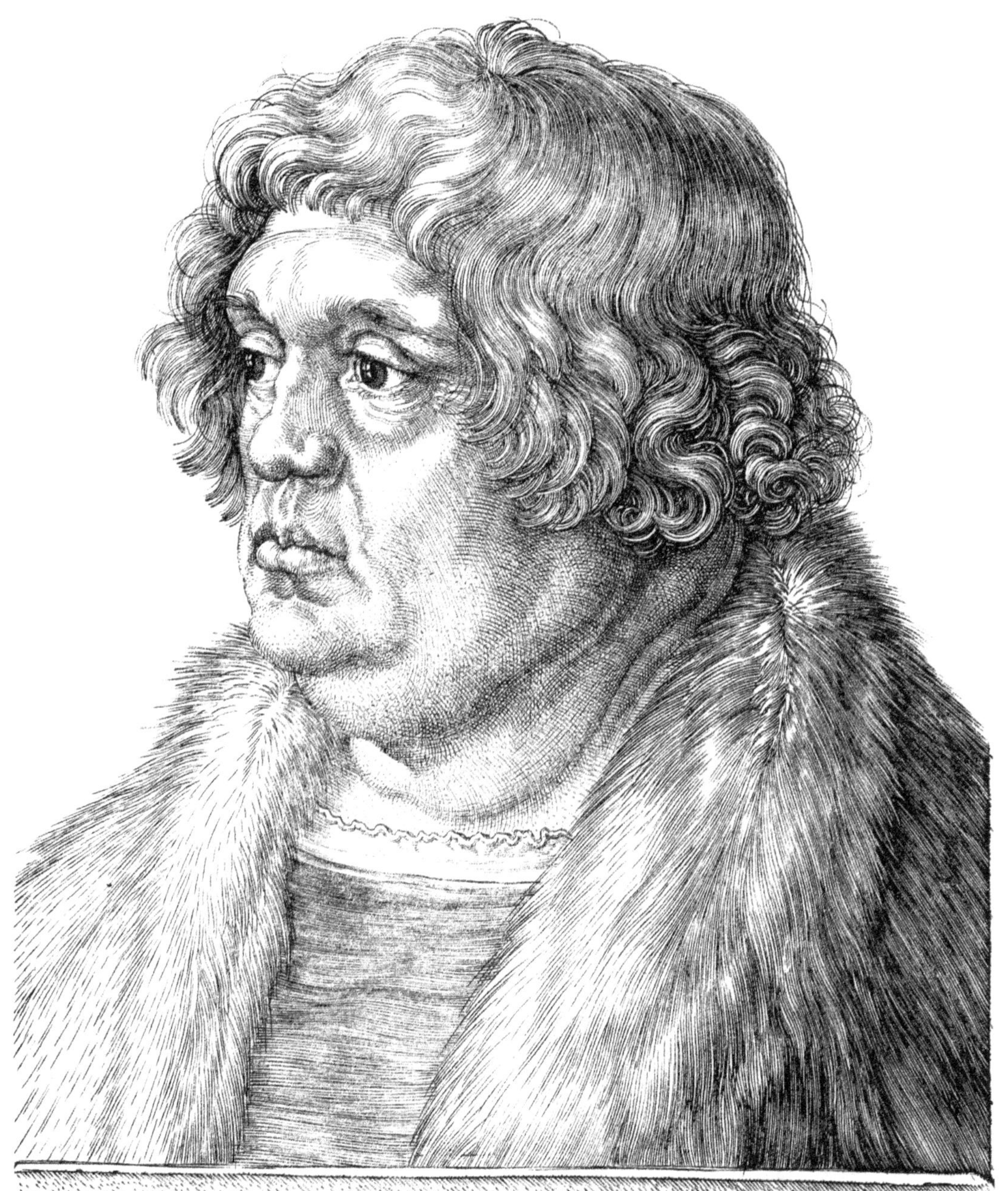

159. Portrait of Willibald Pirckheimer, Albrecht
Dürer, 1524

160

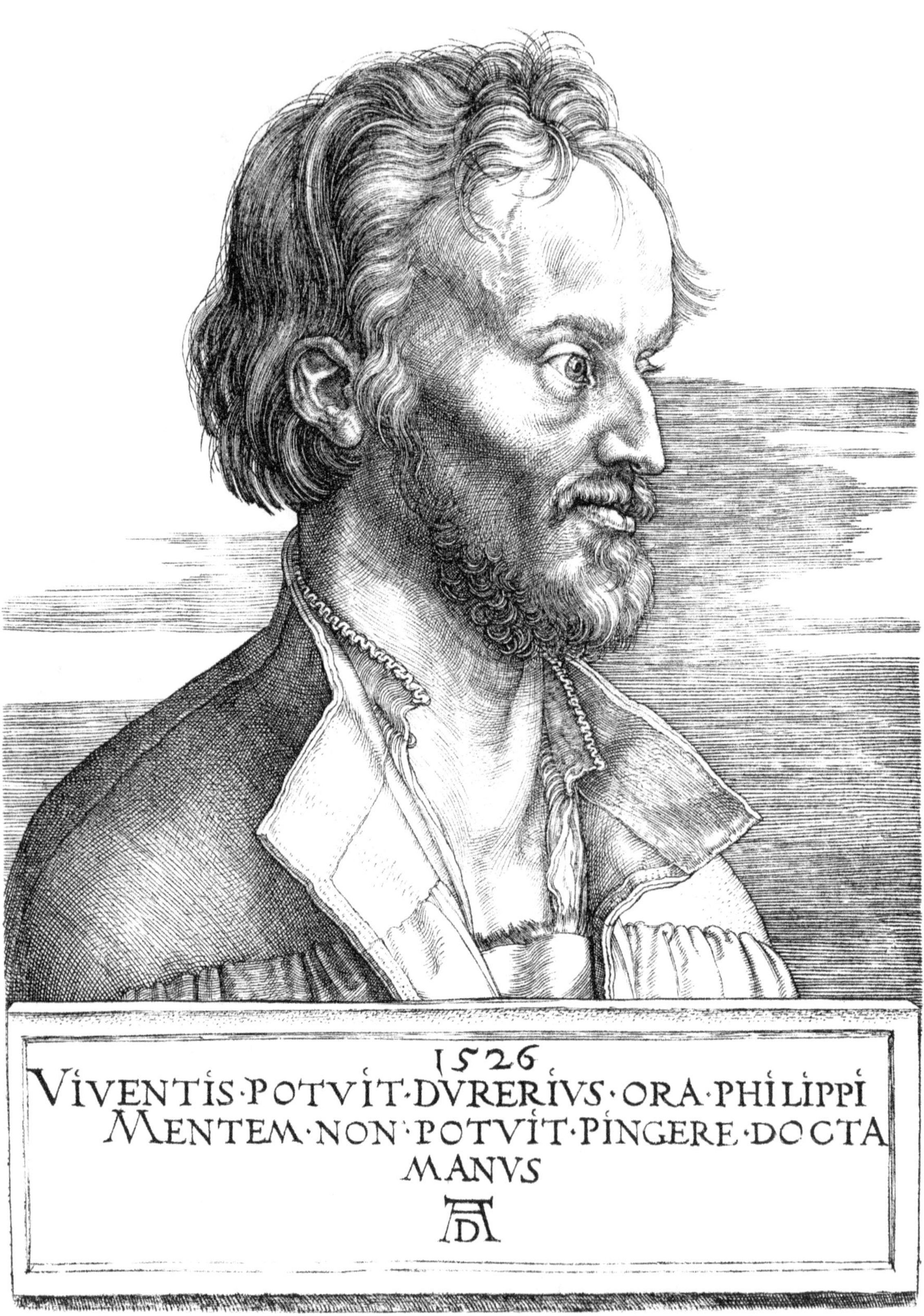

160. Portrait of Philipp Melanchthon, Albrecht Dürer, 1526

161

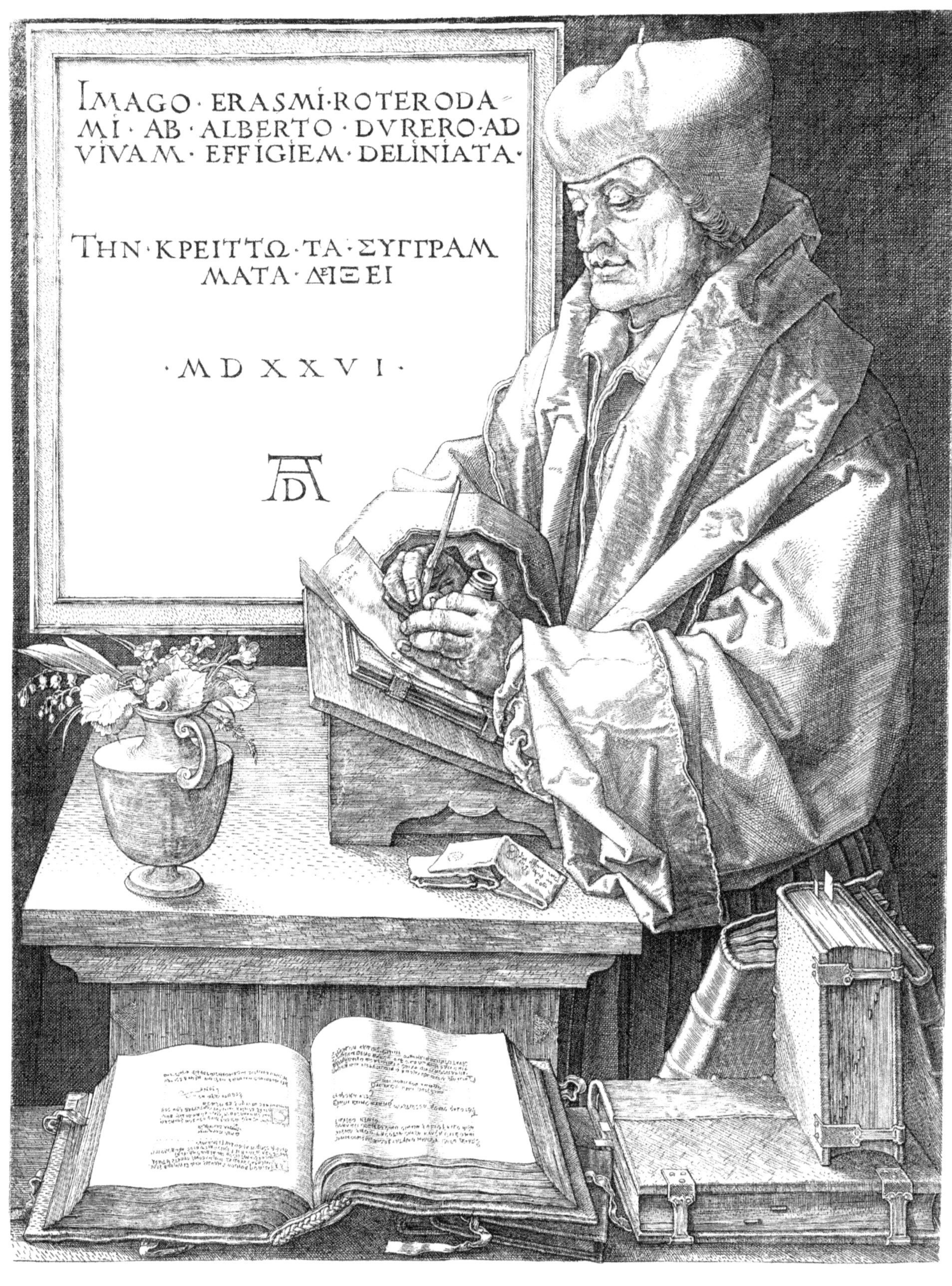

161. Portrait of Erasmus of Rotterdam, Albrecht
Dürer, 1526

162

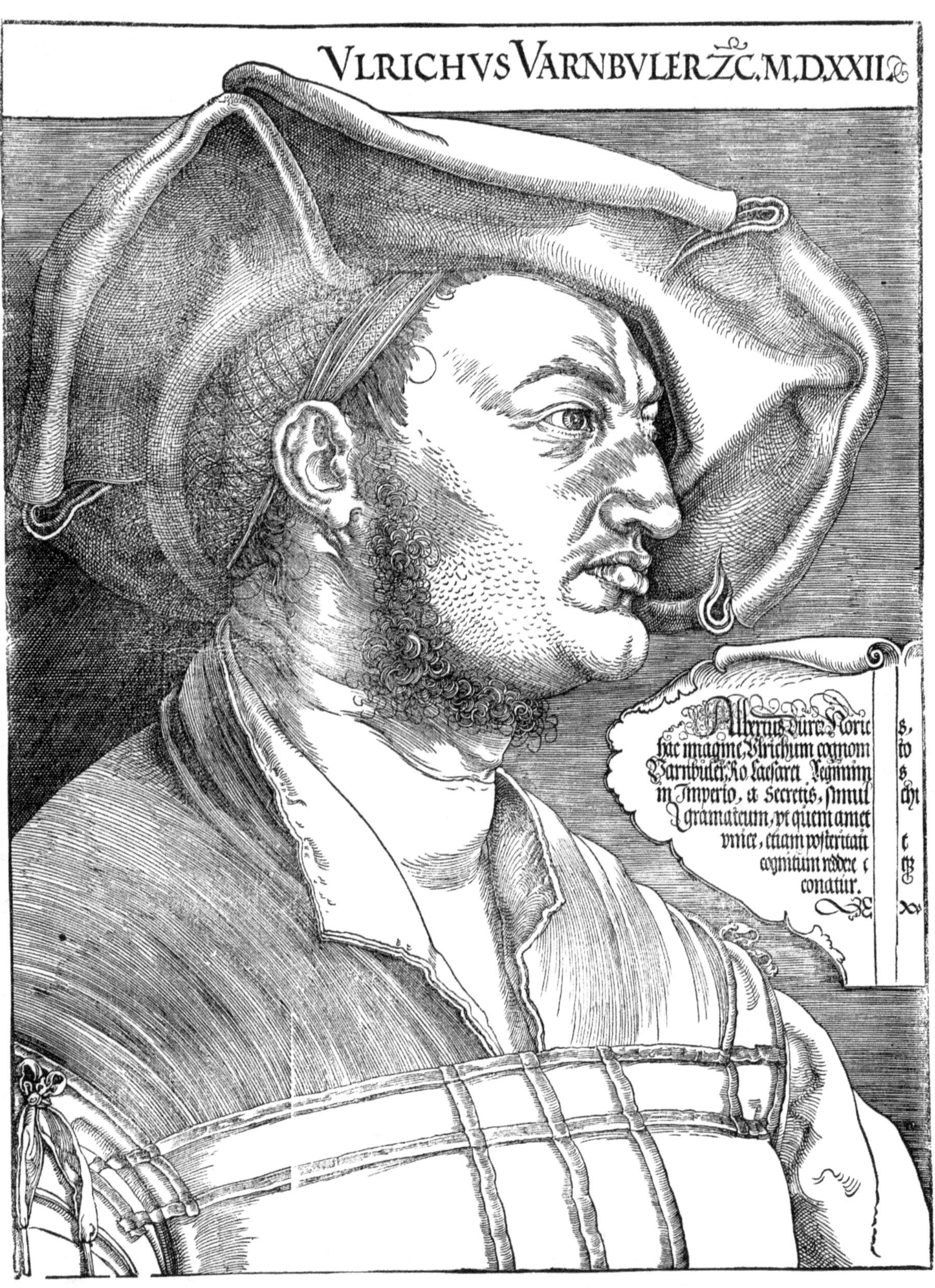

162. Portrait of Ulrich Varnbüler, Albrecht Dürer.
1615 - 1625

07

SUMMARY

Albrecht Dürer stands as a towering figure in the annals of art history, his influence resonating across centuries and disciplines. This carefully curated collection of his etchings, engravings, and woodcuts, meticulously restored by Vault Editions, offers a window into the genius of a man who revolutionised graphic arts. Through his masterful works, Dürer showcased his technical prowess and communicated profound religious, philosophical, and humanistic ideas, making them accessible to a broader audience.

This volume has journeyed through various themes that defined Dürer's work, from his compelling Biblical series, rich in narrative and spiritual reflection, to his evocative portrayals of mythological figures that highlight his grasp of classical ideals. His allegorical pieces, notably the Meisterstiche, reveal a deep engagement with complex concepts and emotions, rendered with remarkable detail and symbolism. The depictions of human figures and animals demonstrate Dürer's keen observational skills and ability to infuse vitality into his subjects. Meanwhile, his contributions to heraldry reflect his time's societal and cultural values, underscoring the importance of identity and lineage during this era.

Dürer's portraits offer intimate glimpses into the lives and personalities of his contemporaries and his self-perception as an artist. These images capture the physical likeness and the spirit and intellect of the individuals, affirming Dürer's status as a master portraitist.

This collection is more than a mere assemblage of artworks; it is an homage to Dürer's enduring legacy. His ability to blend technical skill with profound thematic content has ensured his place as an iconic figure whose work continues to inspire and influence. As you turn the final pages of this book, we hope Dürer's artistry has captivated your imagination and offered insights into the Renaissance era's cultural and intellectual milieu.

Albrecht Dürer's legacy is a testament to the power of art to transcend time and space, speaking to the human condition in ways that remain relevant and inspiring. Though not exhaustive, this collection aims to celebrate the breadth and depth of Dürer's genius, inviting contemporary artists, designers, and enthusiasts to draw inspiration from his unparalleled body of work. May it spark creativity and appreciation for the timeless beauty and intellectual richness that Dürer so masterfully conveyed.

LIST OF ILLUSTRATIONS

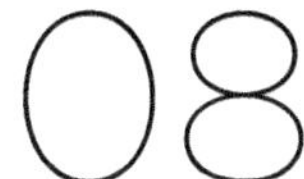

09

DOWNLOAD YOUR FILES

START HERE

Enter the following URL
in your web browser:
www.vaulteditions.com/pages/add

STEP 2

Enter the following password to
access the download page:
sxda736382hdisa

STEP 3

Enter your email address
where requested and submit
your details. A download link
will be sent to your inbox.

TECHNICAL SUPPORT

For technical assistance,
please email:
info@vaulteditions.com

DISCLAIMER:

Vault Editions Ltd. believes that
the images in this book are no
longer protected by copyright
and are in the public domain
after taking reasonable steps to
determine their copyright status.
However, please note that Vault
Editions Ltd. cannot guarantee
that your use of the images will not
infringe the rights of third parties.
It is your responsibility to conduct
your own analysis and satisfy any
copyright or other conditions for
your proposed use of the images.